12/17/19

THE BLACK AND WHITE CLUB
— FIGHT FOR TRUTH —

THE BLACK AND WHITE CLUB:
GENESIS

PETER BERGERON

ISBN 978-1-54398-465-1 (print)
ISBN 978-1-54398-466-8 (eBook)

PROLOGUE

White House, Oval Office, January 17, 1945

Roosevelt put the phone back in the cradle and touched the picture frame on the left side of his desk. He traced his fingers over each photo recalling memories of his four sons, James, Elliott, Franklin Jr., and John, who smiled back in their military dress uniforms. "So, boys, should we do this? Before they could answer, there was a knock on the door, and Grace Tully appeared in the doorway.

"Mr. President, Colonel Buxton to see you."

"Thank you, Grace. Ned, come on in."

Col. Gonzalo Edward "Ned" Buxton Jr. strode into the Oval Office within three paces of the Resolute desk, came to attention, and executed a smart salute, "Mr. President, Colonel Buxton, reporting as ordered."

Roosevelt returned the salute, "I appreciate you coming in Ned. Aren't you a little old to be playing soldier?" He pointed to a chair next to him. It was easier on his back for him to face left when talking.

"I was feeling sentimental Mr. President. I thought I'd put on the old Army greens for this occasion. I believe we all will be putting away our uniforms for good when this War is finally over. Then, it's time to win the peace."

Col. Buxton moved to take a seat. Still maintained a trim figure for a 65-year-old spymaster. His brown hair receded from his forehead, and he slicked it back on both sides, but it was his original color, and he filled out the Army blouse without the paunch of some of his contemporaries. Roosevelt reviewed Buxton's record many times. He was a Colonel in the American Expeditionary Force in World War I and the Commanding Officer of Sergeant Alvin C. York. When the Presidential military order established the Office of Strategic Services (OSS) in June of 1942, the newly appointed Director William "Bill" Donovan named Colonel Buxton as his First Assistant. He was promoted to the agency's Planning Group and Action Principal and became a key figure in all policy and operational decisions. Buxton briefed FDR on many issues, but none more important than this.

"So, Ned," the President began. "Do you think this is the best option for our country?"

"Yes, Mr. President, I do."

"And, Bill Donovan agrees with you?"

"Yes, Mr. President, he does. He would be here today, but we thought it might bring unwanted attention to this issue."

Roosevelt selected the document marked Executive Order 9513 and opened it to the signature page. He placed it on his blotter and ran his hand across the paper to smooth it out. He retrieved one of his Waterman fountain pens. Basil O'Connor gave them to him as a birthday gift. He was an old friend and law partner. I wonder if he would approve.

"You know Ned, on this very desk, in this very spot, I signed the war documents for both Japan and Germany. I hope we're doing the right thing."

"You are Mr. President." Buxton shifted in his chair. His body betrayed his lack of conviction.

Roosevelt scrawled his signature on the page with a flourish he did not feel. He shut the folder and gave it to Ned Buxton, who took it and slipped it into his briefcase. Colonel Buxton rose and walked back exactly three paces in front of the Resolute desk. He prepared to salute.

"Before you go, I want you to take something with you." Roosevelt reached for a small oil lamp to the left of his clock. "Ned, this beacon has sat on my desk for my entire presidency. I call it my light of freedom. It reminded me that all my decisions must be made for the best interest of our country to ensure the radiance of liberty always shines on our nation. I want you to take this symbol. Make sure that your choices, and those that follow you, will always shine the spotlight of opportunity on America."

"Mr. President, we'll always honor the cause of democracy to keep our country secure."

Roosevelt extended it to Colonel Buxton, who put it in his case with the signed document. He came to attention and saluted smartly, "Mr. President, request permission to leave?"

Roosevelt returned the salute, "Godspeed, Ned. Best to Director Donovan when you see him." Colonel Buxton executed an about face and walked into history.

After Colonel Buxton had departed, the President opened another folder on his desk marked Top Secret. On the inside was a medical record for Franklin Delano Roosevelt. He traced his finger over the Diagnosis block, "Adenocarcinoma - Stomach Cancer." At least, I won't live to see the results of this decision, he thought.

1

June 2012 Off the Coast of Colombia

LT Joshua Chamberlain Martin, USCG slammed the dogging handle of the watertight door to the left and exited the center island of the USS OKINAWA. The U.S. Navy's newest amphibious assault ship with a crew of 1060 sailors, an attack force of 1700 Marines, and a contingent of MV-22 tilt-rotor transport aircraft and F-35B SVTOL strike fighters. The quiet of the ship's interior gave way to the sounds of an active flight deck, 844 ft. of choreographed ballet. Josh paused for three seconds and glanced down at the U.S. Coast Guard cloth tag sewn on the left breast of his Navy Working Uniform. He tapped the gold SEAL Trident, over the Coast Guard name-plate, three times for luck. Josh was fighter lean at 6' and 185lb's, his brown hair was cut razor short, and Maui Jim shades covered his green eyes. He walked to the group of men milling about a Navy MS60 Knight Hawk helo. He made a quick head count; eight plus 2, missing one. "We're down one, Chief."

"Yes, LT," Special Warfare Operator Chief Richard "Dick" Dormann said, or "Big Dick" in SEAL circles. "Banana went below to give birth to a Marine. We loaded all the gear and briefed our two guests. They're ready to go."

"Roger, Dick." Josh went over to the two gentlemen standing apart in Navy flight suits. "So, Rob, are you two ready to go?

"We're all set, Lieutenant." Rob shifted his flight helmet under his right arm.

Both men were contractors from Sea Island Security, another name for CIA. It made Josh laugh. Everyone knew they were CIA, and all SEALs had the highest security clearances, but CIA clandestine folks always worked for some defense contractor or consulting firm. A cover your butt move in case something went wrong. No blowback on the spooks. The Agency had no knowledge of this operation. It was Sea Island Security. They also could have come up with a better name. The team dubbed them "SIS" the weak sisters of charity. The first sister, Rob McDonald, was not a weak sister. He was 5'10", 220lbs, bald, and heavily muscled. He was an operator. The other sister, Nick Lacava, had the look of a weak sister. He was about 6'1, rower lean, with a manicured beard, brown styled hair, and an Ivy school look. All he needed was a cardigan and a button-down shirt, and he would be ready for the Harvard/Yale football game with Buffy. They couldn't be a more mismatched pair. Rob was obviously from the CIA paramilitary branch, and Nick was the analyst. The boys nicknamed them Mr. Rob and Biff.

"We got one guy taking a shit, and then we're wheels up." When Josh finished the sentence, the watertight door banged open, and Special Warfare Operator 2nd Class Craig Peel sprinted across the flight deck.

"Let's mount up ladies," Big Dick twirled his right index finger in the air.

The men piled into the MS60 with a call sign of Reaper 1. The Pilots and Crew Chief were already in place after completing their pre-flight checks. Josh took a seat just aft of the pilot and plugged the aircraft communications link into his helmet. The Crew Chief secured the helo side door and took station behind the Co-Pilot.

In his earpiece, Josh heard, "Tower, this is Reaper 1. All pre-flight checks are complete. Request permission to take off to port. 14 souls on board, 2 hours to bingo."

"Reaper 1, this is Tower, you are cleared to take off to port, 14 souls on board, 2 hours to bingo. Take all signals from the LSO."

"Tower, Reaper 1, Roger."

The pilot engaged the engines, and the rotors began to spin. The helo started to shake as the engines ramped up. He pulled on the collective. The chopper lifted off the deck, swayed back and forth, and banked to port with a sudden dip. The pilot applied more power and aircraft gained altitude and turned southeast at 100 knots. It would be a quick trip.

Josh glanced out the side window at the expanse of ocean below. There were occasional white caps, but it was another beautiful Caribbean day.

He spent a lot of beautiful Caribbean days on drug patrols on his first cutter out of the Academy, USCGC SPENCER (WMEC). It seemed like a long time ago. Ten minutes into the flight, they passed down the starboard side of the USCGC YEATON (WMEC 914), the last of the famous class of cutters. The Coast Guard named her after the first commissioned officer of the Revenue Cutter Service, the forerunner of the U.S. Coast Guard. The MS60 made a flyby at 100 knots to show off. The Coasties on deck shielded their eyes from the bright sun and strained their necks to catch a glimpse of the helo as it flew past the weather decks. The Knight Hawk pedal turned to starboard and flew back around to take station about 200 yards off the YEATON's starboard quarter.

"Shark 914, this is Navy Helo Reaper 1. Request permission for Vert Rep, followed by 11 Pax transfer, followed by cargo transfer. Please pass numbers, over," via VHF secure.

"Reaper 1, this is Shark 914, course 350T, speed 7 knots. Wind 270, speed 10 knots, pitch 1, roll 1, cutter ready for Vert Rep, followed by 11 Pax transfer, followed by cargo transfer, over."

"Roger, Shark 914, copy all. All Vert Rep checks complete. Request green deck for a Vert Rep, followed by 11 Pax transfer, followed by cargo transfer."

"Reaper 1, you have a green deck."

Josh saw the green light illuminate on the flight deck light tree as the MS60 started its approach. The helo made a straight glide to the stern of the cutter, and the crew chief called the progress.

"Over the fantail, over the flight deck."

The pilot executed a quick pedal turn to port to catch the wind on the nose and settled into a perfect hover 20' off the deck. No indecision, no hesitation, and no wasted back and forth. The crew chief yanked open the door and tossed a fast rope to the cutter flight deck below.

Josh unhooked his seat harness, unplugged his communications link, and edged over to the helo door. He grabbed the rope with his heat-resistant gloves, swung out the door, locked it between his boots, and slid down the line to the rolling Coast Guard cutter. He checked his descent with his gloves and boots, and landed on the flight deck, with hurricane winds generated by the helo trying to launch him over the side. The downdraft from an MS60 exceeds 100 knots. He powered through the forces pushing him overboard and reached the safety of the ship's hangar. His platoon trailed behind with their uniforms stuck to their bodies by the strength of the rotor wash blowing down on the deck. Mr. Rob and Biff followed the team across the gray non-skid with Chief Dormann bringing up the rear. When the last team member was in the hangar, Josh turned back to watch the cargo transfer. The tie-down crew took a position to receive the cargo offload. He had spent a lot of time engaged in flight ops as a landing signals officer on USCGC SPENCER his first cutter out of the Academy. He was familiar with the operation.

Once the Pax transfer was complete, the crew chief retrieved the fast rope and started the equipment transfer by a winch. He moved black duffle bags and Pelican cases to waiting hands on the cutter. The crew retrieved each piece of gear with a grounding rod to prevent static electricity buildup before it impacted the steel surface of the flight deck. When an equipment bag landed, the tie-down crew fought through the wind to move it inside the skin of the ship, until they finished the offload. For the opportunity to lose your life in a helo mishap, each crew member received an extra $150 in their pay allotment, provided they got eight landings or takeoffs in a month.

"Shark 914, Reaper 1. Mission complete. Request permission to depart?"

"Reaper 1, Shark 914. You are cleared to depart to port. Red Deck."

"Roger, Shark 914. Good hunting." Reaper 1 gained altitude and banked hard to port.

Josh surveyed the hangar. Not much had changed. It felt like home. Bungee cords fixed a Bowflex machine in the middle of the compartment, and the crew stowed two exercise bikes and one elliptical machine in the corner. In addition to being a hangar, it doubled as an exercise room, if the cutter was not carrying a helicopter and detachment. Overhead was a 60' x 60' cargo net holding about 300 orange life preservers for use in migrant operations. There also was a supply of blankets, beans and rice, a tarp for shelter, and two portable toilets. Josh turned right at the sound of a passageway door banging open to see the ship's XO, LCDR Jeff Davis, bound through the door into the aviation space.

"Jesus H. Christ. Look what the cat dragged in, and out of uniform." LCDR Davis was a former Academy rower with short blond hair, a full mustache, and a Scandinavian complexion. "Glad to see you boys made it out of the helo. The H60 always kicks up a lot of wind."

"Afternoon, XO. Thanks for letting us come on board." Josh shook hands with the XO. "This is my team chief, Dick Dormann."

"Morning, Sir." Chief Dormann extended his hand.

LCDR Davis shook his hand. "Welcome aboard, Chief. What can we do to help? We don't have much of a mission brief other than receiving you folks and providing whatever assistance you need."

"XO, we'd like to stow our gear in the aviation stateroom and the hangar," Josh said. "We're required to complete weapon and equipment checks, and we'd also like to look at your RHIB."

"Yeah, no issues, Josh. Let me pipe the BMOW to help with the boat checks." He pulled the black handset from the holder on the forward bulkhead of the hangar and punched in three numbers. "Bridge, this is the XO. Send the BMOW down to the hangar." He hung up the phone. "Prep your gear in the aviation stateroom and here. We don't have any flyboy passengers this trip, so this space is all yours. And Josh, the skipper's waiting for you in the cabin."

"Roger, XO. We'll give you a mission brief in the wardroom in about an hour if that works for you?"

"Perfect. I'll have the OOD pass the word. Let's head up to the cabin."

"Roger, Sir." Josh turned to Chief Dormann. "A flight crew stateroom is through this door on the port side of the passageway. We can operate in there. Have Banana and Sneeds set up the weapons. Miller can look at the RHIB, and Phillips and Boye can prep the mission brief. Make sure Mr. Rob and Biff know the ops update is in an hour, and that they can find the wardroom."

"Roger, Skip."

"Alright, XO, let's go see the captain." Josh and LCDR Davis left Chief Dormann in the hangar and walked through the starboard door on the forward bulkhead of the hangar.

Josh trailed the XO down the passageway through chief's row and officers' country. The fluorescent overhead lights reflected on the highly polished floor, and LCDR Davis inspected two fire extinguishers for damage control petty officer maintenance along the way. Josh smiled. Never seen an XO walk by a fire extinguisher without flipping the tag to see if the damage control petty officer carried out proper maintenance that month. The passageway was immaculate—no dust bunnies, dirt, or boot scuffs. Not bad for a 30-year-old ship, but what you would expect from a ship commanded by CDR Dave Preston.

LCDR Davis stopped in front of the cabin marked by CDR D. R. Preston stenciled in a blue plastic name tag on the door. He knocked twice.

"Come on in," came a reply from within.

LCDR Davis leaned on the door. "Afternoon, Captain. I found a Coastie impersonating a Navy officer back aft."

Josh accompanied the XO into the cabin. The cabin on a 270 was a joke in the Coast Guard fleet. The naval architect who reviewed the finished plans noticed he left off the captain's quarters on the final drawing, so he slipped in an inadequate space to fill the need. The CO's cabin consisted of two compartments with an adjacent head. The office space was tiny with an attached desk on the forward bulkhead, a chair for the captain, one for visitors, and a 4' bench seat on the left as you entered the space. Crammed into the sleeping quarters was a single rack, a recliner, and a wall-mounted TV. There was no room to walk around.

"Josh, how the hell are ya?" CDR Preston shook hands with Josh as he entered the cabin. CDR Preston appeared just like the old teacher of nautical science at the Academy. He was not an impressive figure, but he had an imposing personality. He wore a faded YEATON T-shirt, with blue working uniform pants, and scuffed boots with short, black hair with a little gray, about 150 lbs with mechanic's hands and a grip like a vise.

"Sit down, boys. Anyone want a cup of coffee?"

"I'm topped off, Sir. Thank you." Josh took a seat on the bench, and LCDR Davis sat in the visitor's chair.

The CO sat back down in his chair. "So, what brings you slumming off the OKINAWA to the mighty warship YEATON? Did you miss us?"

"Yes, Captain, nothing like rolling around on a Coast Guard cutter to remind you what it feels like to be a real sailor."

"How does it feel being the first Coastie to make it through SEAL training?"

"I appreciate it every day, Sir. This is my first deployment as a SEAL platoon commander. Always better to be out in the field than training all day. Did you receive the op order from Atlantic Area?"

"Yes, we did. It didn't say much. Rendezvous with the OKINAWA. Embark your team, and provide any assistance needed. Also told me you would have a mission brief."

"Yes, Sir. I wanted to brief you and your command staff in an hour in the wardroom with your approval."

"Yes, that works for me. XO?"

The XO nodded his agreement. "No problem, Captain. We have them working in the hangar and aviation stateroom, and we're preparing for the brief." The XO turned his head to the 1MC speaker as the officer of the deck keyed a mike on the bridge.

"Now for the information of all hands, there will be a command staff meeting in the wardroom at 1500" was announced over the ship's 1MC.

The phone rang, and the CO picked it up on the first ring. "Yeah, I heard it. The XO and LT Martin are with me now. Right. What is the range? 10 miles? All right, I'll be up."

CDR Preston hung up the handset. "Well, gents, duty calls. It seems like a thousand-foot tanker wants to occupy the same water as us."

LCDR Davis and Josh rose to their feet as CO stood to leave. "It was a pleasure seeing you, Josh. Always like to see a Coastie do well. I'll see you down in the wardroom." He pulled his hat off a hook on the back of the door and departed the cabin.

Josh and the XO stepped out of the cabin behind the CO. The XO turned to Josh. "Let me know if you need anything."

"Yes, Sir, I will." Josh turned left back down the passageway to the hangar to look in on the mission preps and scrounge some chow from the galley.

2

Josh stood at the end of the wardroom table in front of the microwave and observed the assembled crew. It was easy to pick out the SEALs among the audience. Months of training, combat, and dedication provided a sense of purpose, and they were the fittest of the group, although the female Coast Guard JG could give them a run for their money. The wardroom was laid out like all famous class 270s in the fleet. The dining table, which also served as a triage and operating room in an emergency, ran fore and aft, with four blue padded chairs on each side, and one chair at each end. An embedded TV screen was to Josh's right showing a profile photograph of CGC YEATON as the first slide in Josh's presentation. SEALs notoriously hate PowerPoint presentations, but they were making an exception for their Coast Guard audience. Against the fore end of the compartment was an L-shaped couch covered in blue cushions facing a 55" TV. Biff assumed the junior officer position lounging on one of the cushions. Mr. Rob stood at ease with the back of his legs touching the couch, waiting for the captain to make an entrance. At 1500, the wardroom door opened, and Captain Preston walked in.

"Attention on deck," Josh commanded. Everyone snapped to attention.

Captain Preston moved to the head of the table. "Seats." A shuffling of chairs followed as everyone sat down.

"So, how is everyone doing on this beautiful Coast Guard day? I'm sure everyone has already done introductions, but how about we go around the room for my benefit. Please state your name, and where you call home. My name is Dave Preston, and I'm from Newport, Rhode Island. XO?"

"Afternoon, Captain. LCDR Jeff Davis, Virginia Beach, Virginia."

"LTJG Linda Sharp, Law Enforcement Officer, San Diego, California."

"Petty Officer Brian Boye, Miami, Florida, SEAL Team 4."

"Petty Officer Bill Phillips, Detroit, Michigan, SEAL Team 4."

"LT Josh Martin, Lancaster, New Hampshire, SEAL Team 4."

"Chief Dick Dormann, Long Island, New York, SEAL Team 4."

"Petty Officer Clint Carter, Charleston, South Carolina, SEAL Team 4."

"LT Pete Nash, Operations Officer, Philadelphia, Pennsylvania."

"LT Scott Peters, Engineering Officer, Seattle, Washington."

"Rob McDonald, Sea Island Security, Etowah, Tennessee."

"Nick Lacava, Sea Island Security, Boston, Massachusetts."

Captain Preston scanned the faces around the wardroom. Impressive group. "Thank you, everyone. Welcome to Coast Guard cutter YEATON. So, LT Martin, how can we help you?"

"Thanks, Captain. Let me begin the briefing."

Josh pressed the clicker. A picture of a semi-submersible flashed on the screen. "As most of you know, this is the latest preferred method of smuggling cocaine into the U.S., either a semi-submersible or a towed cylinder." Josh hit the remote again, and a metal tube about 40' long moving through the water by a cable appeared on the screen. "This baby is towed behind a fishing boat. If law enforcement approaches, the crew cuts the line, and the cargo drifts away. We board the vessel with negative results, and the bad guys return to retrieve their cargo. Both semi-submersibles and towed arrays have limitations because they are vulnerable to air surveillance. They can't dive to avoid detection and are often just cigarette boats encased in wood and fiberglass. But this is the future." A picture of a submarine under construction appeared.

"Is that the Ecuadorian boat?" LTJG Sharp turned her chair to face the screen.

"That's correct. This is a picture of the submarine under construction by the Machecha smuggling ring. They are Kevlar-coated submarines that can submerge to 60 feet, go 10 days without refueling, and glide underwater for up to 18 hours at a clip. They make them in the mangrove swamps of Colombia and Ecuador in isolated outposts with no access to electricity. The Office of Naval Intelligence finally got their first look at one of Machecha's captured submarines. It was a 74-foot-long beast with twin propellers. It had a streamlined hull, diesel-electric propulsion, and a fuel ballast system design. Fortunately for us, one of the technicians working on the sub project notified the Colombian military, and we were able to put these folks out of business."

"I'm assuming there is a 'but' somewhere in here?"

"Yes, XO, there is."

A photograph flashed on the screen of a severe-looking Russian in a naval uniform. "This is Captain 3rd Rank Victor Petrov, formally an engineer for the Russian Navy. Now, he's the 'Constructor de Submarinos' for the La Libertad Cartel. He works for this guy." Another picture appeared of a slight-built Colombian with a thick black mustache. "This is 'El Jefe,' Juan Pablo Rodriguez. He's the head of the cartel and fancies himself the next Pablo Escobar. And this—"

Captain Preston held up his hand. "Okay, Josh, I think we understand your problem. Your team wants to do a snatch and grab on either the submarine builder or the drug lord. Correct?"

"Yes, Captain." Josh put the remote on the wardroom table.

"So, what do you need from us?"

Chief Dormann handed Josh a folder. "Captain, this folder contains a démarche from the Colombian government allowing the Coast Guard to conduct law enforcement operations within Colombian waters for the next seven days. Tomorrow, we request you conduct boardings near the Archipelago of San Bernardo, close to the Island of Mangle." Josh passed the folder to the CO. He opened it, briefly scanned the paperwork, and handed it to the XO.

"What's on the Island of Mangle? I take it we're already close to the location?" Captain Preston arched back in his chair and put his hands behind his head.

"Mangle is about 15 miles west of our current location, which is why we chose this spot for the rendezvous." Josh lifted the remote from the table and flashed to an aerial view of a submarine under construction. "This photograph was taken yesterday over the Island of Mangle. You can see our cartel friends are hard at work getting this sub ready for sea. This is one of seven subs at various stages of completion that we are observing. We can destroy every one, but they'll keep building them. We need to eliminate the builder, which brings us to Petrov. He's the only one with detailed sub construction knowledge."

LCDR Davis finished looking at the Colombian démarche and placed it on the wardroom table. "Why don't you do some of that SEAL shit and grab him at night?"

"We've already tried some of the SEAL shit a few times, XO. We've spent a few wet nights waiting at multiple locations, but the scumbags are smart. They only build during the day, so they can see anyone approaching the beach from miles off. We can't do an air insertion, and they have spotters ringing the island for any submerged approaches. They would spot us as we exited the water. So, that leaves the Coast Guard. Coast Guardsmen are a frequent presence throughout the area conducting boardings. You don't go ashore, so you're not a threat to our boat building folks.

"The plan is to launch one of your boats for boardings near Mangle Island. You start to make inquiries via VHF in the clear. Do alpha checks and conduct some boardings. After a couple of hours of normal operations, you launch your Over the Horizon Boat with my team. We start towards Mangle Island to conduct boarding operations. We'll have a UAV overhead to confirm activity at the build site. Once we have confirmation, we'll make a fast approach, beach the boat, and assault the target. Intel indicates Petrov will oversee work on the submarine tomorrow. We bag him, destroy the sub, and return to YEATON with the package."

"All you need from us is boarding operations and the Over the Horizon Boat?" LT Pete Nash, YEATON's ops officer, asked.

"Correct. That, and bring us closer to Mangle Island." Josh put the remote on the wardroom table.

"All right, gents, I think we have the concept of operations." Captain Preston leaned forward and scanned his officers. "Anyone got any questions? Any problems? XO? Ops? Chang?"

Everyone shrugged no around the table. Captain Preston stood, followed by everyone else. "Another great Coast Guard day, ladies and gentlemen. Let's make this happen."

3

—

Captain Preston always liked mornings at sea, especially when they were in the Caribbean on a beautiful day. His thoughts drifted back to the era of sailing ships and pirates. He stood on the starboard bridge wing and scanned the ocean with his binoculars. The wake and outline of YEATON 2 appeared in his field of vision, as it made its approach to Mangle Island with Josh and his team. "Ops, did the UAV report activity?"

LT Pete Nash stepped to the bridge wing door. "Yes, Captain. They're a go."

"What are we doing with the other boarding team?" The captain turned to look at his ops officer.

"I had them finish the boarding, and they're returning to the ship. I wanted some flexibility in case we have to do something to support this op."

"Roger that. Once we recover the boat, start heading over to Mangle Island. Bring us within three miles of the shore." Captain Preston resumed watching the small boat with his binoculars.

"Aye, Captain." Ops went back to the radar to move the range ring to three miles for their transit to the island.

The radio in Captain Preston's hand buzzed to life. "YEATON, this is YEATON 2. We're hitting the beach."

"Roger, YEATON 2, copy all," YEATON's officer of the deck responded.

"YEATON, this is Sierra Tango actual. We're on the beach making our approach."

"Roger."

Captain Preston kept his binoculars on the island. The tropical foliage was clear against a bright blue sky. He squinted hard as a bright flash of light filled his field of vision, momentarily blinding him. The ship vibrated from the concussive force of an explosion, and the bridge windows rattled in their tracks, followed by the sharp report of detonation. Through blinking eyes, he stared in disbelief at the rising cloud of smoke and debris erupting from Mangle Island. "This is the Captain. Sound General Quarters."

4
—
Present Day

Josh cupped his cards in two hands and flicked the edges with his right thumb to reveal a 6 and 5 of Spades. He sat in the cutoff seat, one to the right of the dealer. His favorite spot. It offered a chance to steal the blinds, punish limpers, or slow play, depending on how the betting progressed. He was seated at his weekly Friday night game in the high rollers room in the brand-new Cape Sands Resort and Casino. The Las Vegas East built in the heart of downtown Boston, fronting the Island End, and Mystic River, just south of Everett. The gleaming symbol of excess was the brainchild of Enzo Davide Bosco, a son of Boston, who moved back East to fulfill his lifelong dream.

The buy-in for the tournament was $110,000: $100,000 for the prize pool, and $10,000 to the house for the dealer, security, room, food, top-shelf booze, and high-price talent waiting in adjoining suites at an additional fee. The game started at 2000, and now it was pushing 2300. It started with 10 players: four regulars, and six tourists. Tourists were usually dead money, but this game was finally down to one tourist and Josh.

Josh studied the tourist across the table, waiting for the first bet. The tourist tried to imitate Johnny Chan from the World Series of Poker fame, right down to the red "All in" T-shirt, white "All in" hat, and dark aviator shades. Two Triad imposters flanked him, straight out of the movies in dark suits, black ties, white shirts, and black shades.

"Mr. Josh? Enzo says you're the one to beat. It looks like tonight is my night." Johnny Chan shuffled his cards and pushed $100,000 in chips into the middle of the table.

"Yeah, you never know." Josh counted his stack. $505,000. He should throw this hand away, but any two cards. He said, "Call," and tossed $100,000 into the pot.

The dealer flipped the burn card to the side, dealt three cards into the center of the table, and fanned an Ace of Diamonds, 6 of Clubs, and 5 of Hearts. Josh stared at Johnny, not the flop, and saw him tilt forward at the sight of the cards. Bingo. He likes his hand. Tourists always have a tell. This gangster wannabe always tilts forward on strong hands and back on the blanks. He must have an Ace, Queen, or Ace, King.

"So, Mr. Josh, are you ready to gamble? Let's play some poker," and Johnny pushed his entire stack across the betting line in front of him. "All in." He sat back with a smile and folded his hands across his chest. The dealer tossed a blue "All In" chip on the table near Johnny's stack.

"Well, Johnny, I have a date, and I don't want you to have an accident on your trip back to the Big Apple. Call."

Johnny flipped over his cards, showing the Ace of Spades and the Queen of Clubs. "I think I'll be driving back to New York in style with my million bucks. Maybe I teach you some style someday."

"Not tonight, Johnny, unless you got a lucky horseshoe up your ass." Josh turned over his hand, revealing the 6 and 5 of Spades.

"Son of a bitch. How can you make a $100,000 call on a 5 and 6 of Spades? Donkey call." Johnny stood and shoved his chair, which banged off the wall and narrowly missed the drink hostess. "This is bullshit. Counterfeit the motherfucker."

The dealer burned a card and flipped the turn card, a Jack of Diamonds.

"Bullshit! Bullshit!" The greasy charade of Johnny Chan started to unravel.

Josh glanced at the two Triads. There should be no guns in the room, as everyone walked through a metal detector to enter the area. He slid back a couple of inches from the table to give him some room to go left, or right if the need arose. Enzo stood behind Johnny with four of his security guys flanking the Triads. Enzo's normal bouncers were Boston College football players looking to make a little money on the side. The bouncers in the high roller room were strictly professional with slightly baggy suits and a bulge in their left breast pocket.

The dealer rolled the next card, a 4 of Hearts. Blank. "Two pair wins." He pushed all the chips to Josh.

Johnny headed to the door with the two Triads in tow. "This is the last time I play this game. You cheated me." He slammed the door to exit the room.

Enzo motioned to his team. "Please ensure Mr. New York makes it out of the executive poker area." The four professionals followed Johnny Chan's crew out of the room.

"So, Josh, another win. Do you want me to put it on your account?"

"Thanks, Mr. Bosco, that will work." Josh's phone vibrated in his left breast pocket. He took it out and pressed the side button. The screen illuminated. Unknown caller. He hit the green accept call button. "Hello?"

"The deal's on. 1000 tomorrow. Braintree Restful Inn and Suites."

"Everything like we talked about?"

"Yeah, Josh, we're set."

"Okay, meet you there at 0950. Reserve a room tonight. Text me the number." Josh hit the red cancel button, and the call went dead.

"Excuse me, Mr. Bosco?" Josh went over to the other side of the room. Mr. Bosco was apologizing to the drink waitress, who was nearly beaned by Johnny Chan's flying chair. Josh leaned in to whisper in his right ear. "Change of plans. Can I receive $250,000 of my winnings in cash?"

Mr. Bosco nodded his head slightly. "Of course. Wait here. I'll have it sent up. Enjoy some of the shrimp and lobster. I had it brought in fresh today." He made a sweeping arm gesture at the extensive buffet lining the back wall.

"Okay, thanks." Josh perused the buffet line. Not too bad. He picked up a plate with the Cape Sand's logo, the outline of Cape Cod, and a different Cape Cod lighthouse at the center. This one had Highland Light. Josh grazed the line. He selected five jumbo shrimp the size of his thumb, a 1½ pound Maine lobster, some steamers, and a bottle of Sam Adams Octoberfest. He carried his plate over to one of the overstuffed, brown leather chairs in the corner, so he had an unobstructed view of the entrance. Hard habit to break. Always protect your back and keep your eyes on the front door. Some things never change, but that was a long time ago. He pulled around one of the serving tables on wheels and set up his food and beer. Not a bad way to wait.

5

—

Agent Chase Britt eased through the Cape Sands parking lot looking for a Blue F150 crew cab with a license plate, MA CGA 05. He was about 5'10", with shoulder-length brown hair, a goatee, dressed in a faded green Army jacket, jeans, sneakers, and a Patriots 04 Super Bowl hat. "Are you sure he didn't park it in the VIP lot?"

"My valet guy says no." Agent Chen Li parked at the entrance to the garage in case they missed the target, and he became mobile.

"How reliable is your valet guy?"

"I arrested him on a heroin possession charge. He provides information, or he gets a 10-year felony charge. He's reliable."

"He hasn't missed the Friday night high roller game in a while. Did he park at the club?" Agent Britt continued to scan the garage.

"No, we got teams watching the club, both in the parking lot and inside. Let me check again." Agent Li spoke into the mike on her radio. "Sierra One, status report?"

"Sierra One, all clear."

"Roger, Sierra One. Sierra Two?"

"Sierra Two, all clear."

"Roger, Sierra Two."

Li pressed her mike again. "Nothing moving, Chase."

"Roger, I'm just about at the end of the VIP lot. Nothing so far. Wait a minute. I think I see it. He parked in the employee executive lot."

Agent Britt stopped at the fender of a white Mercedes convertible and scouted for surveillance cameras. They were located throughout the garage, providing extensive coverage, including the executive parking area. *I should've worn a suit for this gig.* He crouched between the Mercedes and a Red Toyota Prius and frog-walked between both cars, so he was invisible to the cameras. If he stayed low, he should be fine. At the back of the Prius, he could see the back of the Blue F150. He crawled to the rear to check the license plate: MA CGA 05.

"Dragon lady, I got the target."

"Oh, baby, you make me so horny when you talk like that. Tag the car and run the fuck back here, before you get arrested for loitering."

"Roger. Me love you long time." Agent Britt slid under the truck and placed the tracker on the underside of the body near the drive shaft. It would be difficult to recover, but it would also be difficult to detect unless someone physically got under the vehicle.

"Bug's in place. Miller time. I'm coming back to the car."

Josh gnawed on the last shrimp and pulled the tail off as he chomped down. *Tasty*. He glanced at his stainless, silver SEAL watch, his one hold-over from the Navy SEALs. Two grand worth, which he couldn't afford at the time, but accurate down to 3,000 meters. Everyone should have a decent timepiece. Never know when you need to dive down to 3,000 meters. The luminous dial showed 2340. *Time to go if I'm getting lucky at the club.* The girls always look better at quitting time, but the morning sunshine brings a lot of reality to the deal. He took the last sip of beer and set the bottle on the food tray just as Mr. Bosco backed through the door carrying an aluminum suitcase.

"Sorry to keep you waiting. We usually don't have this kind of cash sitting around." Bosco peered at the remains of Josh's dinner. "I trust the wait wasn't too bad," as he handed Josh the case.

Josh took the aluminum container in his right hand and felt the weight, just about 10 pounds: 5 pounds for the money, 5 pounds for the briefcase. "No problem, Sir. Thanks for your help in getting this together. I appreciate it. Could you also make sure $10,000 gets transferred from my account to tonight's staff? They were exceptional as usual."

"Sure, Josh, and thank you. Do you want security to walk you out?"

"No, thanks, I'm going to stop and check on the club. I'll put the money in my safe." Josh stood and shook hands with Mr. Bosco. Bosco had a firm grip and tried to give Josh a little squeeze. Josh squeezed back with a vise-like grip from years as a dairy farmer. He could sense the shock of the older man. Few men could return Enzo Bosco's grip.

"Still working out?" Mr. Bosco asked as he let go of Josh's hand.

"I try to keep the heart pumping. It's difficult to remain on a schedule with the club and new wife, but I'm managing." Josh left through the high roller door and came out into the elevator anteroom. He walked over to the bank of elevators and pressed down.

The lift started its ascent to the high roller floor on the top of the hotel. The Cape Sands Resort Casino consisted of two 50-story towers constructed to look like lighthouses from Cape Cod. The north tower was Monomoy Point Light, and the south tower was Stage Harbor Light. The casino complex sprawled between the towers, complete with a 120-table poker room. Enzo purposely added the extra tables to exceed the 114 tables of the Foxwood Casino, not bad for a shoe salesman from Dorchester.

The elevator doors opened, and Josh walked inside. He pressed 5, and the doors closed to sounds of Earth, Wind & Fire and a photograph of Jeff Foxworthy coming to the Cape Sands' Nantucket Coliseum. Josh pulled his phone from the front pocket of his khakis and snapped a picture of the advertisement. His wife's, Kat's, birthday was coming up, and this could be the night's entertainment, after dinner out. Josh returned the phone to his pocket as the floor dinged, and the number lit on the keypad. The doors slid open. Josh stepped into the elevator reception area where Johnny Chan and his two Triad partners stood, waiting.

"So, Mr. Josh, I see you brought me a refund of my entry fee, plus a little extra for all my time and expense."

Josh took six slow, deep breaths to switch off the fight or flight response and start the tactical decision making of a trained SEAL operator. As had happened many times in the past, the hours of hard training and execution came flooding back. In hand-to-hand fighting scenarios with multiple attackers, always circle counter, or clockwise, to engage one opponent at a time and keep that opponent between you and the rest of the scumbags. Strike fast and strike hard. Disable attackers quickly and reduce numbers. *Glad to see Mr. Johnny is a talker.* They would've had more success if they had jumped him the minute he walked into the space. These guys were not professionals.

"Now wait a minute, boys…you know this place has security cameras everywhere?"

"That is true, Mr. Josh, but Mr. Enzo doesn't pay his surveillance staff as well as I do."

"I guess that also explains how you found me at this exact location."

"Yes, I was getting impatient waiting for you to eat and obtain my money, but it looks like it will be worth it. So, set down my money, make yourself scarce, and nothing bad will happen to you."

During the conversation, Josh assessed the situation. It would not be a fair fight. Three competent fighters to one wouldn't be fair, but one softy and two stooges was really not fair. The only fighter was to Mr. Johnny's right. He was relaxed and balanced on the balls of his feet, ready to strike. The suit to the left twitched like he was going to pee his pants, and Mr. Johnny was all bullshit.

"Mr. Josh, I don't…"

Josh took two steps left and brought the aluminum briefcase to the center of his body with two hands. The fighter made a quick step forward and launched a straight right at Josh's face, hard and fast. Josh raised the case to block the punch and heard the impact as the fist landed on the Kevlar-lined case with the sound of cracking bones. He shook his hand in disbelief at the shock and pain of breaking his hand. Josh stepped left, planted his left foot, and struck down with his right foot in a swift, sharp kick to the outside of the fighter's right knee. He felt the knee give way to the inside, creating a hinge effect, with an accompanying involuntary scream in pain. Josh swung the aluminum attaché with a two-hand strike catching the combatant in the back of the head with a loud crack, and the impact reverberated through his arms. The Triad dropped like a cheap suit from a hanger.

Disable attackers quickly.

Johnny Chan did a two-step jig like the floor was a hot stove top. He tried to shove through the second stooge to the exit door behind him. Josh double-stepped forward and crouched. He swept his right leg, which caught the dancing Johnny behind the left knee and dropped him to the polished tile with a thud and whoosh, as the air escaped out of Johnny's lungs. He sat up in a rebound from hitting the deck, and Josh hit him square in the side of the head with the briefcase. Thwack and Johnny joined his partner on the ground.

Josh hopped over Johnny and advanced on the final stooge, who now scrambled backward and cowered on the wall with his eyes wide, and his mouth working up and down, but no sound was coming out. A dark stain spread on the front of his pants.

He finally found his voice. "Please, no. I just came along for the free food and drink. This was all Johnny's idea."

Josh stopped in mid-strike and relaxed. Never strike the weak. Not from SEAL training, but a commandment from his father many years ago. "You should leave. Unless you want to talk with the cops, and I don't think you want to be here when Mr. Bosco shows up."

"Yes. Yes. Thank you. Thank you very much," and the final stooge flailed out the exit door into the parking garage.

Josh inspected the two sprawled figures at his feet. He checked for pulses on both bodies. He wasn't worried about Mr. Johnny; he didn't hit him that hard. He wasn't sure about the first guy. Both men were breathing, so that was fortunate. No need for unwanted police attention. Josh removed his phone from his pocket. Selected his contacts list, and pressed the number for Mr. Enzo. The phone rang twice, and he came on the line.

"Miss me already? I thought you had a date with a lady friend."

"Yes, Sir. I had a little problem. Mr. Johnny was looking for a refund on his entry fee."

"Shit. Are they still alive?"

"Yes, but they're not awake. One of them is running through your parking garage. You can't miss him. He's the one with the dark stain on the front of his pants."

"Where are you?"

"Fifth floor, Monomoy Tower elevator waiting area. You also have a leak in your surveillance crew. Apparently, you don't pay as well as the New York contingent."

"Yeah, okay, thanks for that. I got security moving your way now. Why don't you take off? You shouldn't be there when they arrive."

"Roger that. I'll be at the club if you need me." Josh pressed the red cancel button, and the phone cut off. He put it back in his pocket and backed through the exit doors into the resort complex.

6

The fifth floor of the casino complex contained conference rooms and offices for the resort executive team and their support staff. Josh ambled past the series of offices and followed the signs to the Champions Club. He approached two glass doors with Champions Club in gold letters embossed on the front with the emblems of the Patriots, Red Sox, Bruins, and Celtics in a circle under the name. Below the circle was written, Joshua C. Martin, Managing Partner. He paid $2 million for his share when he left the Coast Guard back in 2013. His other partner in the Champions Club was the Cape Sands Management and holding company, otherwise known as Enzo D. Bosco. He owned 51%, and Josh the other 49%.

Josh pushed through the glass entryway into the reception area. It was an open space with two couches and some overstuffed chairs on the right, as you came through the doors. The carpet was a thick, blue pile, and the logo of the club was embossed in the center. Gina Hale was his receptionist, and her desk faced the entrance. Various pictures of Boston sports teams covered the walls. A hallway to the left led to some staff offices. There was another set of doors on the right, which opened into the executive office area. Josh strode through them. His office and apartment suite were on the left. On the other side was the office of Eric Bonilla, his club manager.

Josh walked into his office and put the case on his desk, a solid oak antique that Josh had shipped from his home in Lancaster, New Hampshire. It was his father's before he passed. It took four men to move it from the truck to his work setup. It didn't go with the décor, but Josh didn't care. To him, it was a reminder of home and all that it represented. The rest of the suite was arranged in a U-pattern: a sitting area, with a table and four chairs to the left, a couch, and two recliners on the right, facing an 80" TV mounted in the corner. Behind him was an expanse of windows with a clear view of the beach area of the resort.

Enzo had created the Cape Cod experience in Boston. Josh gazed out at the beach with the Boston skyline lit up in the back. The resort complex was two miles of fresh white sand, which fronted a manmade ocean lagoon with the largest wave machine in the world. The lagoon was the old Island End River, which was dredged and converted into this ocean oasis. Of course, it took a lot of money and effort to accomplish the job. But, that was Enzo; money talks, bullshit walks, as they say in New England. In addition to the beach and water, there was also a two-mile boardwalk to go with the beach, complete with arcades, cotton candy, taffy, Italian ice, restaurants, and souvenir shops. You could have the complete Cape experience without the traffic, congestion, crowds, and hassle of getting across the Bourne Bridge. In winter, the ocean sand was transformed into a winter wonderland. The saltwater play area became one of the largest skating rinks in the country. The boardwalk became Santa's playground. There was even a new T-line to connect the Sullivan Square Station to the Cape Sands. You could leave work, take the T, and lose your paycheck in a couple of hours.

Josh sat in his chair, reached under his desk to the right drawer stack, and pressed a button. A safe rolled out of the side with a whine of gears. One of the benefits of an enormous desk—plenty of space. Josh touched his thumb to the biometrics keypad. "Voice verification, please," came the digital reply.

"Fight like you are the third monkey on the ramp to Noah's Ark, and brother, it's starting to rain." The safe door opened slowly. Josh slid the aluminum briefcase inside and said, "Close safe." The door closed with a metallic thunk, as the locking bolt slid into place. He hit the button again, and the vault retreated into the desk.

Josh got up and walked across his office to the back bar located under an empty display case. The exhibit would eventually contain rings from every Boston sports championship: 17 for the Celtics, 6 for the Pats, 3 for the Bruins, and 4 for the Sox. He picked up a glass from the counter and dropped in 4 frozen steel cubes from the fridge underneath. He placed the etched glass tumbler on the bar and poured Woodford Reserve over the frozen cubes. He took a sip and savored the smooth burn of the bourbon. He swirled the smoky liquid, so the cold distributed throughout the drink, and he contemplated the numbered placeholders on the empty shelves: 2007–2008 Celtics, 1970 Bruins, Sox 2004, and Pats 2005. Time to get serious about filling his collection. He felt a buzz in his pants pocket. He pulled the phone out and clicked on the text folder. One text from an unknown number. "Room 212." Another from Eric. "Your date's here."

"Fuck, I forgot."

Josh set the glass down and walked through the door on the right of the office. The office exited into a small corridor, which separated his work area from his living space. On the left side of the hallway was his private elevator. He pressed the down arrow and got in. There were five buttons on the control panel, the number 5, and Sox, Pats, Celtics, Bruins, labels for each of the other buttons. Josh hit the Flying Elvis button, and the elevator started to descend. It opened at Gillette Stadium, at least a replica of the Patriots' home field, complete with the lighthouse and foghorn for third downs.

The Champions Club was four floors of a sports bar, restaurant, and nightclub. Each floor was set up to pay homage to the home team: Bruins were on the first floor, Celtics on the second, Patriots on the third, and the Red Sox on the fourth. Josh edged across the Gillette field, which also served as the dance floor. He avoided cocktail waitresses dressed as Patriot cheerleaders, and the hundreds of partygoers who danced to "Born This Way" by Lady Gaga, rocking from the array of speakers that ringed the field. There were four bars shaped like footballs in each corner of the club. A black and white sign hung over each bar with a different quarter designation. Josh headed to the Second Quarter. His date would be next to the waitress station. He caught sight of his manager Eric, who directed traffic behind the bar on a typically busy Friday night. Eric wore a Red Gronk jersey with tan khaki pants. The club support staff wore Patriot jerseys and tan khakis. Most of the clientele were also dressed in some athletic attire. Josh pressed through the crowd and edged over to the server station.

Eric slid over. "Evening boss, how was the game?" Eric was about 6'2" and built like an NFL linebacker. He had dark black hair, cut military short, with a dark complexion, and GQ looks, which was rare for a former Army Ranger. Eric helped build the club from the ground up.

"Another victory for the sea services." Josh leaned on a barstool with a smile.

"Damn, man, another million bucks. You should quit all this shit and just play poker."

"Then who would keep you out of the barrio, and show you how to drive to work? I hear you Army grunts have trouble locating the latrine at night."

"Pssst, my ass. If it weren't for the lean green Army machine, you squids would have no place to call home. So, your date for the evening is over by Carrie, at the end of the bar, and brother, she's looking fine. White top, leather mini skirt. If you need any help, you just let old Eric know."

"Yeah, I think I can handle it. Send me the night's total, when you close."

"Will do. You have an entertaining night. You staying in the apartment tonight?"

"Yes. I'll leave a sock on the door." Josh bumped his fist twice on the bar top and edged by some BC students waiting to buy a drink. A couple more steps and Josh spotted his date, white top, leather mini; Eric wasn't kidding. She was beautiful with short black hair, a dark complexion, fit body, and model good looks. She was also getting her share of interest from about six guys all vying for her attention.

Josh walked up. "So, beautiful, thank you for waiting for me."

The date glanced at him with dark brown eyes like she was sizing up a purchase. "Are you Josh?"

"Yes, I'm Josh, and I'm here to take you away from this," waving his hand around the bar. "My penthouse awaits."

"You are confident, aren't you, Josh? Maybe I got a better offer from one of my admirers." She tilted her head at the group of guys who pushed closer to her.

Josh reached into his pocket and pulled out a money clip with a fat wad of $100 bills. "Do you think any of these gentlemen have one of these?" He placed the clip on the bar.

"Maybe she's not looking to hook up with her dad tonight," came a comment from a college kid in a white, Super Bowl, Edelman jersey.

Josh took six slow, deep breaths, not to turn off the flight or fight reflex, but to shut off the grab the throat, slam the head on the bar six times, reflex. "Well, Junior, you may be right. But the one certain thing about being an American, you can say whatever you want, but you also must accept the consequences."

Josh nodded his head, and two of his beefy security guys grabbed Junior under each arm and dragged him to the door. "What. What the fuck. You can't do this. I will—"

"So, gentlemen, anyone else want to call it a night?" Josh observed the assembled group of admirers with an amused smile. "No? No takers? All right, you guys have a wonderful evening." He turned back to the beautiful lady. "I guess your other options decided to pursue a different course of action."

"Well, Josh, I think you're my date for tonight. Where would you like to go?"

"I have a place upstairs. Let me buy you a drink in private. The view is spectacular."

Josh gave Eric the bro nod, and he led his date back through the crowd to his elevator. The speakers blared AC/DC "Highway to Hell." Josh danced along with the beat, as his date walked through the crowd. It was an impressive view. They rode the elevator in silence and exited in the hallway between the office and the apartment. "This way, madam." Josh opened the door and led the lady into his inner sanctum.

The executive suite was one expansive room, sectioned off by furniture groupings. A complete kitchen with a center island to the left, a 12' oak dining room table with eight chairs, two double sets of theater recliners facing an 80" 4K TV, and a complete bedroom set with a king mattress, end tables, and two dressers. The bedroom was set back in an alcove, away from the living area. There was a full master bath with a car wash shower. The shower was a 4' x 8' gift to sailors everywhere. It was a tiled stall with two overhead, oversized, sun shower heads, nine shower jets, three to a side, and one handheld. You just fired it up and walked into heaven. It was a significant improvement after living with years of two-minute sea showers to conserve water. It was a way of life on Coast Guard cutters. Turn on the water, soap up. Turn off the flow, shampoo your hair. Turn the faucet back on, rinse off, two minutes max.

"Fantastic place, sweetie." The date went over to the expanse of floor-to-ceiling windows, which lined the right side of the room. "What a view! I think my price just went up."

"Can I pour you a drink?"

"No thanks. I'm an all-business kinda girl. Can I have the $5,000? I like to receive my money up front."

Josh walked over to the bed. "Come over here and take a look at something. I've got a proposition for you."

The date strolled over and stood next to Josh. "What kind of proposition do you have in mind?"

"Consider this." Josh pushed on the bed near the stack of bills with his hand

She glanced at the money. There was a bunch of $100 bills fanned out in one pile, a wooden coat hanger, and a wad of $100 bills wrapped in a $10,000 band. "So, what am I looking at, sweetie?"

"Here's the deal." Josh went over to the bed and picked up the coat hanger. He took it over to the bathroom door and hung it on the metal hanger bolted to the door. "If you can stand here for 20 minutes, holding the coat hanger with two hands over your head, while on the towel hook, I'll pay you the $10,000 for your night's gratuity. If you can't, you're only paid $1,000. Or, you can have the $5,000 straight up, as we've previously agreed."

"All I have to do is hold a hanger over my head for 20 minutes, and you pay me ten grand. You got a deal, sweetie." The lady kicked off her shoes, strolled across the room, and grabbed the hanger with both hands. "Okay, stud, ring the bell."

Josh took his phone out his pocket and called up his boxing app that tracked the minutes for each round and rest period. He set the time to 20 minutes and hit start. The time started to count down. 19:59, 19:58, and he placed it on the floor, so his escort could watch the seconds tick down to $10,000.

Josh walked over to his date and undid the buttons on his shirt with each step. He kept his eyes on the prize and watched her eyes, which were firmly closed. He got close and brought his lips to her lips, gently brushing them with the tip of his tongue. Her breasts caressed his abs, and he moved a little back and forth to bring some friction to her nipples. The scent of fresh flowers on a bright spring day filled his nostrils. He began to apply some pressure with his tongue, to find her eager mouth, and he found clenched teeth.

"You didn't expect me to make it easy, did you?" She breathed through gritted teeth.

"No, that would take the fun out of it."

The hanger flew across the room, clanged against the windows, and tumbled to the floor. "Fuck me now, stud." Josh could feel her hands grab the back of his head, as her mouth found his tongue circling his with anticipation. She jumped up and wrapped her legs around his waist. He caught her firm ass with both hands.

"Let's go, stud. You better be worth 4,000 bucks."

Josh glanced at the time, as he headed to the bed: 11:43. 8 minutes, 17 seconds. Best time yet.

Agent Li smacked Chase in the arm. "Wake up. Lights out."

"What?" Chase sat up in his seat.

"He just turned off the lights."

"What time is it?" Britt rubbed his eyes to clear the sleep.

"0200."

"Are we calling it a night?" Agent Britt moved his seat from recline to upright and sat back.

"Yeah. He's not going anywhere until tomorrow. We got the tracker in place, so we know when he moves. The CI said the buy was set for 1000 at a tourist hotel in Braintree. We can catch a couple of hours of sleep and nail sailor boy tomorrow." Agent Li started the car and shifted into drive.

7

Becka Kendall turned right on Birmingham Avenue, from Route 17, and eased to a stop, three cars back, from the Birmingham Gate Entrance to Naval Air Station Jacksonville. Only the far-right lane was open. The Naval Petty Officer on duty checked IDs with a handheld scanner and waved people through when they passed the screening. He was dressed in a blue, Navy, camouflage uniform. He waved her up with his right hand. She hit the button on the door, and the glass rolled down.

"Evening, ma'am," Third Class Petty Officer Curtis Johnson said.

"Evening, Curtis. I see you got stuck with the mid-watch again." She gave him her ID card.

"Yes, Ma'am, but I like the quiet." He checked her military ID card and handed the card back to her. He snapped to attention and rendered a sharp salute.

Becka took her ID and returned the salute. "You have a quiet night, Curtis."

"Thank you, Ma'am."

Becka drove through the checkpoint, leaving the window down. The night breeze sent a chill down her spine, and the fresh air felt invigorating. It would be another 12 hours until she felt fresh air again. She turned right on Allegheny Road, left on Akron Drive, and pulled into the gravel parking lot of the Navy Munitions Command. She parked next to a 1979, gray, F150 pickup. *I guess Max has the shift tonight.* The Navy Munitions Command was a series of prefabricated buildings, which now contained office spaces. She stepped out of her new Toyota Camry; her boots crunched on the small stones underfoot. She stared at the sky awash in stars like a million pinpricks in the fabric of the universe with the light of heaven shining through. She located the Big Dipper, followed the two stars that formed the edge of the cup, and found the North Star, made a wish, and headed to work. She bypassed the Navy munition buildings and made a straight line for the haunted house, about 50 yards from the parking lot through the grass. It was a stone, medieval-looking building about 40' by 60' with brown shutters and no windows. The only light was a single dome light over the door, with a #4 covered in green patina. The stone mausoleum wasn't alone. There were 24 identical buildings lined up behind it, but #4 was the only one with a light. It was also the only one with a two-man security team in the woods, which bordered the building. She scouted the tree line. No movement, but they were there. They checked in every hour with the Intel team for an "Ops Normal."

She took her Common Access Card out of her pocket, inserted the chip into the reader next to the door, and punched in 8823. The door buzzed. She pulled it open and walked into a dark room. The door shut behind her with a metallic clank as the locking bolts slid back into the wall, and overhead fluorescent lights blinked on revealing a 10' x 10' concrete room with a gleaming tile floor. A single camera mounted from the ceiling pointed at her. There was another door slightly left of the elevator bank. She took her cover off, exposing a short blond haircut, green eyes, standing tall at 5'2¼". They wouldn't let her put the quarter inch on her ID. She waved at the camera. There was a sound of electric gears rolling as the locking mechanism released, and the 4-inch-thick steel door swung open. She walked through and entered another space with a set of elevator doors.

She stepped over to the elevator entrance; L to 5 across the top in bright red lights. She pressed the down arrow on the left side of the elevator bank. Kind of redundant, since down was the only direction. The doors opened, and she entered the car. She took a key from around her neck and inserted it into the emergency key slot. She turned it right, then left. The doors closed, and the elevator descended, passing floors 1 through 5, which were stocked with Mark 50 torpedoes, and then another 200' below the bottom floor. The doors opened into another 10' x 10' anteroom with another security camera on the bulkhead and a biometric palm reader to the right of the door. She put her right hand on the purple fluorescent outline of a hand. The reader emitted a bright flash of a photocopier, and a green light illuminated on the console. There was a loud metallic thunk, and a blast-proof door pivoted open. She entered the most sophisticated intelligence collection operations center in the world, which did not belong to any government agency.

"Hi, Becka," Max Lindy turned around in the supervisor's chair. "Any plans for the weekend?" Max was also a USN officer with LCDR Oak Leaves on his collar. He was about 5'10", brown hair, 180 lbs, with a small gap in his front teeth when he smiled.

"I'm here for the entire weekend, so not much other than sleeping." She tossed her cover on the desk, which also had a gold oak leaf on the front. "Anything going on?"

"Naw, all quiet. White 55 is going to buy heroin at a meeting in Boston, tomorrow at 1000. I let the boss know. Nothing else going on. The regional centers are handling everything else."

"Okay, I got it. Enjoy your day."

"Roger that."

"On the floor, this is LCDR Kendall; I have the watch."

"Aye, LCDR Kendall has the watch," the team responded in unison.

The team was made up of six intelligence analysts, divided by geography, to cover the entire United States. They supported the regional centers, which were set up in every major American city.

Max got up from the supervisor's chair and went to grab his Navy windbreaker. Becka sat down. She put her CAC card into the computer monitor, and the comprehensive, integrated intelligence feed of the U.S. government came up on her screen:

Buxton D-Wave on Line

HUMINT	TECHINT	NSA	SCOTUS
GEOINT	MEDINT	DOD	White House
MASINT	Intelligence Portal	CIA	DIA
OSINT	Cryptanalysis	FBI	DOS
SIGINT	Meteorological	DEA	Cabinet

Optrint	DHS	States	
Spy satellite	FININT	DNI	Local
TEMPEST	CYBINT	Congress	Universities
Traffic analysis	Omni	Labs	
NASA	Industry	FAA	ATF

8

—

Josh opened his eyes and checked the clock on the nightstand: 0600. He rolled over and stretched his hand across the pillow to see if the date was still here. The bed was empty, but his hand hit a small box wrapped in alphabet paper with a blue bow. He pulled the box back. "Hey, sweetie, what is this?"

Mrs. Katherine "Kat" Montgomery Martin emerged from the bathroom combing her damp hair. She was wearing a forest green polo shirt of the Cape Sands Resort, with tan khakis, and a name tag with KAT and Front Desk Supervisor across the bottom. "What is what?"

"This box." Josh held it up.

"Why don't you open it and find out?" She came over and sat next to him on the bed.

Josh ripped open the paper and found a small box, which was half pink and half blue. He lifted the lid. A baby pacifier was nestled in both pink and blue tissue paper. "You're kidding me. Are you pregnant? Really?"

"Yes, I am. I went to the doctor's office yesterday for a blood test. I got the results last night, while I was waiting for you. Drinking club soda, with lime, I might add."

"This is so fricking unbelievable." Josh reached out and embraced Kat, feeling the warmth of her body and the fresh fragrance of her hair. He kissed her on the mouth and started sliding down her neck.

"Wait a minute, daddy. Mommy has to go to work." Kat got up from the bed. "And speaking of work, you still owe me the extra four grand. My arms are killing me from holding up that frigging hanger."

Josh stretched over to the nightstand, picked up $4,000, and handed it to Kat. "I didn't hear any complaints about last night. It was a pretty good date night if you ask me."

"No complaints, just business. I need to buy some baby things for the house. What are you doing today?"

"I have a meeting at 1000, and then I will come back to the club to handle last night's receipts."

"Did you win any money at your poker game?"

"Yes. I had Enzo put it in our account."

"You know, we could just give up all this crap, and live a healthy life. You could travel and play poker, and I could play housewife and raise babies."

"Come on, Kat. We've been over this before. I need to settle things before I can move on."

"Well, hurry up and finish things. Your child is going to need a daddy, and I don't want to raise him in our current life." Kat turned and walked back to the powder room to put on eyeliner and lipstick.

Josh rolled out of bed and went to the kitchen for some coffee. The maker went off at 0600. Real Kona from Hawaii. Josh filled a cup, walked over to the counter, and retrieved the wireless house phone. He dialed the club restaurant and ordered breakfast. Two eggs over easy, whole wheat toast, and bacon, with fresh orange juice. He sat down at the kitchen table and flipped up the cover of his laptop. He opened his browser and clicked on ESPN to check yesterday's sports news.

Kat walked out of the bathroom, through the apartment, and stopped at the table. "Okay, I'm heading out. Call me when you leave the club. Maybe we can meet for lunch if it isn't too late."

"Will do. Have a fun day." Josh stood and kissed Kat on the forehead and put his hand on her stomach. "Take care of my baby. Love you."

Kat kissed him on the lips. "Love you too." She stepped out of the apartment to the elevator for the trip down to the first floor.

After Kat left, Josh walked back to the bedroom to retrieve his cell phone. He punched up the number for Benny. Benny picked up on the second ring.

"Yeah?"

"This is Josh."

"Morning, boss."

"Are you there?"

"Yup. Checked in last night. Paid cash. Two nights."

"Did you hear from the sellers?"

"Course, man. Chino called me this morning. They'll be here at ten. Everything is cool. You're gonna pay me for this, right?"

"Sure, Benny. You'll get paid. Now don't leave the room."

"What am I going to do for food?"

"Order out. I'll pay for it. See you a little before ten." Josh hung up.

The Monday Night Football theme song started playing over the apartment sound system, and a green light flashed over the entry door. *Food's here.* Josh walked over to the door and opened it. A Patriot cheerleader named Amber, according to her name tag, stood in the doorway. She was carrying his food tray with a copy of the *Boston Globe* and *USA Today*. The world was digital, but Josh preferred paper.

"Morning, Mr. Martin." Amber was a perky college student with long brown hair, green eyes, a beautiful smile, and a rocking bod. "Where do you want me to put the tray?"

"Please set it down on the kitchen table near the laptop."

"Yes, Sir!" Amber bounced over to the table and set his breakfast down. "Anything else?"

"No, I'm fine. Thank you." Nothing kills the fantasy like a "sir" from a college student. "Here you go, Amber." Josh slipped her a $100 bill.

"Sir, I can't take that. You're too generous."

"Trust me, Amber. I want to do it. Spend it on books."

Amber took the money. "Thank you so, so much. I really need this."

"No problem. Please send someone up in an hour to retrieve the tray."

"Yes, Sir," and Amber almost skipped to the door.

Josh sat down and worked his way through breakfast, another cup of coffee, and finished both papers. Not much had changed in the world. People were still doing bad things to each other, and politicians still talked bullshit. Josh checked his watch: 0830. Time to head out.

9
—

Special Agent Chen Li glanced at the faces around the table. Chase was on her right; he was still sporting the Army fatigue jacket with the Pats hat. Everyone else was wearing DEA raid jackets with bulletproof vests, except the Braintree police sergeant, who was in uniform. They assembled in the executive conference room at Crazy Larry's Furniture Super Store, which was across the street from the Restful Inn and Suites. The boardroom consisted of a 16' cherry conference table with six chairs on a side and two executive chairs at either end. There was a coffee station set up along one wall, with a small refrigerator, which contained water and soda. Various pictures of Crazy Larry's corporate life adorned the walls. The scent of furniture polish and lunch filled the air. One of the trash cans was full of empty takeout food containers.

"All right, boys, here's the deal. This is the target." She passed out a surveillance photo of Josh exiting the Cape Sands Casino, along with his official Navy SEAL portrait. "The target's name is Joshua Martin. As you can see, he was a former Navy SEAL, before he became a criminal. So, he's very dangerous. Exercise extreme caution. If we must put him down, we put him down. No sentimentality for his service. We think Mr. Martin is one of the largest heroin dealers on the East Coast. He only buys in quantities of one key and up with no street network, so he's impossible to pin down. We think he's fronting for a syndicate in Canada. We finally got a break."

She handed out another photo, which was a mug shot of a black male. "This is Benjamin Norris, aka Benny. Benny is about five foot nothing and around a buck fifty. He's also a three-time loser. We arrested him last month on a possession charge, which would send him away for a long time. In exchange for making the charge go away, he offered up Mr. Martin. We've chased this guy for months, so let's nail him. He has a lot of money, and he's a close friend of Enzo Bosco, so if we screw this up, he'll walk, and we'll chase wetbacks on the border. No offense, Alonzo."

"None taken." Special Agent Alonzo Deltoro "Zo" was a Mexican American, who just transferred from the U.S./Mexican border, and he chased wetbacks.

"Benny checked into Room 212 at the Restful Inn and Suites last night," Agent Li continued. "The room is located right here at the front of the hotel." She put her finger on a red x on an overhead shot of the hotel, which was blown up and displayed on the conference table. The Restful Inn and Suites was a cheap, two-story hotel in the shape of an L. It catered to out-of-town tourists and families who wanted an inexpensive place to stay with easy access to Boston. It was right off I93 and close to the Braintree, Red Line Station. "The room fronts the parking lot, so they'll have a clear view of anyone coming up Elm Street from the highway exit. Elm Street is a dead end, so there's only one-way in."

"Mr. Martin is going to purchase one kilo of heroin from these two gentlemen." She pulled out two more mug shots from a folder. "This outstanding citizen is Andre Pino. His street name is Chino." The mug shot showed a small Mexican with a dark complexion, smiling at the camera with a single gold tooth for a right incisor. "Chino is the number two for the Centre Street Kings in Jamaica Plain. Notice the right gold tooth. All the members have one with a C engraved on the face. It makes it easier for us to identify who's who in the zoo."

"Yo, Zo, these guys are giving all you Latin studs a bad name, man," Special Agent Dakota Fields, DEA said. Dakota was black as the Ace of Spades, with bright white teeth, which showed when he smiled. "Back in Chicago, these motherfuckers would be shining my shoes."

"No shit. We don't claim them in the brotherhood of the Latino."

"Are you boys done measuring your dicks?" Agent Li leaned back with her hands on her hips. "We've got work to do."

"No contest, boss. I've seen both dicks, and Dakota got him beat by a wide margin." Agent Alec Rollins laughed.

"I concur," agreed his partner David Thorton. "Wide margin."

"Fuck you guys. White boys don't even enter the contest."

"All right, you morons, let's return to business. You can have a circle jerk party when we have these assholes under wraps." Li tried to sound authoritative while suppressing a laugh.

"This pendejo is Vincent Casas. He's the real deal." Li passed his passport photo around the table. "He's Colombian and here on a 90-day tourist visa. He's a soldier for the La Libertad Cartel. The Centre Street Kings work for La Libertad. They rotate cartel soldiers, every 90 days, to keep an eye on business. As you gentlemen so eloquently put it, the gene pool is not too deep in the Centre Street Kings neighborhood."

Sergeant Brendan Mooney studied both mug shots. "How can we help?" Brendan was a 12-year veteran of the Braintree Police Department, of Irish descent, and he had no love for Feds, but even less for drug traffickers. He had the look and haircut of a Marine.

Li addressed Sergeant Mooney. "First, thanks for helping out with this. I know it was on short notice."

"No problem, Ma'am," which brought a smirk from Agent Britt.

"Okay, here's the plan. Benny is already in the room. Martin is supposed to arrive at 0945 with the money, about 250 thousand in cash. Chino and Casas show up at 1000 with one kilo of H. When we've confirmed that all players are at the party, Agent Britt will enter the lobby and secure the front desk, so they can't make any calls in the event they're dirty. He will also obtain the master key from the clerk."

"Sergeant Mooney, your guys will close off Elm Street at the base of the hill. No one in or out. Also, another unit will close off the rear parking lot exit to the street in case things go wrong and the bad guys make it that far. Once we have the road secured, the five of us will cross from Crazy Larry's to the back stairwell entrance of the hotel here." She put her right index finger on the aerial photo at the back of the building under a small overhang. "We'll go to the second floor and meet Agent Britt, who will have the on-duty manager in tow. The only rooms occupied near 212 are 215 and 216. Thorton and Rollins, you will clear 215 and 216 with the manager, and remove all the cleaning staff, if they are on the floor. Then, Thorton, you watch the elevator and front stairs. Rollins, you have the back stairs. Got it?"

They both nodded in unison.

"Dakota and Zo, you'll make the entry with Chase and me. We'll take Martin and Benny. You guys wrap up Casas and Chino. Any questions?"

"How are we going to do the entry?" Dakota asked.

"We have a no-knock warrant, but I'd prefer an easy entry. I'll knock on the door as housekeeping. If they open the door, we do a tactical entry. If there is a sliding bolt on the door, Chase throws in a flashbang, and we take the door. Any questions?"

"How come the minorities are doing all the work, and the white boys are playing escort duty?" Zo hooked his thumbs in his belt.

"Because two white dudes will move the occupants of the rooms faster than a black dude and a Mexican in this part of town without a lot of questions."

"Also, Thorton and I will be exercising our supervisory skills in case you guys need some help and oversight in executing a takedown," Agent Rollins added.

"Supervise this." Agent Zo grabbed his crotch with his right hand. "You and Thorton better bring a pad and some paper, so you can take notes on the proper way to do a takedown."

"My man." Dakota did a fist bump with Zo.

"Any real questions?"

"No, we're set, boss." Agent Zo laughed. "We're just pulling your chain."

"Anyone? Okay, let's earn a paycheck." Agent Li closed the folder, and went to the fridge, and pulled out a bottle of water.

LCDR Becka Kendall picked up her third cup of coffee and took a sip. *Wow! Excellent coffee, strong and black.* The light on the top of her computer flashed red. She set the coffee down, tapped enter, and the base intelligence screen came on with DEA letters blinking on her screen. She moved the cursor to DEA and left clicked.

***Warning — DEA was granted a no-knock warrant to take down scheduled heroin buy between White 55 and members of the Libertad Cartel.

"Shit." Becka picked up the STE phone and punched in a number. The caller picked up on the second ring.

"Director."

"Good morning, Sir, this is LCDR Kendall. We just got a DEA warning notice on White 55 in Boston. They received a no-knock warrant to take down the heroin buy between White 55 and the La Libertad Cartel."

"What is the time frame?"

"1000. We have about 90 minutes. Do you want us to warn him off?"

"Who is the cartel contact?"

"Vincent Casas."

There was a pause on the line. "Let it proceed. I'll call Boston."

"Yes, Sir." She put the phone back in the cradle and typed "clear" on her keyboard. The warning flashed off.

10

Josh walked out of the apartment into his office. He wore jeans, a buttoned-down, light blue, Lands' End shirt, and white sneakers with a black leather motorcycle jacket in his right hand. He walked over to his desk and laid the jacket on top and pressed the button under the edge. The safe slid out of the side and locked in place. Josh pressed his thumb on the biometrics pad. "Voice recognition, please."

"Fight like you are the third monkey on the ramp to Noah's Ark, and brother, it's starting to rain." The safe door opened with mechanical precision. He pulled the case out of the interior and set it on the floor. He then removed a color picture with smiling faces from a different time. Fighting men, sitting on a couch. Chief Dormann was holding a framed picture of a monkey dressed as Jules Winnfield, from *Pulp Fiction*, gripping a Dirty Harry .44 cal AutoMag with the saying, "Fight like you are the third monkey on the ramp to Noah's Ark, and brother, it's starting to rain." Josh traced his fingers across the photo—Chief Dormann, Banana, Sneeds, Phillips, Boye, Miller, and Carter. Gone, but not forgotten. Brother, it's starting to rain.

Josh slipped the image back into the safe and withdrew a Glock Model 22, in .40 cal Smith & Wesson, and a Sig Sauer P938, in 9mm. He also took out two fully loaded magazines for the Glock with Federal, Hydra-Shok, Jacketed Hollow Point, 180 grain ammunition. He was using 135 grain, 9mm, Hydra-Shoks in the Sig. He didn't need any spare clips for the backup. He set both pistols and clips on the desktop and opened the bottom, left-hand drawer. He lifted out a custom-made Craft, black, horizontal shoulder holster with a thumb break, cross-shoulder harness, and a double magazine pouch for the Glock, and a standard belt clip Sig holster for the P938. He stood and inserted the Sig into the holster and clipped it inside his belt in the small of his back. He gathered the Craft shoulder rig and placed his left arm through one loop, and pulled it around his back, and slipped in his right arm. He picked up the Glock and ejected the mag, checked it for 15 rounds, and ran his left index finger over the tab on the right side of the Glock, which indicated a round in the chamber. He slammed the clip home and tucked it into the holster, securing the thumb break. He picked up both magazines and inserted them into the pouches, and slipped on the black leather jacket, shrugging his shoulders to put everything in place. The combination of bulky, black leather jacket, black leather holster, and black gun helped with concealment. No need calling attention to yourself walking through a casino with a gun, even with a Massachusetts concealed carry permit. Josh stood, zipped up the jacket about 8 inches, and exited his office.

The trip through the casino to the employee parking lot was uneventful. Josh activated the unlock button on the key fob to his blue F150 with a CGA 005 license plate. The truck lights flashed, the horn honked, and the doors opened. Josh climbed into the cab, put on his seatbelt, and got his sunglasses from the overhead holder over the console. He pressed the ignition start button. 700 HP rumbled to life. Nothing like the feel of a Shelby F150. For $100,000, it had better feel amazing. Josh slipped it into drive and rumbled out of the parking garage.

Agent Li lounged at Crazy Larry's, when her pocket started saying, "Me so horny, me so horny. Love you long time. Me so horny, me—" Li snatched the phone out of her pocket and pressed the green accept key. "Agent Li."

"Tango just got in his truck and departed the garage. We're about four cars back. Do you want us to follow him?"

"Negative. We know where he's going, and we don't want to spook him."

"Roger. We're turning off now."

"Thanks for the help." Li signed off the phone. "Okay, boys. Showtime."

"Hey, Rollins? There are some notepads over there on the end of the table. I want to make sure you guys take detailed notes on how the men take down a scumbag."

Rollins stood and gave Zo the finger. "Why don't you take this?"

"I would, but we have some real police work to do." Everyone piled out of the conference room.

Josh cleared the casino and got on the I93 south. Traffic crawled on the northbound lanes with all the daily commuters trying to enter the city. One thing about Boston—the traffic sucked, along with Boston drivers. The trip to the Route 3 interchange went fast. He took a left at the Elm Street exit and headed up the hill to the Restful Inn and Suites. He parked the truck in a space near the entrance and walked into the lobby.

"Yo, paisan, how are the wife and kids?" Josh waved to the small man behind the counter. He set the silver briefcase on the floor.

"Mr. Martin, what a pleasure. My family is fine. How is the Mrs.?" Beppe was the owner and operator of the Restful Inn. He was a third-generation Italian with dark black hair, brown eyes, and a black mustache. He reminded Josh of Geppetto from Pinocchio. Beppe walked from behind the check-in desk and gave Josh a bear hug.

"She's fine, Beppe. In fact, I'm going to be a daddy." He slapped Beppe on the back.

"You are? That is indeed excellent news, my friend. You and Kat must come over for dinner to celebrate."

"We will, but only if we can sample some of Oscar's famous homemade wine."

"Of course, of course, it will be a fun time."

Josh slipped a plain brown envelope out of his jacket pocket and handed it to Beppe. "This should cover this month's rent."

Beppe took the envelope and walked back behind the counter and put it in a drawer. "Thank you for this. We couldn't make it without your help. Your friend is in Room 212, as you requested."

"Thanks, Beppe. Two more foreign gentlemen will be joining us. Please make sure the cleaning ladies are not on the second floor from 10 to 11."

"I already took care of it. Please be safe, my friend."

"Always, Beppe. You know that." Josh picked up the case, tapped the counter twice with his knuckles, and headed up the stairs from the lobby to the second floor. He turned left at the top of the stairs and walked down the hallway to the fifth door on the left. An engraved red, small, plastic placard with 212 in white letters hung to the right of the door. He knocked twice.

"Who is it?" came a voice from the other side of the door.

"Benny, open up."

The door cracked open, and a black face peered out. "Mr. Martin. Morning, boss. Let me unlatch the door." The door closed, and a chain rattled as Benny slid the latch out of the track. The door opened again, and Josh walked into the room.

As you entered the room, a bathroom with a tub/shower combo, sink, and toilet was on the right, and a full-length mirror hung on the left. Deeper into the main room were two queen beds with white bedspreads across from a luggage table, a TV, a hanging coat closet, and a mini fridge. A cramped worktable, with an internet connection, desk chair, and desk lamp were on the far wall next to a window which looked out on the parking lot. The curtains were open. Benny had ESPN's Sports Center on the TV. He wore jeans, red Converse sneakers, and a Patriots T-shirt with "Fear the Hoodie" written on the front.

"Nice shirt." Josh went over to the first bed and placed the briefcase on it. He entered the code, popped the latches, and raised the lid to reveal 25 stacks of banded $100 bills in $10,000 denominations. They appeared like brand-new bills printed fresh this morning. Benny gasped as he stared at the pile of cash. Josh took four stacks out of the case. He handed one stack to Benny and tossed the other three on the queen bed farthest from the door.

Benny's eyes got as wide as a kid at Christmas when he first sees Santa Claus. "Thank you, Mr. Martin."

"Don't spend it all in one place, Benny, and don't blow it on drugs."

"No, no...I won't." He continued to stare at the bills in disbelief.

"All right, Benny, now you can earn it." Josh checked the time: 0950. "When our friends arrive at 1000, I'm going sit on the desk with the curtains open so that I can see the parking lot. You're going to handle the transaction. Did you bring the test kit as I asked?"

"Yes, Sir. Here it is." Benny stepped over to the bed and retrieved a NIK® drug test kit for heroin from under the pillow. He put it next to the money case.

"What about the scale?"

"On the counter in the bathroom."

"Okay, that will work. Now, when the gentlemen enter, show them the money, and ask to see the drugs. When they hand them to you, weigh them on the scale. It should be 2.2 lbs. I don't mind being heavy, but light is not acceptable. Got it?"

"Yeah, I got it. Light is no good."

"After you weigh it, test a small amount with the kit. If the crystals turn a dark, olive green color, we're in business. Tell them they can have the cash. If they change any other color, you dive on the floor between the wall and the box spring. We clear?"

"Crystal."

"All right. Kill the TV." Benny got the remote and turned off the TV.

Agent Britt sat in a white rented Kia Sorento at the far end of the parking lot, with a clear view of the hotel entrance. Josh arrived, parked, and entered the hotel. Beautiful fucking truck, scumbag. Chase spoke into his radio, "The first scumbag is in the building."

"Roger," Agent Li replied.

"Control, this is Braintree patrol unit. Black Cadillac Escalade just exited the highway and is heading up Elm Street."

"Roger. Britt, did you copy?"

"Roger. They're turning into the parking lot now. They're parked, and they're getting out of the car. They're our boys. One gang banger and one GQ wannabe. They're entering the hotel."

"Roger. All units, this is Control. Execute, execute, execute."

11

Josh stared out the window. The black SUV turned into the parking lot and took a slot in the back. Two Hispanic males exited the vehicle. They appeared like Chino and Casas. "Okay, Benny, showtime. Do you remember everything?"

"Yo, man, I'm ready. I got this." Benny wiped his hands down the front of his jeans and tapped his chest twice for luck.

Josh continued to scan the parking lot. A white male got out of a white sedan at the far end of the parking lot and headed to the entrance. He was wearing a green Army fatigue jacket and a red baseball cap. He scanned the area, as he walked across the parking lot like he was looking for a problem. Two Braintree, black-and-white patrol units also started up Elm Street and then turned 90 degrees, blocking the road. Four officers got out of cruisers and drew their side arms. They took position behind the cars, covering the Elm Street exit from the hotel. Fuck me; this is going to suck. It was starting to rain. Josh slipped his hand into his jacket, unsnapped his holster, and took out a pair of Moldex impulse earplugs and set them on the desk next to his right hip. Showtime.

Three raps tapped on the door. Benny eased off the bed and walked to the door. He cracked the door open and recognized Chino's smiling face with a right gold incisor with the letter C.

"Cho Benny, let us in."

Benny opened the door. Both Chino and Casas walked past Benny into the room. Their eyes immediately settled on the money in the briefcase. Chino wore baggy jeans with a red bandana in the left back pocket, a white wifebeater, and a green Boston Celtics ball cap worn sideways on his head. Casas wore a custom-tailored gray suit, white crisp shirt, red tie, black leather, cap toe shoes with a brown leather legal case in his left hand. He was cleanly shaven with dark black hair that was cut short and parted on the right. He could have stepped off a runway in Milan or New York. He also had a slight bulge under his left armpit.

"Cho Benny, you all business. I like your style. Who's your friend on the desk?" Chino glanced across the room at Josh.

"This is Mr. Jones. He's my financial backer." Benny waved his hand over the money.

"Buenos días, Señor Jones." Chino put his left hand on Casas's shoulder. "This is Mr. Garcia. He's my attorney in these transactions."

Josh nodded his head slightly. The clock in his head told him things would go sour soon. Still had some time for them to sweep the floor and prepare for the tactical entry.

"So, Chino, you can see our money, can I see your product?"

"Sure, no problem." Chino turned to his partner and held out his hand.

Mr. Garcia twisted the snap on the leather satchel and opened the flap. He reached in and pulled out a bag of white powder wrapped in thick plastic. Favorable sign. If it were brown, or black, we'd have a problem. He gave the bag to Benny.

"Thanks, my man. Let me weigh this shit to make sure I'm getting my money's worth, and then I'm going to check it. You can count the money." Benny walked into the bathroom.

Chino walked over to the case and counted the stacks of money. He also selected a couple of stacks at random and fanned through them to make sure they were all hundred-dollar bills, and not ones, or paper. He handed Mr. Garcia a stack. He grabbed a hundred out of the wad and set it on the luggage table. He took a marker out of his jacket pocket and marked it on the hundred.

"They're real." Mr. Garcia put the marker back in his jacket.

Benny stepped out of the bathroom. "2.2 pounds, Mr. Jones." He went over to the bed and pulled a small sample tool out of his pocket, pierced the plastic, and removed a tiny amount of powder. He picked up the NIK kit, opened the top, and placed the tip of the sampling tool in the upper part of a glass ampoule, which contained the chemical reagent. He tapped the heroin into the ampoule, resealed the top, and gave it a shake. It turned a dark olive green.

"Now that is what I'm talking about. Motherfucking awesome. We're happy. Mr. Jones, what do you think?"

There was a rap on the door. "Housekeeping. Do you want me to clean up?" said a female Asian voice from the other side of the door.

Everyone froze like a bunch of kids getting caught smoking at school.

12

At the execute signal, Agents Li, Deltoro, Fields, Rollins, and Thorton ran across Elm Street from Crazy Larry's to the back entrance of the Restful Inn. Sergeant Mooney got into his cruiser and pulled out of Crazy Larry's and blocked the back parking lot entrance to the hotel. He also radioed his patrol units to block Elm Street. He exited his vehicle, drew his sidearm, and positioned himself behind his cruiser, keeping the lot and the rear entrance in front of him.

Agent Li got to the second-floor landing and stopped to catch her breath. She drew her sidearm, a Glock 17, in 9mm, and held it down to her side. The other agents stacked up in a line down the stairs. She peered through a small window in the exit door. The L section of the floor was empty. She pushed on the entry bar for the door with slow, steady pressure, and the bolt clicked open. She pushed a little further and cracked the door about an inch, then peered left down the central hallway. It was also clear. Too clear. No housekeeping carts. She eased the door farther open, stepped through, and motioned the rest of the team. The smell of cleaning fluid filled her nostrils, and a rivulet of sweat edged down her neck. She went behind the corner wall and pointed her gun down the hallway in case things went to crap in a hurry. Fields got behind Li, on the corner, and Zo stayed in the exit door with his gun trained down the hallway.

"You guys set?" Agent Li was prepared to move.

"Yeah, we're ready." Agent Thorton shifted the grip on his gun.

"Okay, see you on the other side." Agent Li nodded.

Agents Thorton and Rollins quick-stepped down the hallway with their guns trained on Room 212. They reached the end of the corridor and were met by Agent Britt. A small, dark-haired man was behind him. Must be the front desk clerk. The clerk had a key card in his hand. They went to Room 215, across the hall, and one down from 212. He slipped his key in the door and entered the room. He was soon followed out by an older white couple, and Thorton and Rollins escorted them down the stairs. Britt had called from the lobby to explain the situation and to make sure everyone was ready to vacate their rooms. They did the same thing for Room 216, and they exited with a young college kid dressed in a Harvard sweatshirt. Once the civilians were out, Agent Britt gave a thumbs-up to indicate all clear.

Agent Li holstered her gun, walked down the L portion of the hallway, and found the cleaning ladies' supply closet. She opened the door and pushed two carts out of the way and snagged six folded, white towels from a stack on the shelf. She got a whiff of Dial soap. The towels should block the view of anyone in the room looking through the door. She walked back down the hallway.

Thorton and Rollins were on the lobby entrance side of the hotel to prevent anyone from making a run for it if they made it out of the room. If for some unknown reason, they made it to the back stairway, they would find the Braintree sergeant positioned behind his vehicle. Fields and Zo were on the right side of the door. Britt leaned on the wall slightly left of Li. Agent Li shuffled a little left of the door to get out of the line of fire in the event some asshole decided to shoot through it. Fields had the hotel pass key in his left hand. It was a green plastic card with a picture of the Restful Inn on the front. He would activate the door, turn the knob, and Agent Li and Britt would be the first through the door with Fields and Zo close behind.

Agent Li held up the towels with her left hand and blocked the peephole. She had her gun in her right. Britt reached his fist between Li and the wall and rapped three times on the door.

"Housekeeping. Do you want me to clean up?" Li used her best Chinese hooker accent.

The report of a gunshot thundered from the door followed by another two in rapid fire, and a third. "Fuck me." Agent Li dropped the towels and stepped back behind the wall. She nodded at Fields. He slipped the card into the door slot and pulled it out. The light turned green. He turned the knob, and Li hit the door with her left shoulder, felt it give way, and moved into the room. "Federal agents. Let's see some hands." *Britt better be on my ass.*

At the sound of the knock, Josh picked up the ear plugs from the desk and put them in each ear. They allowed him to hear conversation but eliminated any loud, impulse noise like a gunshot or flash bang. He eased off the desk, feeling the wood scrape his ass. He reached into his jacket and gripped the reassuring form of his Glock 22. He drew his weapon and the scene unfolded in front of him.

Casas pulled his Beretta. Benny, with his mouth open and a blank look on his face, tried to figure out what was happening. Chino moved to the door to see what was going on. Josh knew what was going on. The door was about to bust in, and a bunch of motivated tact guys would come through it, or a flash bang would sail in, and ruin everyone's day. He dove to the floor next to the bed and landed on his left shoulder, winced at the impact, and rolled on his back. He brought the Glock up, found the front sight, and aimed around the edge of the bed. The bed should give him some cover if bullets started flying. Not much, but better than air.

A shot echoed in the room, more like a dull thud through the ear plugs, and a spray of red hit the wall up high. Fucking Benny. A shadow moved at the end of bed, headed in his direction. Josh inched closer to the bed frame to reduce his target profile and force Casas to expose himself, before getting off a shot. The muzzle of a Beretta 92F started to appear around the bottom of the mattress, the mouth of the barrel wide, angled down, to send a bullet to its target. Cold, impersonal, no feeling…just a tool. A gray suit followed the gun muzzle, centered perfectly in Josh's sight picture. No need for six deep breaths now. It was all training and muscle memory. Thousands of training rounds fired for just this moment. Josh squeezed back on the trigger and felt the recoil in his hands, wrists, arms, and shoulders in precise coordination, never losing track of the front sight. Again, same muscle memory, the recoil bounced the sight up and to the right. He centered the sight picture on a blurred face and squeezed the trigger again. Two to the chest, one to head; he could do the drill in his sleep. Total time less than a second.

Two .40 cal, Hydra-Shok, 180-grain bullets caught Casas straight in the chest and disintegrated his heart and internal chest cavity. The force of the rounds propelled him backward. The ammunition—designed to expand all their energy within the body with no exit wounds—did their job. The third Hydra-Shok entered his face, just above the bridge of his nose, snapped his head back, and jellied his brain, as the rest of his body flailed back like a rag doll thrown against the wall. He slammed into the TV, smacked the wall, and slid down, wedging himself between the wall and TV with a loud crash. The water glasses next to the TV fell to the carpet and skidded near Josh's feet. A red stain bloomed on the front of his pressed white shirt, adding to the GQ outfit, and a "What the fuck?" look was frozen on his face.

"Let me see some hands. Federal Agents!" Agent Li shouted. Josh tossed the Glock 22 on the bed and raised his hands over the bed from the floor.

"Gun." Agent Britt raced around the foot of the bed, pointing his gun at Josh. "Don't move, asshole." Britt reached for Josh's arm to turn him over, stepped on a water glass at the foot of the bed, and started falling on top of Josh. The automatic in Agent Britt's hand exploded in a ball of fire, and a bullet zipped by Josh's head and thwacked into the nightstand, sending wood splinters into his cheek.

"Fuck me." Josh rolled to his right to move away from the falling Britt and wood splinters. Britt fell face first on the carpet, and the air rushed out of his lungs. Josh reached for the small of his back and drew his Sig P938 backup. He rolled back to his left, and grabbed the hair on the back of Agent Britt's head, and pulled the gasping Britt on top of him. He locked him in a rear naked chokehold with his left forearm. He pointed the P938 down the side of the mattress and lined up the front sight on a Chinese female in a DEA raid jacket with a gun pointed at him.

"Drop the gun, asshole. You got nowhere to hide." Li was sucking air. "We got this place locked down."

"Not today, sweetheart. So, round up your folks, and hustle your ass out of the room, or I'm going to punch this POG's ticket."

"You got nowhere to run, Mr. Martin. Why don't you put the gun down, before anyone else gets hurt?"

Josh tightened his forearm around Britt's neck, feeling him gasping for breath, as he choked off his airway. His face turned a bright shade of red as blood stopped flowing between his heart and brain. "You really should move, or your partner here is not going to make it."

"Okay, okay, we're leaving. Everyone out." Li backtracked around the bed and followed everyone out of the room, pulling the door closed behind her.

Josh rolled to his left on top of Agent Britt, pinning him to the floor. He put the P938 back into his holster and grabbed Britt's right wrist and twisted his arm behind his back in an armbar. He released the chokehold, and Britt gasped for air. He kneeled to the right of Britt, continuing to twist his right arm in an armbar. He pulled Britt's handcuffs from the small of Britt's back, hooked his right wrist, and tapped his left shoulder. Britt put his left arm behind his back, and Josh cuffed him.

Josh stood and picked up his Glock from the bed and put it back into its holster. Benny's body sprawled in a pool of blood between the beds with most of his face gone. Chino was nowhere to be seen, so the Feds must have taken him. One less asshole to worry about. "Okay, POG, on your feet." Josh hauled Britt up to standing. Britt had a red smear on the side of his face, where it hit the carpet. "You should have that checked. I'm not sure when they cleaned the carpet, but I bet you got a case of something."

"Fuck you. Putting your ass in a cell is going to bring a smile to my face."

"Well, not today, sunshine. Why don't you slide your sorry butt over here?" Josh pinched Britt's arm above the elbow and steered him over to the door. "Sit down."

"What?"

"Sit down, on the floor, before I put you on the floor."

Britt leaned on the door and slid to the floor. "You and I have a date when I'm out of here."

"Yeah, I'm not too worried. So, shut the fuck up, before I knock you out." Josh leaned over to the first bed, pulled the bedspread off, and draped it over Benny. He pulled the spread off the second bed and covered Casas and the TV. He walked over to the computer desk and ripped the internet access cable out of the wall and walked back to Britt. He tied a bowline loop in one end of the cable and cinched it through Britt's cuffs. He attached the other end to the doorknob. If someone were going to do another tactical entry, it would not go well for the Army's finest.

Josh took his cell phone out of his jacket. "What's your partner's cell phone number?"

"1-800-Eat-Shit."

Josh kicked Britt square in the gut, and he let a gasp of air and pain. "One more time. What's your partner's cell phone number? I don't want them doing another tactical entry with you tied to the door. Two hours, and we're out of here. Max. What's her number?"

"781-848-7755."

"Thank you. Now wasn't that easy? What's your partner's name?"

"Agent Li."

Josh punched up the numbers on his phone. She answered on the third ring.

"Yeah?"

"Agent Li?"

"Yeah, who's this?"

"This is Mr. Martin on the other side of the door."

"Well, what can I do for you, Mr. Martin on the other side of the door?"

"Your agent is handcuffed and tied to the entry door. If you try any tactical entry, I'll use him for target practice. I only need two hours. I'll surrender in two hours."

"Two hours? Okay. Two hours. See you at 1235." Agent Li signed off.

Josh punched in another number and put the phone to his ear. "I got a problem. DEA raided the party."

"That's unfortunate," the caller said. "Where are you?"

"I am at the Restful Inn off I93 and the Route 3 interchange. I'm in Room 212, with two dead guys, and a DEA agent handcuffed to the door."

"Fuck."

"Yeah, my thoughts exactly."

"How much time you got?"

"Two hours. 1235."

"Okay, wait it out. We're rolling now. We'll be there as soon as we can."

"Roger." Josh pressed the red off button.

"So, war hero, how do you plan on getting out of this?"

"Right through the front door, POG. Right through the front door."
Josh stepped into the bathroom and shut the door.

13

Josh flushed the toilet. Washed his hands in the sink, dried them on a hand towel, and walked out of the bathroom, waving his hand in front of his face. "Man, you might want to give that awhile."

"Ah, man, you stink. You're killing me…wow!" Agent Britt tried to burrow his face into the floor.

"Man, you Army guys like burying your faces in the carpet. Do you play for the other team?"

"Fuck you," came the muffled reply.

Josh checked the time on his phone: 1105. "It won't be long now."

"I hope not. I need some MOPP gear in here."

"Come on. That smell must make you feel like you're back in the Army."

"How do you know I was in the Army?"

"I saw you walk across the parking lot from the white Kia. You walk like a soldier."

"Ah, fuck, you knew we were coming."

"Yup. Casas over there gave me no choice. He blew Benny away the minute you knocked on the door and announced housekeeping, and then he was coming for me."

"Tell it to the U.S. Attorney."

"Housekeeping? What genius thought of that? Must have been the Asian chick's idea. She sounds like a Bangkok hooker. There were no housekeeping carts on the floor. You should have used a food delivery guy."

"Well, you can give some tips to other cons in federal lockup on tactical entry techniques, or maybe you'll have new friends on death row. I'm sure you know that death during the commission of a felony is considered homicide, even if you didn't pull the trigger. I'm guessing buying a key of heroin is considered a felony, both Benny and Casas are deader than shit, so I bet you meet both counts."

"Yeah, sounds about right."

"Of course, when I'm out of these cuffs, I'm gonna kick your ass, so you might not make it to holding."

"Now that, we can agree on, POG. I'm not making it to holding."

At 1205, there was a rap on the door. "Mr. Martin, this is Special Agent Cory Randolph with the FBI. I have a warrant for your arrest. Would you please open the door?"

"Sure. Let me move the doorstop first." Josh slid the internet cord off the door handle and helped Agent Britt to his feet. "Why don't you wait in the bathroom?" Josh grabbed Britt's arm and ushered him into the bathroom and closed the door. He walked over to the bed and pulled his Glock out of the holster and set it on the bed, and did the same for the P938. He stepped back over to the door.

"Agent Randolph?"

"Yes," came the reply from the other side of the door.

"I put the doorstop in the bathroom. He's still handcuffed. Both of my firearms are on the bed. I'm unarmed. I'm coming out with my hands up."

"Okay. Open the door slowly. Walk out of the room with your hands over your head. Walk across the hall, place your hands on the wall, and assume the position."

"All right, I'm coming out." Josh turned the knob and slowly opened the door, catching it with his right foot so that it wouldn't close. He put his hands over his head and walked out of the room. Suits, DEA raid jackets, uniformed officers, and a lot of guns, all pointed at him, crowded the hallway.

Two of the suits stepped out of the crowd and pushed him to the wall. One suit frisked him and removed the magazines from his holster. The other suit twisted his right arm behind his back, and the cold steel of a handcuff snapped on his right wrist, followed by the left. While this was going on, the second suit read him his Miranda rights.

"Do you understand these rights?"

"Yes, Sir." Josh felt two strong hands on either elbow, as suits one and two pushed him through the crowd, which parted, as he walked down the hallway to the lobby entrance.

"This isn't over, dickhead. You and I have something to settle," Agent Britt shouted. Followed by an argument with the Asian hooker, which Josh couldn't follow.

Josh was escorted down the stairs, through the lobby, by the two FBI agents, with Special Agent Randolph bringing up the rear. They walked to a dark blue Chevy Tahoe parked near the entrance. The suits put Josh in the backseat, and both escort agents got in the front. Agent Randolph got in the back next to Josh. They started the vehicle, took a left out of the parking lot, down Elm Street, past the Braintree roadblock, and up on I93 headed into the city. Once they were on the highway, Josh leaned to the right, and Agent Randolph opened Josh's cuffs with a key. Josh rubbed them to improve circulation.

"Kinda tight there, Chris?"

Special Agent Chris Anthony turned back from the front passenger seat. "Sorry, Josh, I had to make it look real for our DEA friends. The Asian chick was really pissed when the boss showed her your warrant, and she got a call from her SAC."

The driver, Special Agent Owen Quinn, glanced in the rearview to see Josh's expression. "What did you do to the agent in the room? It didn't sound like you guys will catch a Sox game anytime soon."

"I was all set to surrender, and Agent Grace stepped on a water glass, fell on me, and nearly shot me in the head. Everything just kinda went to shit after that."

"So, tell me exactly what happened." Randolph was an African American from Detroit, Michigan. He was about 6'0, 225 lbs, with a round face, a receding hairline with a touch of gray at the temples, and a black mustache. He had the look of a federal judge. He was pushing 50, and his best field years were behind him. He was an ASAC at the FBI field office in Boston.

Josh turned to face his boss. "I set up a buy with the Centre Street Kings using Benny as the go-between. I knew the cartel swapped out soldiers, so I wanted to meet the new guy. Everything went fine until the DEA showed up."

"Any idea how they found out?" Agent Randolph shifted in his seat to face Josh.

"No idea, boss. If I were betting, I'd say the DEA got something on Benny, and he flipped. The minute the DEA knocked on the door, the cartel guy knew something wasn't right, and he shot Benny in the face. Chino had a deer in the headlights look, so he didn't know anything was going down; it wasn't him. After the cartel guy shot Benny, he was coming for me. I ducked down behind the bed in case the DEA crew blew the door or threw in a flash bang. Mr. Cartel walked around the bed, pointed a gun at me, so I put two in his chest, and one in his head. He dropped behind the TV. The DEA blows in, and Agent Britt, I think, falls on me. Did we identify the cartel guy?"

"Yeah, his name was Vincent Casas. He came in on a flight from Caracas to Logan last Tuesday. He's also the son-in-law of the head scumbag Juan Pablo Rodriguez. I don't think he'll send you a Christmas card this year."

"Oh, that's not going to help us." Josh slumped back in his seat. "Is my cover blown?"

"Too early to tell. We'll check with our sources and the intel guys to find out, but I don't know. Until we're sure, you need to go to your safe house. Time for the Cash Man to take a vacation. Stay with your club owner cover, so people don't start asking questions."

"Sounds like a plan. What about my truck and guns?"

"Our guys are going to process the scene, so they'll bring your firearms back to the office. We'll do ballistics on them for the investigation. You can pick them up, or I'll have someone drop them at your house. Agent Jensen is dropping your truck at your place. Keys will be in the center console."

"Roger that."

"We're going to drop you at Exit 13. I called Kat and told her to meet us at the McDonald's. You head home and wait for my call."

Agent Quinn signaled right, a sign of weakness in Boston traffic, took Exit 13, made a right at the end of the ramp, and another right into the McDonald's parking lot. He stopped in front of a green Ford Explorer.

"Okay, take some time off from buying drugs and stay off the streets. Spend some more time at the club, until we sort this out."

"Will do, boss." Josh pulled the latch on the door and hit it open with his forearm, stepped out, and pushed the door closed behind him. He waved at Kat and got the are-you-all-right look in response. *No baby-celebration sex tonight.* He walked over to the Explorer, opened the door, and climbed in. "Honey, I'm home."

14

Big Papi, complete with David Ortiz number 34 jersey, gold chains, Sox b-ball cap, and white satin sweatpants, paced his office, which was the back storage room at Marley's Jerk Chicken Restaurant on Centre Street in Jamaica Plain. Big Papi, real name Jason Brown, was Jamaican, not Dominican, but he resembled the Sox legend at 6'2", 258 lbs, so he adopted it for his street persona. He carried a two-tone Marucci Ash bat on his right shoulder. It was an authentic, game-used, Ortiz bat. He paid three grand for it on eBay. It now had a couple of dings, some dark stains, and a tooth mark.

"Are you sure Chino said that?" Big Papi made a couple of practice swings, flexing the bat with his wrists.

"Yeah, boss." Runner stepped back to move out of bat swing range. He'd seen the faces of a few rival gang members who were on the receiving end of the Marucci, and he wanted no part of it. Runner was a wiry street kid from El Salvador. His parents came to the U.S. when he was 9. His first arrest for possession was at age 12. He dropped out of school at 14. Now, he ran drugs from dealers to buyers for the Centre Street Kings.

"This is bad, real bad. Fuck me." Big Papi switched the bat from his left to right shoulder and mimicked a swing in between. Runner edged further back, bumping against the wall. He didn't want to be Big Papi's next home run. "Cartel dude is dead?"

"Yeah, boss, Chino said. 5-0 hit the buy. Cartel dude blew away Benny, and then the Cash Man smoked the cartel dude. Two to the chest, one to the head. Real professional. Didn't hesitate." Runner edged a little left and felt the doorknob in the small of his back.

"Same Cash Man we've done business with before?"

"Chino says, the same guy. Always buys with a suitcase of Benjamins. Don't say shit. No problems."

"Fuck me." Big Papi leaned in and swung the bat. Thwack. The bat smashed through a box of canned tomatoes, sending cans flying across the floor and bouncing off the wall. One can put a dent in the drywall to the left of Runner's head. Runner ducked to the right and covered his head. "I don't need this shit. You got a phone?"

"Yeah, boss." Runner gave him his cell phone, trying hard to stop his hand from shaking.

Big Papi snatched the phone. "This a burner?"

"Yeah, boss."

"All right, move your ass the fuck outta here. I gotta think."

Runner turned and pulled the door. He went through it in a flash like he was running from the police with a kilo of H. He yanked the door shut behind him.

Big Papi set the bat and phone on his desk, an old gray office model, which was full of dents and faded paint. He pulled his office chair around and sat down. *I got to call. I don't call...he finds out? I'm dead. I call...tell him the news...he doesn't like it? I'm dead. Something's not right. 5-0 didn't just show up. Somebody snitched. Benny? Cash Man? Chino? One of my guys?* Big Papi picked up the bat and moved it around like he was loosening up for an at-bat at Fenway Park. He put the bat back on the desk and picked up the phone. He punched in the emergency number and hit send. There was a series of clicks, and then a voice came on the line.

"Yes?"

"I need to talk to the El Jefe."

"You sure?"

"Yes, motherfucker, I'm sure."

"Such language, Jason," Juan Pablo Rodriguez said. "What's so important that you interrupt my family time?"

"Sorry, Mr. Rodriguez, but we have a problem."

"We? No problem here. You must have a problem."

"Yes, Sir. I have a problem." He rocked back and forth in the chair. He could feel the sweat running down his back. "We had a deal set up today. Your friend was at the location. It didn't go well. The DEA raided the place."

"Did they arrest my friend?"

"No, Sir. They killed him." Silence on the line. "Mr. Rodriguez, are you there?" He stared at the phone to see if the line was still open. The call was still on. More silence.

"I'm here, Jason. Listen carefully. I'm going to send someone to meet you within the next two hours. He'll have my instructions. Do you understand?"

"Yes, El Jefe."

"Two hours." The call went dead.

Big Papi stood and chucked the cell phone against the wall, where it split into three pieces. He picked up the autographed David Ortiz bat and slammed it three times on top of the desk. "Fuck, Fuck, Fuck."

15

The ride from McDonald's to home was uneventful and quiet. Not the best sign. Kat always got quiet when she was pissed. She took I93 south out of the city, and Route 3 south, at the Route 3/193 interchange. Traffic started to build, but it wasn't too bad. They cruised right by the Elm Street exit without a peep. No "Hey, honey, I just spent the morning up the hill at the Restful Inn. I nearly got killed, and I blew a guy away." Josh kept his eyes out the window, not saying a thing, like a kid that got picked up at school by his mom for getting expelled. Kat took Exit 18 to South Weymouth, Mass, and left on Shea Drive. She entered the old South Weymouth Naval Air Station. Home was officer housing. They drove by an A-4 Skyhawk jet mounted on a pedestal in a small park called the Shea Memorial Grove, named for Reservist CDR John "Jack" Shea, who was killed in action when the aircraft carrier WASP sank during WWII. At least he got a memorial. If Grace's bullet went 6 inches to the left, old Josh wouldn't receive a jet Memorial. Past the plane memorial, Kat took a left on Glendening Terrace and pulled into the third driveway on the left, "The Base Commander's House."

Naval Air Station South Weymouth had been an operational United States Navy airfield from 1942 to 1997. The War Department first established it as a regular Navy blimp airfield during World War II. During the postwar era, the base became part of the Naval Air Reserve Training Command, hosting a variety of Navy and Marine Corps reserve aircraft squadrons and other types of reserve units. The facility was closed in 1998, by the Base Realignment and Consolidation program approved by Congress. The First Coast Guard District in Boston took over the base housing for enlisted folks and five executive homes for officers.

An Army Brigadier General, who worked logistics for the Defense Logistics Agency, occupied the first quarters with his wife, Ellen. The second house was empty. Andy and Jennifer White had just departed on Permanent Change of Station orders. Andy finished a tour as CGC SPENCER's commanding officer. His next assignment was in DC at Coast Guard HQ. The fourth house was a Coast Guard captain assigned to the district office, and the house on the end belonged to Master Chief Jim Dempsey and Marie. Josh and Kat occupied the old Base Commanding Officers House nicknamed the "Big House." It was a sprawling five bed-rooms, three baths, WWII era home complete with butler's pantry and a bell system to call the help. It was too much house for the two of them, but the FBI picked up the tab, so like any efficient bureaucracy, the Coast Guard billed the FBI full price on the largest house.

Josh opened his door and stepped out of the Explorer. Kat had already walked around the front of the car and entered the house. Josh was just about ready to follow her in for the inevitable discussion when he saw his truck and a black Chevy Tahoe coming down Glendening. His truck pulled into the driveway, parked behind the Explorer, and the Tahoe followed behind. Lester Johnson, from the FBI forensics team, stepped out of the truck.

Lester called to Josh, "It shimmies a little at 140, but not too bad."

Josh walked over. "I didn't think you lab gremlins could drive over 55."

"Only when we drive an agent's private vehicle." Lester appeared more like an NBA power forward than a scientist. He took a jump shot and arced the keys to Josh, who caught them with his right hand.

"Thanks for bringing it over, Lester. I thought Agent Jensen was going to do it."

"He was supposed to, but I volunteered. Not every day you experience the thrill of driving a Shelby, especially a truck. Are you doing okay?"

"Yeah, I'm all right, but you guys may have to come back with a full team. I haven't spoken to the Mrs. yet."

"That should be fun. Marty brought your weapons back to the office. You can pick them up anytime. We processed them both. You only fired the Glock, correct?"

"Yes, three times. All the rounds are in the Colombian."

"Who shot the nightstand?"

"DEA Special Agent Grace, I don't know his real name. He stepped on a water glass and put a round into the nightstand about 6 inches to the left of my head."

"That would be one Special Agent Chase Britt." Lester laughed. "He wasn't too happy with the FBI."

"He can stand in line on that one."

"You got that right. Liam and I got to drive back to the hotel to finish up." He jerked his thumb in the direction of the Tahoe. "Let me know if you need anything."

"Will do, Lester. Thanks for coming out."

"No problem, boss." He gave Josh a wave and climbed into the Chevy. They backed out of the driveway and headed out. Josh gave them a wave and walked over to the house.

There were two ways into the house. The front door and the back service entrance. Josh walked around the Explorer and opened the back-screen door and stepped into a small hallway. The old butler's pantry, complete with a dumbwaiter and a call bell, was on the right. They used it as a bedroom as it also came with a full bath. He closed the door behind him and was greeted by the scratching of nails, trying to find traction on a tile floor and a blur of fur.

Syrin, the war dog, rounded the corner through the kitchen and headed straight for him. He kneeled and caught her full in the chest. "Who's my best girl?" Josh playfully grabbed her snout to happy growls. Syrin wagged her butt and licked his face. Nothing like coming home to unconditional love. Syrin was a Belgian Malinois; a favorite breed of Navy SEALs. Similar to a German Shepherd, but smaller to accommodate the rappelling and parachuting requirements of SEALs. SEAL Team 4 had Cairo, the war dog when Josh was assigned there. Josh trained Syrin in all facets of a military working dog, including explosive/drug detection and officer self-defense. She was also the perfect defense asset for Kat. No one would want to walk into the house unannounced.

"Sit." Syrin stopped playing and sat at rigid attention. "Find mommy." Josh snapped his right arm and index finger out. Syrin took off and tore through the kitchen. Her nails scratched on the tile floor, attempting to get traction. Josh could hear Syrin barking from back in the house, and Kat saying, "Syrin. Knock it off. Syrin, sit."

Josh walked into the kitchen, which was small by today's standards, and into the formal dining room. The dining room opened into an expansive living room with a massive stone fireplace on the left. He heard Syrin barking and Kat laughing from the sunroom. He walked through the living room and entered the sunroom on the left, past the fireplace. The sunroom was set up like a greenhouse with a roof, and floor-to-ceiling glass on three sides. Kat was on the ground wrestling with Syrin, who licked her face.

"Order your dog off me, Josh." Kat laughed between licks. "Syrin, stop it."

"Are you ready to talk?" Josh suppressed a laugh.

"Yes, yes, make her stop." Kat rolled over and covered her head with her arms. Syrin danced around Kat, nudging her with her nose.

"Syrin, come." Syrin stopped playing with Kat, came over to Josh, and sat down. "Good dog." Josh scratched behind her ears.

Kat climbed off the floor and sat in one of the green recliners. They had the room set up with two green recliners and a small table between the two. They had floor lamps behind each chair, and a hammock swayed at the end of the room. Kat staged various potted plants around the space to give an outdoor vibe. Josh called it the jungle. It was Kat's favorite room in the house.

Josh dropped into the other chair. "Release." Syrin relaxed and lay down at his feet.

"So, are you going to tell me what happened?" Kat flopped in the chair, and her hair was a mess.

"I thought you didn't want to know."

"Well, now, I need to know. We're going to be three, so 'we' gotta start thinking as a family. I was okay with the SEAL stuff. I know you had to seek justice, by joining the FBI, after the loss of your SEAL team. I put up with the undercover crap, but I can't see bringing a child into this world, and we're doing it. I don't want to raise this kid without a dad. So, what happened today, that got you dropped off, and we had to come straight home?"

Josh stared at the floor. He felt her eyes on him. Not wanting to look at her, and not knowing how to start. He patted Syrin on the head, and she licked his hand. Finally, he glanced at Kat. *God, she's beautiful.* His mom was right. He did marry up.

"I've been posing as a major heroin buyer on the East Coast for a syndicate in Canada. We've been buying from a street gang in Jamaica Plain called the Centre Street Kings. They sell for the La Libertad Cartel. They're the scumbags responsible for the ambush of my SEAL platoon in Colombia. We're building a RICO case to take down the street gang, all the La Libertad members in the U.S., and obtain a warrant for the arrest of Juan Pablo Rodriguez, the head scumbag in Colombia."

"Jesus, Josh. You're kidding me."

"It gets better."

"Aw shit." Kat sat straight up in her chair.

"Today, I was at a buy with a member of the street gang and one of the cartel soldiers. Everything was going as planned until the DEA raided the room."

"Are you serious?"

"Yup, you can't make this shit up. So, some female DEA agent poses as housekeeping and knocks on the door. The cartel guy knows something is up, so he shoots my CI right in the face. No discussion, just boom. Brains on the wall."

"Oh, Josh." She put her hand on his knee.

"Then the asshole starts coming for me. I'm already on the floor, behind the bed, in case the DEA starts shooting first and asking questions later. Shithead comes around the bed. Points a gun at me, so I smoke him. Two to the chest, one to the head."

"Oh, baby, I'm so sorry." Kat reached over and climbed into his chair. He took her in his arms and squeezed her tight.

"And, it gets worse. After the DEA hits the door, I have my hands up in the air. The arresting agent steps on a water glass, shoots the nightstand about 6 inches from my head, and falls on top of me."

Kat lifts her head off his chest. "Really?"

"Really."

"Then what happens?"

"I take the agent hostage. Call Randolph. He comes with a warrant for my arrest, and here I am."

"So, what now?"

"I don't know. We need to find out how this plays with the cartel and the street gang."

"Are they after you?"

"No baby, no one is coming for me." He phrased it with more conviction than he felt. "Randolph told me to lay off the streets until I hear from him. I can catch up my honey-do list."

Kat climbed off Josh, pulled him out of the chair, and kissed him full on the mouth. Josh could feel the stirring of little Josh, but it was kinda early.

"When things settle down, we need to talk future. For now, why don't you fire up the grill and make some steaks? Junior is hungry."

"Now we're talking. How do you know we're having a boy?"

"Women's intuition." She slapped Josh on the ass. "Now go make momma some food."

16

———

Big Papi rocked back and forth in his chair and checked the clock on the wall. He just finished a jerk chicken lunch. The remains sat on a paper plate in the center of his desk next to the two-tone Marucci. The restaurant may not look like much, but the food reminded him of home in Kingston. *If you're going to die, you might as well die full. Plus, I need my energy. If I'm gonna die, a couple of those motherfucking Colombian pricks are coming with me.* He felt a buzz in the pocket of his pants. He reached in, pulled out his phone, and punched the green phone button. "Yeah?"

"They're here," came the reply on the line.

"How many?"

"Eight."

"Eight motherfuckers?"

"Yeah."

"They strapped?"

"Yeah, heavy."

"How many we got?"

"Sixteen. Four across the street in the Suds and Bucket, two on the roof, six with me in the restaurant, and four outside; two on both sides of the door."

"They got the AKs?"

"Yeah. In the laundromat and on the roof."

"Okay, show the motherfuckers in. Anything fucks up, kill 'em all."

"Yeah, boss."

There was a knock on the door, and a well-dressed, bald, white dude with the build of an MMA heavyweight fighter, who'd been in a few brawls, walked in. He wore a gray Brooks Brothers suit, a white shirt, red tie, and black wingtip shoes. He had a cell phone in his right hand. "Mr. Brown, I think this call is for you." He handed the phone to Big Papi, who rose from his chair to retrieve it.

Big Papi stared at the caller ID. It showed Unknown. "Hello?"

"Daddy, is that you? There are some men with mommy and me. Can you come home, daddy? I'm scared."

"Listen, baby; you got—" The line went dead. Big Papi felt the blood drain from his face and his hand crushed the phone. He fought the urge to grab the Marucci and beat this suit-wearing pecker-head into the floor.

"So, Mr. Brown, I believe we've got your attention," Mr. Gray Suit said. "Mr. Rodriguez isn't happy that his son-in-law got killed on one of your deals. He'd like you to make restitution. He wants you to return the kilo of heroin you lost, plus the $220,000 involved in the deal."

"All this for a kilo of H and 220K? I can pull that outta the safe."

Mr. Gray Suit held up his right hand. "Not quite. Also, Mr. Rodriguez would like you to kill everyone who was in that hotel room. The DEA agents, your buyer, and your Mr. Chino."

"Are you fucking crazy? You want us to whack two DEA agents. Man, the Feds would be on us like a fat kid on a Ho Ho. Plus, we don't know how to find the Cash Man. He always gets in touch with us."

"I'm afraid, Mr. Brown, those are Mr. Rodriguez's terms, and they are non-negotiable."

"Well, fuck you! Why don't I just tune you up and—"

Mr. Gray Suit threw a straight punch into Big Papi's throat, and a quick right leg sweep, which caught Big Papi behind the left knee, sending him crashing to the floor clutching his throat, gagging, trying to breathe. Mr. Gray suit then grabbed the Marucci off the desk and made a sharp swing, which struck Big Papi flush on the right knee, with a loud thwack of wood on bone. Big Papi bit his lip, so he didn't cry out.

"Now listen here, you little cockroach," Mr. Gray Suit said. "We allow you to operate. We could work with any other gang in Boston, and stomp you like the insignificant insect you are. In fact, I'm going to do it. Stomp you like a bug. Kill every Jamaican pendejo on the block, fuck your wife, and sell your kid to the pedophile down the street." Mr. Gray Suit's face turned red and spittle formed at the edges of his mouth. He pulled back the bat to hit Big Papi again.

"Wait, wait." Big Papi gained his voice and held up his hand to ward off the blow. "We'll do it. We'll do it. We'll kill them all."

Mr. Gray Suit stopped his swing and ran his hand over his suit to smooth out any wrinkles. "Excellent, Mr. Brown. Mr. Rodriguez will be happy we came to an agreement."

"What about my family?"

Mr. Gray Suit pulled a phone out of his left inside pocket, punched the send key, and spoke into the receiver. "We're all set." He signed off and put the phone back in his pocket. "There. Your family's now safe and under our protection. They're going for a ride with my friends until you've completed all your tasks. Are we understood?"

Big Papi nodded his head. "Yeah, we're clear."

"Now, I believe you have some things in a safe for me?"

"Yeah, let me call one of my guys, and he'll bring it." Big Papi crawled off the floor into his chair. His right knee throbbed with the slightest movement. "Runner? Run your skinny ass in here," he yelled.

The door opened, and Runner burst through the door. "Yeah, boss." Runner glanced sideways at Mr. Gray Suit holding the Marucci. No one held the boss's bat unless he wanted to find it upside his head.

"Go find Big Dog and tell him to give you 220K and a kilo of H outta the safe. Then, give it to our Colombian friends."

"Yeah, boss. 220K and a kilo of H. Got it. That it?" Runner was anxious to get the fuck out of there, away from the muscled white dude with the bat.

"Yeah, now git."

Runner flew through the door like his ass was being chased by the Po Po and slammed it shut behind him.

"I need to ask one favor." Big Papi shifted in his chair to ease the weight off his knee. "I don't know the Cash Man, and I don't know how to locate him. Can you guys help us out?"

"That seems like a reasonable request, Mr. Brown. I'll see what we can do. Anything else?"

"Home addresses for the Feds would also speed things up."

"Glad to see you are motivated, Mr. Brown. I'll call you." Mr. Gray Suit put the bat back on the desk and walked out of the office.

—

17

"Hey, baby, how do you want your steak cooked?" Josh turned the steaks with tongs.

"Medium rare. Do you want a Cabernet or Merlot?"

"I'll drink the Duck Horn Cabernet." Josh touched the steak with his finger. *Feels like medium rare to me.*

"Okay, are you just about done? The corn, baked potato, and onion are finished."

"Yeah, I'm coming in." Josh backed into the house carrying a silver platter with two-inch-thick strip steaks, seasoned with Zach's steak rub and Montreal seasoning.

"I put us in the dining room."

Josh walked into the dining room and set the platter on the table. "We're eating fancy tonight."

"Of course, we are. We're going to be a mommy and daddy, and daddy made it home today. So, we've got a lot to be thankful for. Now say grace." Kat lowered her head and reached for Josh's hand.

They held hands as Josh said grace, and then he poured himself a glass of wine and toasted Kat with her glass of grape juice. "To new parents. God help the baby." If Josh ever had to have a last meal, this would be it. The only thing missing was chocolate cake. Strip steak, fresh corn on the cob, baked potato, and an onion cooked with a beef bouillon cube. It was a recipe passed down from his Uncle Ed.

Halfway through the meal, Kat set her fork on the plate and stared at Josh. "How do you do it?"

"How do I do what, sweetie?" Josh chewed a mouthful of steak and followed it up with a sip of Cabernet. *Excellent wine.*

"You were almost killed today. You shot someone, and now we have a fabulous meal, and you're my normal, sweet husband. How do you do that?"

Josh took another swig of wine, swished it around in his mouth, and set the glass down. "The shrink's term it compartmentation. You learn it in SEAL training. When I'm working, I don't bring home with me. There is no room for home during operations. And when I'm home, I don't carry business with me. There is no place for all the bullshit around you. I call it my switch. So now, I'm thinking only about you, and the baby, and how much of a super mom you're going to be."

"How did I marry such a sexy man?"

"Yeah, you did win the lottery."

"And modest, too."

They finished the meal, and Syrin came over and put her head in Josh's lap.

"What do you want?"

Syrin nudged his hand at the question.

"Someone hungry?"

Syrin answered with a bark.

"I take that as a yes."

"You know. Someone is in for a rude awakening when we bring a certain something home." Kat tilted her head toward Syrin.

"Naw, she'll be a good big sister. Won't you, girl?"

Another bark and she pushed his hand again with her snout.

"Okay, girl, let's go." Josh stood and went into the kitchen to feed her, and Kat cleared the table.

"Feed the dog, and then Mr. Lottery Pick gets to do the dishes." Kat brought some dishes into the kitchen and set them on the counter.

"Yes, dear." His dad told him the secret to a happy marriage were six words. *Yes, dear, and you're always right.* Kat added two more to the last phrase: *as usual.* So far, they worked like a champ.

After finishing the dishes, Josh walked through the living room on the way to his office, which was left of the front door, as you walked into the house. Kat was curled up on the sofa with Syrin. She had a small fire going in the fireplace, and she was watching *Wheel of Fortune* on TV. She viewed it every night. She came from old family money, but she just might win 10K! He leaned over and gave Kat a kiss on the cheek and patted Syrin on the head.

"Let me know if I win." Kat had both of their spin IDs written on a piece of paper and taped on an end table next to the couch. "I gotta check my email, and then I'll be in."

"Okay, sweetie." Syrin didn't even move her head.

Josh walked into his office. There was an enormous cherry desk facing out with a leather executive chair. Kat found the desk at an auction and had it professionally restored. It was beautiful. She gave it to him for his birthday. It also weighed a ton. It took two men and a boy to move it into the house. The office had two bay windows, which faced the front of the house, and two more, towards the side driveway, so there was always plenty of light. Various awards from the Coast Guard, Navy, and FBI hung on the walls. He also had two barrister bookcases with lead glass doors on the front, which dated from the 1920s. They were from his grandmother's estate. They contained various collectibles from his many travels overseas, including a jade dragon from Hong Kong, a boatswain knife from CGC SPENCER, his first SEAL trident, and his Bible from the Coast Guard Academy. The chaplains at the Academy gave all the swabs engraved Bibles after they reported for swab summer. "Please, God, let me put up with this bullshit," Josh had written on the inside cover.

Josh sat in his chair and adjusted the pictures on his desk. There were only two: a shot of Kat and Syrin in an embrace on a trip up the Maine coast, and a photo of SEAL Team 4, sitting around a fire on a beach in Aruba, posing arm in arm, saluting with raised beer bottles. The only other items on the desk were a glass top to protect the wood, a notepad, and a custom pen. Josh had it made by Lau Lau creations in Hawaii from koa wood. A 32" computer monitor took up the most space. Josh reached under the desk and felt a Glock 22, in .40 cal, Smith and Wesson, secure in its mount. He needed to make some changes when the new baby comes. He pressed the power button on his Razer custom computer. One of his old shipmates from CGC SPENCER made it for him. A screen saver photograph of

Siberia in the winter flashed on the screen along with the security password prompt. He typed in Third M0nk3Y, and the Google search bar appeared. He logged into AOL, clicked on the mail icon, scrolled to spam, selected it, and there it was.

On Josh's first day as a rookie FBI agent, he had received an email with the words "SEAL Team 4 Open Now" as the subject line. When he opened it, there was a message and some instructions.

Agent Martin, as a veteran and a patriot who has suffered a tragic loss, you were selected to receive actionable law enforcement intelligence information for your regional area of operations. The information will arrive every Saturday at 1900 via Cyber Dust. You will have 15 minutes to copy the information. You cannot save it, or print it, in its original form. You can copy, paste, and print. You cannot reference this information in any court proceedings, and you cannot base any law enforcement action on this information. You must develop your own evidence using this information. You can pass this information to any other law enforcement agency, but you cannot reveal the source of your information. If you violate any of these restrictions, you will stop receiving this intelligence. You can ask questions, request additional information, or seek clarification by hitting reply to the daily message. Your identifier is White 55. Weekly messages will be in your SPAM folder. Look for a B and W in the subject line. An advertisement will appear on your screen. Click on a small bw logo somewhere in the ad. We'll pass alert information when it's available. A two-beep tone will proceed it.

"Fight like you are the third monkey on the ramp to Noah's Ark, and brother, it's starting to rain."

Josh clicked on Crazy Larry's Warehouse Sale, and an ad for No Interest Financing at Crazy Larry's appeared on the screen. He located the bw underneath a coffee table. Sometimes it was like finding Waldo, but tonight it was easy. He selected the bw, and a single page document appeared. It was always titled daily brief with no indication of day or time. The information was brief, but it was consistently accurate. Mr. Evan Bloomfield, from Southside Bank and Trust, is embezzling money from the bank. He has the proceeds in an off-shore account in the Cayman Islands, Account #78865413. Mr. Leroy Johnson robbed, and killed, the store clerk at the

ABC Liquor store in Braintree, Mass. His present location is at his aunt's house at 178 Broad Street, Braintree, Mass. Massachusetts State Senator Mrs. Ellen Fairchild is taking kickbacks from Morgan Construction for the development of the Boston Waterfront. Josh copied the information into a Word folder and printed it out.

He opened the right-side drawer of his desk and pulled out one of six burner phones he kept in a box in the front of the drawer. He dialed a number, and Detective Ryan Hollis from the Braintree Police Department answered on the second ring.

"Detective Hollis."

"Bernie Mac, how are you doing?" His name may be Hollis, but he was an identical twin of the late comedian Bernie Mac.

"Who is this, and how did you obtain this number?" Detective Hollis sounded annoyed.

"Don't squish your panties in a wad. This is your favorite federal agent."

"Joshua Chamberlain Martin, my favorite general, how are you doing this evening?"

"Better than you, by the sound of your greeting."

"Yeah, sorry about that. I didn't recognize the number, and my chief's on my ass over a liquor store robbery and murder. We got nothing. No prints, a shitty eyewitness description, no video, and the punk ass dropped the gun at the scene. A piece of shit Smith and Wesson .38 with no history. Son of a bitch shot the clerk right between the eyes, and he has a wife and two little kids."

"Yes, I heard. I can help you out with some information."

"Oh, man, you got something?"

"I do. Same rules apply."

"I know. I know. I got it. This is an anonymous tip, and I have no idea where I got it."

"Okay, your perp's name is Leroy Johnson. He's holed up at his aunt's place, 178 Broad Street, Braintree."

"You're a lifesaver. No idea how you find this shit, but you're the best. Next beer is on me."

"You're welcome, Bernie Mac. Let me know how it goes. Can't remember the last time I had to buy a beer in a cop bar."

"Will do, Josh, and thank you." Hollis rang off.

Josh removed the battery from the phone and dropped both in the trash. He refreshed the computer screen and hit reply on the Crazy Larry spam email. He typed:

Subject: White 55

Please provide any updated information on recent activities of La Libertad Cartel and Centre Street Kings in the Boston Metropolitan area.

(Send)

Josh signed off the computer. He pulled the single printout of the message from the printer and put it on his desk. He would contact the bank fraud and corruption guys tomorrow.

Josh pushed away from the desk and killed the light switch on the wall as he left his office. "So, can I buy the new Sage fly rod from Cabela's?" Josh went over and sat next to Kat on the sofa, trying to wiggle in between Syrin and the cushions.

"Not unless your initials are H.A."

"What was the final puzzle?"

"Popular view. She wasn't even close. Anything interesting in your email?"

"Not unless you want some new furniture. Crazy Larry is having a warehouse sale."

"We have enough furniture. Although we will need baby stuff. Are you ready to go upstairs?"

"Outstanding idea. I'm exhausted."

"You kill the fire, and I'll meet you upstairs." Kat climbed off the sofa with Syrin close behind and headed upstairs.

Josh went over to the fire and knocked it down with a poker. He closed the screen and followed Kat up the stairs. *Things are going to sort themselves out in the next couple of days. One way or another.*

18

LCDR Kendall checked the op center clock on the wall; still a few hours left in her 24-hr shift. There was an office in the back with a rack and a full bath. She had caught a nap over lunch. It was still a long day. They always did the turnover at night, so it reduced visibility on people coming and going at the Navy Munitions Command. She picked up the phone and hit the director's line. He picked up on the third ring.

"Evening, Becka. How is the world tonight?"

"All quiet, Sir. We just got a request from White 55 for updated info on the La Libertad Cartel and the Centre Street Kings. Can we pass the information on the meeting between the cartel and the CSKs this afternoon?"

"Do we have anything specific?"

"Yes, Sir. Jason Brown, aka Big Papi, called El Jefe and broke the bad news about the DEA raid on the buy and the death of his son-in-law Victor Casas. El Jefe sent a contingent of eight cartel members to meet with 16 gang members to discuss the way forward. We have nada on the meeting, no electronic or communication devices. We couldn't access any video, and no satellites or drones were in the area. Also, the cartel snatched up Big Papi's wife and daughter, and they're still holding them."

"All right, let him know they met, and that Big Papi's family is in play. A meeting with 24 players means something is up. Tell our folks to keep looking. Also, did he take any action on the information we passed?"

"Yes, Sir. He called a Detective Ryan Hollis on one of his burner phones and relayed the information on the robbery/murder suspect in the liquor store event."

"Okay, sounds fine. I hope you have a quiet night. Call me if anything changes on the cartel event."

"Yes, Sir." Becka hung up the phone. "Hey, Jimmy?"

"Yes, Ma'am," the Northeast analyst said.

"Send White 55 the meeting information."

"Roger, Ma'am. Include information on the family?"

"Yes. Send it all."

"Roger." Jimmy typed into his computer screen.

"Hey, honey, your phone's beeping." Kat was sitting in bed reading the latest Reacher novel. "Sounds like a work beep."

"Okay, I'll be right in." Josh finished brushing his teeth and spit into the sink. He gargled with some mouthwash, and spit that into the sink. He ran some water, swished it around to clear the toothpaste and mouthwash, and shut off the water. He walked out of the bathroom into the bedroom.

The bedroom was set up with a king-size oak bedframe, with drawers underneath, on the wall opposite the bathroom. There were nightstands on either side of the bed with over-the-shoulder lights mounted on the head-board. Kat had a solid oak dresser on the wall, on the left side of the bed, and an antique writing desk she used as a makeup table. The desk was also from his grandmother's estate. It was made from the remnants of a spinet piano. His highboy armoire was to the right of the dressing table. There was no walk-in closet, so they each used the closets in the other bedrooms for hanging stuff. Plus, Josh kept some suits and clothes at the apartment in the casino. An 80" 4K TV was mounted on the wall opposite the bed with a small entertainment center below for the cable equipment and the Blu-ray player.

Josh walked over to his side of the bed, picked up his phone, pushed the side screen button, and swiped his security pattern. A message appeared on the screen. Eight cartel members met with 16 Centre Street King members at 1600 for 57 minutes. No further intel was available on the meeting. The cartel also picked up Jason Brown's, aka Big Papi's, family, including wife Theresa, and 8-year-old daughter Nichole. No other intel available.

"Shit." Josh cleared the message.

"What's the matter? Girlfriend not happy you're not at the club tonight?"

"Yeah, she can't believe I'm in bed at 8:30 on a Saturday night."

"Sucks getting old."

"I showed you old last night, baby. I gotta make a call. I'll be back in a minute." Josh stepped into the bathroom and closed the door. Josh opened his contact list and pressed the number for Agent Randolph.

"Hello?"

"Good evening, Sir. This is Josh Martin. Sorry to bother you so late."

"No problem, Josh. What can I do for you, and how was the ride home?"

"The ride home was quiet."

"You still married?"

"Yes, Sir."

"What's on your mind?"

"I just received some information on the La Libertad Cartel and the Centre Street Kings."

"From our anonymous friends?"

"Yes, Sir."

"And?"

"There was a gathering today at 1600, between the cartel and the gang members with about 24 players. The cartel also picked up Big Papi's wife and daughter."

"Shit. Any mention of you?"

"No, Sir. Our friends didn't have any eyes or ears on the target."

"Okay. I'll pass this to our kidnapping and organized crime folks. Why don't you swing by the office around 1000 on Monday, and we can decide what we're going to do?"

"Yes, Sir. See you then."

19

"Runner! Move your skinny ass in here." Big Papi's leg was propped on a blue plastic milk crate, and he had an ice pack strapped to his right knee. It was already swollen with a dark purple hue. He popped a couple of Oxi, which took the edge off the pain. He would make a doctor's appointment in a couple of days when all this shit got back to normal. If it ever did.

Runner pulled the door open and stuck his head in. "Yeah, boss?"

"Find Big Dog and step in here."

"Yeah, boss." Runner pushed the door shut.

"Yo, Big Dog, the boss wants to see us," came through the closed door.

A couple of minutes later Big Dog walked through the door, all 6'6", 300 solid pounds of Nigerian nightmare. Black as a lump of coal, from Abuja, the capital of Nigeria, real name Taylor Lanier. He stared at Big Papi's knee on the crate. "Yo, boss, you shoulda let us stuff all them Colombian bitches into their fancy Escalades and set them all on fire." He went over and sat in a gray chair; back by boxes of red beans. Runner stood because no one asked him to sit.

"They picked up Theresa and Nichole." Big Papi stared at the ground.

"They what?" Big Dog clenched and unclenched his fists at the news.

"The Colombians picked up Theresa and Nichole, before our meeting. They handed me a phone with Nichole on the line. They're going to hold 'em until we finish some tasks."

"Motherfuckers. What tasks do those bitches want us to do?"

Big Papi peered at Runner. "If you repeat this to anyone, they're going to find pieces of your skinny ass all over Boston."

"No, boss. I won't say anything." Runner took an involuntary step back to distance himself from the bad news.

"In addition to the 220K, and the kilo of H, they also want us to smoke the two DEA agents who raided the hotel room, the Cash Man, and Chino." Big Papi watched Big Dog's reaction.

"They want us to smoke Chino. What the fuck for?"

"The Colombian prick was Rodriguez's son-in-law."

"Oh, shit." Big Dog leaned forward in the chair and rocked back and forth, thinking of a solution.

"Yeah, oh shit." Big Papi shifted his leg on the milk crate and glanced at Big Dog. "So, what do you think?"

"Chino's got to go." Big Dog rose off the chair and moved back and forth. Thinking. "He's easy. We can do him inside, or outside if he makes bail. The hard part is the DEA assholes and the Cash Man. We don't know the DEA agents, and no one knows the Cash Man. We always dealt with Benny, and Benny's a stain on the wall."

"Our Colombian friends will provide us the names and addresses of the DEA agents and the Cash Man." Big Papi rubbed his thigh to keep the circulation going.

Big Dog stopped pacing and watched his boss. "What do you want us to do now?"

"Put a cap in Chino's ass. If we do him inside, no problem. If we do him outside, we need proof that we got rid of him." Big Papi lifted his leg off the crate and eased it to the floor. "Fucking leg cramps when I put it up and hurts like a motherfucker when I put it down."

"What kind of proof? Like a selfie or a finger?"

"Both. Also, round up our 12 best shooters. We need to off all these fuckers in one drive-by, or they'll put them in some protective custody shit, and we won't get another fucking chance."

"Okay, boss. I'm on it." Big Dog glared at Runner. "Not a word to anyone, or I'll bury your nappy head under home plate at Fenway Park. Motherfuckers be sliding over you forever."

20

Fall Sundays in New England were all about football, Dunkin Donuts, brunch, and the Sox if they made the playoffs. Quinn Christy sat in a back booth at O'Toole's, on Broad Street, in Downtown Boston. Quinn was your typical Irishman from Southie with curly brown hair, a ruddy complexion from too much Guinness, and freckles. He savored his corned beef and Irish breakfast with his Sunday *Globe*. He was partway through an article on Tom Brady and deflate-gate, when he muttered, "Fuck Goodell."

"Exactly, Fuck Goodell." A muscular bald man in an impeccably tailored gray Brooks Brothers suit stood next to Quinn's table.

Quinn glanced up. "Can I help you, pal?"

"I believe you can, Special Agent Christy," Mr. Gray Suit said.

"Do I know you?"

"No, but I know you, and we both work for the same southern employer. May I please sit down?"

Quinn made a quick, nervous scan of the bar—only two regulars sitting at a back-corner table, and Alyssa the waitress. He motioned for Gray Suit to sit down. "Do you want something to eat?"

"Coffee would be fine." Mr. Gray Suit slid across the green leather bench into the booth.

"Alyssa?" Quinn motioned for the waitress. "Can you bring us two coffees, please?" He nodded at Mr. Gray Suit. "How do you like your coffee?"

"Black is fine."

"Make them both black." Alyssa nodded across the bar.

Quinn turned back to his guest with a slight smile and whispered, "What the fuck are you doing meeting me here?" Quinn scanned around the bar.

"Relax, Agent Christy," Mr. Gray Suit said. "I got four guys outside the bar to prevent any interruptions or prying eyes."

"Great and stop calling me Agent Christy. I don't advertise my occupation. Not the best for business."

"Okay, Quinn, and you can call me Mr. Smith."

Alyssa walked over with two steaming mugs of coffee and set them on the booth table. "Can I bring you gentlemen anything else? Would you like some breakfast?"

"No thank you, darling," Mr. Smith said. Alyssa swayed her hips walking away. "I can think of something else, but it doesn't involve breakfast."

"Why are you here?" Quinn slid one of the mugs over to him. "Besides to hit on the wait staff?"

"We need a favor." Mr. Smith reached for the other mug of coffee.

"And, we need to do this in person?" Quinn touched the edge of the mug to gauge the temperature. It was hot.

"Yes, I don't trust anything electronic." Mr. Smith took a sip of coffee. "Not bad. How's the food?"

"The food is excellent. Can you tell me why you are here ruining my Sunday morning?"

"Of course, Quinn. Your agents raided a hotel room in Braintree yesterday. Two individuals were killed."

"And, this involves me how?"

"One of the individuals killed was Vincent Casas. He's Mr. Rodriguez's son-in-law."

"Oh, fuck." Quinn stopped eating. "I have no input on tactical operations. That was handled by our Chief of Operations. I didn't hear about it until after the fact."

"So, you can help us now. After the fact."

"Absolutely. What do you need?"

"I need the names, and addresses, of the two DEA agents who were in the room when Vincent was killed, and the name of someone called the Cash Man."

"Are you fucking crazy?" Quinn leaned forward and lowered his voice. "I can't give you that."

"Can't or won't? It would be unfortunate if some certain pictures of you and an underage Chinese girl found their way to your wife and daughter.

What is she, a junior at MIT now? What a great school. I'm sure all her friends would love to know that her father is a pedophile. Plus, what about the retirement account our employer set up for you? I think your superiors at the DEA would frown on that."

"Okay, okay. Fuck me. When do you need it?" Quinn slumped back on the bench.

"Yes. Fuck you is a good way to put it. Let's say we have lunch tomorrow, back here around 1200. I like the vibe, and I like the waitress."

"I don't know if I can provide all that in 24 hours."

Mr. Smith slid from the bench and took another sip of coffee. "Damn good coffee. Of course, you can, Quinn. I have faith in you. Plus, your life depends on it. See you tomorrow at noon." He stepped over to the bar and pushed a fifty across the counter to Alyssa. "Don't spend it all in one place. Thanks for the coffee."

"No problem." Alyssa stared in disbelief at the fifty on the bar.

Mr. Smith walked out, into the bright noisy street.

21

Josh stepped out of the shower. He just got back from a 5-mile run around the base with Syrin. He toweled off in front of the mirror and flexed his six-pack abs. Mr. Lottery Pick has still got it. He slipped on some gray boxers and walked over to his armoire. He put on his Brady jersey, jeans, a pair of low-cut hiking boots, and a tan, leather, calfskin jacket. "Hey, honey, are you ready?"

"Yes, I'm down here, waiting on my woman." Kat stood to the right of the landing and looked up the stairs with her hand on the railing.

Josh bounded down the stairs and hit the bottom with a flourish. He waved his hand over his body from head to toe like a model on *The Price is Right*. "This, my dear, does not happen by accident. Perfection takes time."

"Oh, please. I think Brady's less maintenance than you. I don't know how you did it in the military, let alone the SEALs. Let's go, while I'm young. I want to arrive before the tailgate spread is picked over." Kat went into the kitchen and got a milk bone out of the container and gave it to Syrin.

They took the truck and cruised into the city. Everyone was already at the game, their favorite bar, or watching the game in their living room on a big screen TV. Josh preferred to check out the game at the club. He enjoyed the atmosphere, and the fellow camaraderie of other Pats fans, as the Pats kicked the crap out of some team. Today, it was the Bengals. Plus, he always made sure the club put on a fantastic spread. He charged a hundred bucks a head, but that included the game, all you could eat at the tailgate spread, and all the beer you could drink on tap. These events always sold out, and they always made money.

Josh pulled into the high roller parking garage on the second floor. The line was already six cars deep. Nick, one of the valets, spotted Josh and walked over. Josh and Kat got out of the truck.

"Good morning, Mr. Martin. How do you think the Pats are going to do?"

Josh handed Nick the keys wrapped in a $20 bill. "Kick some Cincinnati ass as usual. Come by after work, if you have the time. I'll make sure you are treated right."

"Thanks, Mr. Martin. I will."

"Watch out for my baby, Nick." Josh rubbed the side of his truck.

"Always, Mr. Martin. We park it next to Mr. Bosco's car in his private section of the garage."

"Good choice, Nick. We'll see you later."

Josh put his arm around Kat, and they walked into the casino, over to the club elevator bank, and hit the up button. They rode up one floor to the Pats entrance and stepped into the Mecca for Pats fans in the Boston area.

The dance floor in the center of Gillette Stadium was now full of tables, chairs, and people. The four bars in each corner of the club were three deep with thirsty fans looking for the free beer on tap. Four huge, 12' x 18' TVs hung from each wall. All the VIP rooms were converted into stadium suites for the game, complete with catering service and private bathrooms; 1,540 customers were on a waiting list to reserve the suites for the game at $10,000 a pop, which didn't include food or liquor.

"Hey, sweetie, I'm going to head to our suite. Junior is hungry." Kat rubbed her tummy.

"Okay, babe. I want to check with Eric to make sure everything is ready, and then I'll be over."

Kat leaned over and kissed him. "Love ya."

"Love you too. See you in a bit." Kat walked away. *Not bad for a country kid from Lancaster, New Hampshire,* he thought.

Josh walked over to the Second Quarter Bar, which was Eric's usual hangout. No sign of him. He stopped Amber, who was carrying a tray of drinks.

"Amber, have you seen Eric?"

"He's over by the entrance door working on some issue." She moved through the crowd to her table.

Josh walked over to the entrance and spotted Eric talking to a middle-aged couple with two boys dressed in Edelman and Vollmer jerseys. The hostess staff checked IDs to verify drinking age. If you were of age, you got a blue band. Underage, you got a bright red band. No band, security threw you out. The line snaked out the door. Prepaid tickets were on the right. Walk-ups were on the left. For VIP/suite patrons, there was a separate entrance on the other side of the club. No sense mixing with the riffraff.

"Hey, Eric. How are things going?"

"Hi, boss. This is Mr. and Mrs. Tremont," Eric pointed to the couple, "and their sons Jason and Peter." Eric was in jeans and a Troy Brown throwback jersey. "They have a ticket to Mr. Bosco's suite, but the reader indicates a counterfeit."

"Mr. Tremont, Mrs. Tremont, nice to meet you. My name's Josh Martin. Let me see what I can do." He extended his hand.

Mr. Tremont shook Josh's hand. "Thank you, Josh."

Josh pulled out his cell phone, walked a few steps away, and punched up Mr. Bosco's cell number. Bosco answered on the third ring.

"Go Pats."

"Good morning, Sir. This is Josh Martin."

"Morning, Josh. Why are you calling me and not making money?"

"I'm making money, Sir. Always. I'm at the front door with a Mr. and Mrs. Tremont plus two boys in Pats jerseys. They have a ticket for your suite, but our scanner says counterfeit."

"Counterfeit? I'll have to check with our guest services. Give it to Kat. Tell her to run it down before next week."

"Yes, Sir. What about the Tremonts?"

"Send them up. They're friends of the family."

"Yes, Sir. Will do."

"And Josh, I need to see you after the game. We can meet in your office. Don't bring Kat."

"Yes, Sir. See you then." Josh killed the call. *Don't bring Kat. What was that all about?*

Josh turned back to the Tremonts. "Well, good news. Mr. Bosco says to send you up. Eric, would you please find someone to escort the Tremonts to Mr. Bosco's suite?"

"Sure thing. If you'd follow me, I'll take you up myself." Eric started moving the Tremonts through the crowd.

"Eric, can I have the ticket? Bosco wants Kat to look into it."

"Here it is." He handed Josh the ticket.

Josh found Kat in their suite hitting the food spread. The pre-game was on TV. The suites were set up as a mini-movie theater with ten double recliners, in black leather, formed in a semi-circle, facing a projection wall with ten speakers arrayed around the room for a stadium surround-sound experience. A full buffet bar ran across the entire back wall with a mini fridge stocked with soda, beer, water, and ice. Today's menu was shrimp, hot dogs, hamburgers, ribs, chicken wings, potato salad, coleslaw, and an assortment of chips. There was a small reception area to the left, behind the recliners, with a couch, an overstuffed chair for conversation, and the private suite bathroom.

"Are you gonna leave some shrimp for me?" Josh scanned the buffet spread.

"Hey, a girl's gotta eat. Plus, I'm eating for two." Kat took a bite of shrimp. "The shrimp is really good."

Josh walked over to Kat and leaned in close. "Who do we have this game?"

"Hector and Marie from accounting. Joyce from guest services, and her date, not sure of the name. General Page and Ellen from two doors down, and Jim and Marie. Jim and Marie are caught in traffic. They were late getting off the base."

"Thanks, babe. Hey, before I forget, Bosco wants you to look into this." Josh handed Kat the Tremont ticket.

"What is it?"

"Some guests of Bosco showed up at the front entrance with a counterfeit ticket. He wants you to look into it. No idea why anyone would counterfeit one of our tickets. I can think of easier ways to make a buck. What's good on the line today?"

"Everything's good, but the shrimp is really fantastic. Eric bought it fresh off the boat."

Josh made a plate of ribs, shrimp, coleslaw, and potato salad, and he grabbed a beer from the fridge. He walked over to his recliner with Kat. "General Page, Sir, welcome. I'm glad to see the Army has landed."

22

—

Thirty miles west of Boston, Chino pulled up a plastic chair, getting ready to enjoy the Patriots game in the day room at the Concord Correctional Institution, located in Concord, Mass. All federal detainees are the responsibility of the U.S. Marshal Service, regardless of which federal agents arrested the individual. The Marshal Service then contracts with state and local agencies to provide holding cells for their detainees. Chino wasn't arraigned yet, because they were still debating what to charge him with, or whether he may turn federal witness against the Centre Street Kings if they charged him with felony murder.

The day room in the federal holding wing was institutionally sparse. A gleaming, waxed, green-and-tan tile floor reflected the glare of the overhead fluorescent lights. Thirty plastic, stackable, school chairs were spread out in front of a single TV mounted on a moveable AV cart. All non-violent federal detainees could view the Pats games every week if they earned the privilege the previous week. It was a big motivator.

Chino sat in the back with two other Centre Street gang members: Victor Ramirez, aka Slim Shady, and Oscar Paredes, aka Double Deuce. Victor was a small Mexican with jet black hair, dark eyes, and a fondness for Eminem music. Oscar was a street kid who grew up in Jamaica Plain. His parents both emigrated from Jamaica. His father was one of the founding members of the Centre Street Kings. He was killed in a drive-by on October 22, when Oscar was eleven. Oscar tattooed two dice on his right forearm with a pair of twos in honor of his father. Both players had gold, right incisors with the letter C.

"Yo, man, good to see you guys. I thought I was gonna have to chill by myself. I can't believe the crazy shit in the hotel room. Fucking knock on the door and bam, cartel dude smokes Benny, and bam, white dude smokes the Colombian. Next thing I know, I'm in the back of a van headed to this motherfuckin place. At least we can see the Pats kick the Red BB gun all over the field. What did Big Papi say about all this shit? Did he find me a lawyer?"

"Fuck, I don't know." Oscar leaned over to talk with Chino. "We're doing some bidness on the corner, and some G-men roll up in two black rides. Say something about federal warrants for Victor and me, and boom, here we are with you. I never did see Big Papi."

"Why don't you three homos shut the fuck up, so I can enjoy the game?" A big black dude, a few chairs in front, turned to look at Oscar.

"Why don't you come back here and suck my dick like yo momma did?" Oscar got up and kicked the chair clear from behind him. It skidded across the room.

"What did you say to me, nigga?" The black dude also pushed his chair away, got to his feet, and glared at Oscar. He moved his head side to side and flexed his muscles, which rippled under his shirt.

"Yo, Oscar, man. Sit down and shut the fuck up. That dude will mess us up." Chino grabbed Oscar's shirt to pull him back.

"Nah, man. This dude needs to be taught some manners." Oscar picked up one of the chairs next to him and hit the black dude over the head, knocked him to the ground, and the day room erupted into a brawl with chairs and fists flying.

Victor pulled a shank made from a sharpened spoon and masking tape from the front of his prison pants. He grabbed the back of Chino's head and stabbed him eight times in the throat. Warm blood flowed over his hands as he worked the shank into Chino's throat, and then the trickle of warmth turned into a spraying fountain as he hit the jugular. Chino was dead before he hit the floor.

23

The Patriots set up in the victory formation with 54 seconds left in the game. They were beating the Bengals 35-17, another notch in the Brady Hall of Fame career. Josh leaned over to whisper to Kat.

"Can you close up here, and help Eric with the changeover? Bosco wants to meet with me after the game."

"Do you know what he wants?"

"No idea."

"Okay, you go ahead. I'll handle things here."

"Thanks, babe. See you in a bit." Josh stood to leave. He walked over to General Page. "Thanks for coming, General. I need to go check the books." They shook hands.

"Thanks for having us, Josh. Always good to get away with friends."

"You bet, Sir. See you back at the ranch." Josh left the suite.

The crowd was pretty thick, as people still basked in the glory of another Patriots victory. The free drinks and food ended with the last play of the game, so the bar was backed up with fans trying to get the last free beer, as the game clock over the bar ticked down. Josh found Eric and told him he was meeting with Bosco in a couple of minutes. He pushed through the crowd to his private elevator and nodded to security guarding the door. Everyone wanted to go for a ride on the elevator when they were drunk.

Josh walked to his office and headed over to his bar. He got two glasses and filled them with four stainless steel ice cubes from the fridge and put them on the conference table. He retrieved a bottle of Woodford Reserve Master's Collection, Sonoma-Cutrer Pinot Noir finish, from the top shelf, and set it next to the glasses. He took a chair, which faced the windows and his office entrance, and enjoyed the setting sun over the skyline of Boston.

"Hey, Josh, you in there?" boomed Enzo Bosco.

"Yeah, boss. In here."

In walked Enzo, who looked like the second coming of Bob Kraft, dark blue suit, two-tone light blue shirt with a white collar, red power tie, and white sneakers. "Oh, good, you're all set up. Pour me two fingers." Enzo sloughed off the suit jacket and tossed it on one of the chair backs, stripped off his tie, and tossed it over the jacket, and sat down in the chair opposite Josh.

Josh poured two fingers over the cubes in each class and slid one over to Enzo. "To another Pats victory." Josh lifted his glass to toast.

"To another Pats victory." Enzo clanked glasses with Josh. They both took a sip. "Man, good stuff." Enzo licked his lips, so he didn't miss a drop.

"Yes, Sir." They both set their glasses down. "So, what can I do for you, boss?"

Enzo stared at his glass for a second and swirled the cubes around. He took another sip and set it down. He looked straight at Josh. "Josh, you know I look at you as the son I never had, so this is really tough, but I'll get right to it."

Josh could feel the "Oh shit" rising in the pit of his stomach.

"I just found out this morning. You've got another day job. Is that true?"

I guess 4 billion bucks buys you quite the network. Josh mulled his answer. "Look, Sir, you know I've always been honest with you, but I can't answer that question."

"I guess you just did. We did a thorough background on you before I let you buy the half interest in the Champions Club and run it. So, someone did a good backstory on you, which can only be done by a few government agencies. Answer me one thing: was the money real?"

"Yes, Sir. The money is real and almost the entire backstory. The truth sells better than fiction. You just eliminate a few key details. The money was an inheritance from my grandfather. He was one of the founding members of the Bank of Boston." Josh took another sip of bourbon. "I have to ask you, Sir, does anyone else know? This is important."

"No. No one else knows. Jesus Christ, Josh, you know what kinda business we run here. Not everyone is clean in the strictest interpretation of the law, and some of my investment partners wouldn't approve of a federal agent as an employee, let alone a partner." Enzo pushed out of the chair and went over to the window to look at the city. The sun was just about below the horizon, and the lights of the city twinkled like stars in heaven. "This is quite the view, isn't it?"

"Yes, Sir. It's quite the view. Where do we go from here?"

"My accountants worked up the value of the club this morning. We cleared 6 million last year, after taxes. With a 6x multiplier, the club is worth 36 million. 49% of that is around 18 million. The club's success is mainly due to your efforts of building the staff and running the operations, so I added a 2 million severance package."

"Are you firing me, boss?"

Enzo walked back from the window, sat back down in the chair, and took another sip of bourbon. He reached over and pulled his suit jacket off the chair. The tie fell on the floor. He reached into the jacket, took out a printed check, and tossed it across the table to Josh. Pay to the order of Joshua C. Martin, $20,000,000 and no cents.

"I'm not firing you, son. I'm giving you a choice. Resign from the day job you don't have and come work for me full time or accept this buyout and continue to serve your country. We remain friends, either way." Enzo looked at Josh.

Josh stared at the check in disbelief. That was a lot of fucking money. Not a bad return on a $2 million investment, but this was his dream job. But that kind of money would buy you freedom and time. Freedom to do what you wanted, and time to do it, without worrying about where your next meal was coming from, not that he had worried about money for a long time.

"Can I have some time to think about it? I need to talk to Kat and figure some things out at my moonlighting gig."

"Of course, I expected that." He stood and drained the bourbon. He set the glass on the conference table, picked his tie up off the floor, and gathered his suit coat. "How much time do you need?"

Josh put his hands on the conference table and pushed himself up. "A week should do it, Sir." They shook hands.

"Okay, Josh. Say hi to Kat for me. She can keep her job if you decide to continue to work for the Feds." Enzo strolled out of the office. Josh heard Enzo greet some of the cleaning folks in the hallway.

Josh finished his drink and took both glasses over to the sink. He rinsed them and set them on the counter. He walked out of his office and headed back down to the club to find Kat. They had a lot to talk about. Halfway to the club, Josh heard the distinctive two-beep alert on his phone. He looked at the screen. Chino, aka Andre Pino, killed 1325 today at Concord Correctional Institution by known gang members. NFI. The screen then went blank.

"Son of a bitch! Why whack Chino?"

LCDR Max Lindy picked up the phone on the watch center desk on the second ring. "Good evening, Director."

"Did you pass the information to White 55 on the murder of Andre Pino?"

"Yes, Sir. We just sent it."

"Anything else available?"

"No, Sir. Just the subjects involved in the murder were Centre Street King gang members."

"All right, thanks. Have a good watch."

Max hung up the phone. He went back to the football game on the op center TV. The Jets still sucked, the cross of being from New York.

Josh got back to the club and found Eric and Kat chatting at the Second Quarter bar.

"You know she's married, right?" Josh walked up and leaned on the bar next to Kat.

"I was just seeing if she was interested in a better offer." Eric was drying glasses and putting them back in the trays.

"Yeah, she might be shopping around. She's going to need a sugar daddy to support the new bambino." Josh leaned over and kissed Kat.

Eric stopped drying glasses. "You're shitting me. Kat's pregnant?"

"Yup, she's no longer a virgin." Kat blushed at the attention.

"Out fucking standing. I guess that explains the ginger ale. When's the blessed event?"

Josh gave the reserve salute, which was a shrug of the shoulders and a stupid look on his face.

"Leave it to the squid to not know what's going on. Probably doesn't even know how it happened." Eric laughed. Josh scratched his forehead with his right middle finger extended.

"May 10th. We won't know the exact due date until my follow-up appointment in the third month." Kat spread her fingers on her tummy.

"Well, congratulations. Great news. You guys will make outstanding parents. At least, one of you will." Josh kept scratching his forehead with his middle finger.

"If you boys are finished, it's time to get momma home to bed. No jokes, boys."

Eric grabbed Josh around the head and kissed him on the forehead. "Outstanding, bro. You'll make a great dad, and Uncle Eric will be here to teach him, or her, all the things they shouldn't do." They fist-bumped. Josh put his arm around Kat, and they walked over to the elevator.

Kat checked Josh with her hip. "What did Enzo want?"

"I'll tell you in the truck."

24

Big Papi watched the Packers and Cowboys game in the main dining area of Marley's Jerk Chicken and not in his back office. The restaurant consisted of 16 tables for four, spread out in an open area. There was a counter to the left, as you entered the restaurant, for takeout orders and for the hostess to seat you, and a full bar on the back wall. The place was mostly empty, with four couples spread out enjoying a slow Sunday evening. The takeout business was brisk, with drivers coming and going with boxes of takeout, and the phone rang all the time. Football Sunday was always the best day of the week. If he wasn't making so much money off heroin, Big Papi could make a decent living off the restaurant business. It did make a good front for conducting business.

Big Papi also had some house rules. No bangers could eat in the restaurant; takeout only. No business takes place in the restaurant, only the back offices, which were two in addition to his storeroom office. Paying customers in the restaurant, takeout customers, and anyone within a two-block radius was untouchable. Residents quickly learned the safest person in Jamaica Plain was a customer of Marley's Jerk Chicken restaurant. Plus, the food was fabulous. Big Papi arranged for his Aunt Clarice to immigrate from the island 3 years ago. She ran the kitchen, and she was an old-school cook. There were 4 degrees of hot sauce on the counter to add to your chicken order: Tourist, Medium, Hot, and Local. Even Big Papi couldn't eat the local.

Big Papi was eating the chicken special and drinking a Red Stripe when Big Dog walked through the door and over to Big Papi's table. He lowered his considerable bulk into the chair opposite Big Papi.

"How's the leg?" Big Dog looked at Big Papi.

"Still motherfucking hurts. I've been popping the Oxi, which takes the edge off. Any word on Theresa and Nichole?"

"No, boss. We got everyone looking, but no sign. They must have moved them out of the city, or we'd know."

"What about the other thing?" Big Papi took another bite of chicken and licked the sauce off his fingers.

Big Dog leaned over the table. "Our friend went on vacation this afternoon."

"You're sure?" Big Papi wiped his fingers on his napkin and tossed it on the restaurant table.

"Yeah, boss."

"That was fast." Big Papi took a sip of beer. The cool hops went well with jerk chicken. Reminded him of the islands.

"Ask, and ye shall receive." Big Dog leaned back in the chair. "How's the chicken?"

"You want some dinner?"

"Sure."

Big Papi held up two fingers and then pointed to Big Dog. Aunt Clarice nodded from behind the counter. One #2 Special with a Red Stripe coming up.

Nick parked the truck on the front curb when Kat and Josh walked out of the casino. Nick tossed the keys to Josh, who caught them with one hand, and then he held the door for Kat.

"Thanks, Nick." Kat climbed into the truck. Nick pushed the door shut and scurried around the front of the truck to get the door for Josh. Josh handed Nick a folded twenty.

"Thanks, Mr. Martin."

"You're welcome, Nick. Enjoy your evening." Josh climbed into the truck, and Nick shut the door. Josh wound through the casino complex past the shoreline. The beach area was already converted from summer to fall foliage, and the water was now the largest skating rink in the world. A variety of lights lit the rink to create any image or mood. It was now bathed in a soft glow like moonlight, and hundreds of couples skated hand in hand. "When I Need You," by Leo Sayer, played from the speakers throughout the beach front.

"You need to take me skating." Kat watched the skaters gliding in the glow of the rink's lights, as they drove by.

"I can take you skating in Switzerland tomorrow if you want." Josh turned on the defroster to clear the front windshield.

"What are you talking about?"

Josh handed her the check.

"Holy shit. What is this?" Kat turned to look at Josh.

"Enzo's offer for our share of the club." Josh checked his left side mirror and pulled into the traffic.

"Why would he make an offer for our share of the club?" Kat put the check on the center console and sat back in her seat.

"He found out I have a second job." Josh exited the casino traffic and headed south on I93.

"How did he find out?"

"No idea, but 4 billion bucks buys you a lot of access." Josh kept to the far-right lane, so he could just follow along with the traffic. Not interested in fighting with Mass-holes today.

"What are you going to do?"

"Not me…we. What are we going to do?" He kept three seconds behind a gray Dodge truck.

"Well, this is a lot of money. What did he say?"

"Basically, having an FBI agent as an employee would not be good for business, since the casino lifestyle is kind of a gray area in the eyes of law enforcement. So, we have two options. I resign from the FBI and go work for Enzo full time, or we sell him our ownership in the Champions for 20 million. The 20 million is about two million over the club's valuation. He's giving it to us as a severance." Josh couldn't hang behind the Dodge truck any longer. He stepped on the gas and felt the 700 HP Ford surge forward. He cut left in a break in the traffic and then scooted back right to get in front of the Dodge.

"Feel better?" Kat checked her right-side mirror to look at the Dodge.

"Yes, much better. Order has been restored to the universe."

"Can Enzo do this?"

"Yup, if it's 'a fair and equitable offer,' which would explain the 2-million-dollar kicker. No doubt about it being fair and equitable." The Dodge truck was now tailgating. Josh kept an eye on the road and the rear-view mirror.

"I guess your friend doesn't like the new order in the universe. So, how much time did he give us?" Kat watched the Dodge close on the rear bumper in her mirror and gripped the armrest on the door.

"One week, and you get to keep your job either way." Josh braked to move the Dodge back.

"Well, that was nice of him. I planned on giving my two weeks' notice anyway. I'm ready to be a full-time mom."

Josh headed south on Route 3 with the gray Dodge still on his tail.

"What do you plan on doing with your friend?" Kat watched the Dodge move side to side in her mirror.

"Watch and learn, sweetie. Call Detective Hollis." The phone rang through the truck speaker system three times.

"Detective Hollis."

"Ryan, this is Josh Martin." Josh checked the truck in his rear mirror. Dickhead turned on his high beams.

"Hey, General, what can I do for you?"

"My bride and I are headed home from the game at the casino, and we picked up an aggressive driver. They're right on my ass now. Gray, Dodge, truck. I can't see the license plate because they're so close."

"Where are you?"

"We just got on 3 south from I93 and hit traffic. We're bumper to bumper in the far-right lane, just passing Best Buy."

"Okay, I'll get someone moving your way."

"Thanks, Ryan."

"Sure thing, Josh. You have a good evening." The call ended.

"You're such an ass." Kat let go of the armrest and relaxed.

"No, I'm just keeping America safe from the scourge of Dodge trucks. You know, don't let your friends grow up to drive Dodges."

Josh kept an eye on the passenger side mirror, as the traffic bumped along at a crawl. He couldn't see the front end of the Dodge because it was so close to his bumper. He could see that he was #1 in the eyes of the Yankee fan driving the Dodge. He was tempted to stop quick. Get out. Smack the driver a couple of times, and get back in. He finally caught sight of the flashing blue lights coming up the right-side shoulder. The lights danced off the stop-and-go traffic like a light show at Christmas. The Braintree cruiser stopped running up the shoulder when it came abreast of the Dodge truck, then cut in behind the Dodge.

"Driver in the gray Dodge truck, pull your vehicle to the side and keep your hands at 10 and 2 on the steering wheel," blared from the cop's PA system. The Dodge edged out of traffic to the breakdown lane.

Josh powered down his driver side window and gave a wave to his #1 fan.

"Such an ass." Kat laughed.

Traffic finally started to clear, and they made it back to the Air Station. Josh honked twice in honor of CDR Shea, as they passed the A-4 Memorial, and he swung into the driveway. Syrin bounded out the back door when they opened it. She wagged her tail and barked her happy bark.

"Who's a good girl?" Josh wrestled with Syrin. "I'll take the excited lady out for a walk before she pees on the floor."

"Okay, this tired lady is headed up to bed." She went into the house.

Josh headed over to the empty lawn next to the house. Syrin ran around the yard looking for squirrels, or anything else, that may want to play. Josh got a tennis ball out of the truck and threw it for Syrin; time to burn off that excess energy after being cooped up all afternoon. Josh's phone vibrated in his pocket. He slid it out. The caller ID said, Detective Hollis. He hit the accept button.

"Hey, Ryan, thanks for the help earlier."

"No problem. I just called to thank you. The guy we stopped had an outstanding bench warrant for non-payment of child support and aggravated assault. You're making me look like a hero."

"Glad I could help. Any movement on old Leroy?" Josh took the ball from Syrin and tossed it again.

"We're getting ready to move on him. I'll let you know when we got 'em."

"Thanks, Ryan. I'm thinking that beer is starting to look like steaks at your place."

"Roger that. You have a good night, General." Ryan ended the call.

"Syrin, come." Syrin ran to Josh at a sprint and stopped in front of him. "Good girl. Now let's go in and tell mommy that daddy is not an ass."

25

Josh rolled out of the rack at 0500 for his daily 5-mile run. Kat was curled up in the sheets, snoring like a sailor after a three-day bender. Must be pregnancy related. He slipped out of the bedroom, so he didn't wake the sleeping she-beast, and walked into an adjoining bedroom to get dressed. Syrin followed him out. He put on his running clothes, a T-shirt with Coast Guard on the front, running shorts, Nike Air Max shoes, and headed downstairs. It was still dark and chilly, so he grabbed a Navy hoodie before he ran outside. The crisp fall air always woke him up.

"Come on, Syrin. Let's go." They headed out into the pre-dawn darkness, left on Glendenning, and then left on Shea into the heart of the old base. He followed the same route every morning. Through the base to the airport tarmac, around the runway, and back through the base to home. He clocked the distance with a GPS at 5 miles. Some people would not like running through an abandoned military base in darkness, with a ghost around every corner, and a mugger in every shadow, but most people didn't run with a hair missile. With a nose 40 times more sensitive than a human, and twice as fast as a fit human, Syrin would smell a ghost a ½ mile away, and run him down, before Josh even knew he was there.

Josh could make the loop in under 35 minutes if he wanted to push it, but he usually finished in 45 minutes at a nice 9-minutes-per-mile clip. He appreciated the solitude of a morning run with a dog. No cartels, no drugs, no crime, no casinos, no decisions, and no drill instructor screaming in your ear. They cruised past the hangar at the entrance to the airstrip, where Aerosmith once made a music video and held a concert, and then through an open gate to the airfield. Nature was doing its best to reclaim the strip, with grass shooting up between the cracks in the asphalt. They finished the circumference of the airfield, ran back through the gate, and headed home.

Syrin always beat him and bounded up the front steps to do her victory dance, which was also the "mommy must be up by now, feed me" dance.

Josh pushed through the front door and stopped to listen. Everything was quiet, except for Syrin panting. The she-beast must still be sleeping. Josh stripped off his hoodie, draped it over the staircase banister, and headed into the kitchen. He hit brew on the coffee maker and fed Syrin. When Syrin was finished, and nosing the bowl around the floor to get the last mystery nugget under it, Josh gave the command, "Fetch." She made a beeline for the front doggy door and was gone. Thirty seconds later, she was back with the Boston *Globe* and *USA Today* in her mouth. "Release."

He took the papers from Syrin. She laid down on the kitchen floor. Josh finished both papers, two cups of coffee, and a bagel. He looked at the clock on the microwave: 0715. Time to get the she-beast up. "Syrin." Syrin sat up at attention. "Go get mommy." Boom, she was off down the hall, nails scratching the floor, tearing up the stairs, and bounding into the bedroom.

"God dammit, Josh. Get your dog off me. Syrin, no!" came screaming from above.

Josh called, "Syrin, come." Another bound across the bedroom, quick paws on the stairs, tear down the hallway, and Syrin stopped in front of Josh. "Good girl." Josh stroked her on the neck. "Release." Syrin went into the living room to find her bed for her morning nap.

"You could just wake me up normally, ya know," Kat yelled from the top of the stairs.

"No fun for Syrin in that. Do you want breakfast?"

"No, I'm just going to have cereal this morning. I ate too much yesterday."

"Okay. I'm going to take a shower and head to work."

"All right, I gotta find my robe, and I'll be down."

Josh headed into the butler's pantry to take a shower.

26

Josh wheeled the truck into the parking garage at One Center Plaza. The yellow arm lifted, and he pulled in. He parked in space 465, paid for by Katherine Montgomery; 520 bucks a month for a space he rarely used. *I should get into the parking garage business. Low overhead with loan-sharking rates,* thought Josh. On the plus side, it was close to the Boston Common and downtown venues, so they used it when they went to dinner or the theater. The monthly rate also gave them 24/7 access, which was good for undercover work. He could come to the office at oh dark thirty without any hassles and no printed tickets of his comings and goings.

Josh got out of the truck and checked his tie in the side mirror. Perfect. He got his computer backpack off the rear seat and headed into the office. He wore a dark blue Zegna suit, white shirt, maroon tie with small diagonal stripes, and black leather Johnston and Murphy cap toe shoes. He looked more like a Wall Street investor than an FBI agent. That was the point, and only one person on the sixth floor knew he was an agent.

The FBI main office encompassed the entire sixth floor of One Center Plaza. The Special Agent in Charge was Howard "Hammering Hank" Mathers who made his bones fighting corruption in Chicago. In addition to the Boston office, Hammering Hank was also responsible for 10 resident agent offices scattered throughout New England, and the FBI Law Enforcement Office, near the Boston waterfront, on Atlantic Avenue.

Josh "officially" visited One Center Plaza two years ago, when he met Hammering Hank during an introduction meeting for Operation Trifecta. Operation Trifecta was an undercover FBI operation to identify an intelligence leak and mole in the Boston DEA office, disrupt the New England operations of the La Libertad Cartel, and dismantle the Boston Street gang called the Centre Street Kings. Two years, and countless hours of investigative work, down the drain in one Saturday morning. Josh hit the elevator button for the fifth floor.

The FBI also leased the entire fifth floor of One Center Plaza, but they did not advertise it. In fact, the entire floor was devoid of markings. There were no listings on the building directory, and the entire fifth floor was devoid of labels—no names, office suite numbers, or contact phone numbers. All deliveries went to the sixth floor with attention, "Mail Room."

Josh stepped off the elevator and walked right to a single set of glass doors. He pushed through the doors into a small anteroom with two plastic chairs on either side of the glass doors, a small window with a speaker mounted on the base, and a single door to the left. A cute redhead with the look of an intern sat behind the window.

"May I help you?" the voice behind the counter asked.

"I have a 1000 appointment with Mr. Randolph." Josh checked his tie to make sure it was in place.

"Please have a seat. Someone will be with you shortly."

Josh took a seat in the first chair to the left of the glass doors and put his backpack at his feet. *$5,000 suit and I'm getting it wrinkled waiting outside the principal's office. I guess this is what failure feels like.*

The door buzzed, and Agent Chris Anthony walked out. Chris was from Arizona, with a muscular build, a faded tan, a thinning brown hairline, and a brown mustache that was new. He was dressed in a dark blue sports coat, light blue shirt, blue tie, khaki pants, and penny loafers with no penny in the loafer. Fashion in the FBI was boring at best.

"Damn, Josh, you clean up pretty good, but I think our only intern position is filled." Chris tilted his head left towards the pretty redhead.

"I'm actually here as a consultant to the FBI to provide fashion advice." Josh gave Chris the once-over. "Penny loafers. Really?" Josh lifted himself out of the chair with the armrests, and they shook hands.

"It's casual Monday. I'm setting a new fashion trend." Chris modeled his shoes.

"Well, I wish you luck with that. Is the boss in?"

"Yeah, he's in his office. I'm supposed to take you back."

They walked back down a hallway with two large conference rooms on the left and a series of offices on the right. The walls on both sides were covered with photographs of FBI cases and operations. There were no markings on any offices, including Agent Randolph's, which was a large corner space at the end of the hallway. Chris knocked twice on the door.

"Come in."

Chris turned the knob on the door, pushed it open, and stuck his head in. "Josh is here, Sir."

"Great. Send him in."

Chris stood back and let Josh walk by. "Good luck."

"Thanks, Chris." Josh walked into the office.

27

The office was large with a full conference table to the left, surrounded by eight chairs, and a small seating area with four black leather chairs around a small coffee table to the right. *The Wall Street Journal, Boston Globe, Washington Post,* and *The New York Times* were all arrayed on the coffee table. Four more padded wooden chairs were set up in front of Randolph's large cherry finish desk in the center of the room. A lighted bookcase ran along the entire width of the office behind his desk. There was a door to the left of his desk, as you faced it, which led to a sleeping area and private bathroom. The office was notable for its lack of personal mementos. There were the obligatory pictures of the President, Attorney General, FBI Director, and Hammering Hank, hanging on the wall to the right as you walked into the office, but nothing of Agent Randolph's personal life, mainly due to the fact Agent Randolph did not exist. There were five Assistant Special Agents listed for the Boston office of the FBI, and Agent Randolph was not one of them. He reported straight to the director.

Agent Randolph walked around his desk and extended his hand. "Good morning, Josh. How was your weekend?"

Josh shook his hand, not a bad grip for an old man. "Pretty good, Sir. Pats won. Always a good weekend in Boston when the Patriots win."

"Let's set up over here." Agent Randolph motioned to the conference table. He sat down at the head of the table facing the door, and Josh pulled out a chair and sat to his left.

"Do you want some coffee?"

"Yes, Sir, that would be great."

"How do you take it?"

"If it's good coffee, black."

"Oh, it's good coffee. I'm friends with our liaison in Costa Rica, Rich Lowell. He sends me a shipment of the local stuff every month. Do you know him?"

"No, Sir."

"He's a good guy. If you ever take a vacation to Costa Rica, give him a call before you go. He'll hook you up."

The door opened, and a woman about 55, with blond hair cut short, a red skirt, and white top straight out of the Talbots catalog, stepped into the opening.

"Ellie, can you get us two cups of coffee, black, from the personal stash?"

"Of course, Sir. Also, your two guests are in Conference Room 1."

"Thanks, Ellie."

The door closed, and Ellie departed to get the coffee.

"Buzzer under the conference table?" Josh shifted in his chair to face his boss.

Agent Randolph tapped the table twice. "Saves me from having to yell, and I can discreetly get rid of guests who overstay their welcome. Ellie is Ellie Marks. She's been with me for about ten years. She came with me from DC, when I transferred up here. Did you hear about Chino?"

"Yes, Sir. I got a text on Sunday. Can't figure out why the Centre Street Kings would want to get rid of one of their own. Any luck on finding out how the DEA found out about the buy?"

"We can ask them in person. The two agents from the incident on Saturday are the guests in Conference Room 1."

"Are they cleared for the other stuff?" Josh reached for his backpack and pulled out a leather portfolio. He set it on the conference table.

"Yes, I had them cleared by our folks and our other friends."

"Speaking of which, I got the weekly intel dump." Josh opened the top zipper compartment on his backpack and pulled out a manila folder. He passed it over to Agent Randolph, who opened the folder and scanned the sheet of paper.

Mr. Evan Bloomfield, from Southside Bank and Trust, is embezzling money from the bank. He has the proceeds in an offshore account in the Cayman Islands, Account #78865413. Mr. Leroy Johnson robbed and killed the store clerk at the ABC Liquor store in Braintree, Mass, and he is hiding at his aunt's, 178 Broad Street, Braintree, Mass. Massachusetts State Senator Mrs. Ellen Fairchild is taking kickbacks from Morgan Construction for the development of the Boston Waterfront."

"Did you contact someone at Braintree PD?"

"Yes, Sir. Detective Ryan Hollis. We've done business before. He knows the drill."

"Okay, I'll pass the rest of this stuff up to the sixth floor." Agent Randolph put the paper back in the folder and put the folder in his leather executive notepad.

There were two knocks on the door, and Ellie walked through with a tray of two steaming mugs of coffee. She set the tray to the left of Josh and placed coasters in front of Josh and her boss, and then put a coffee mug on each.

"They are hot, gentlemen. Fresh out of the pot." Ellie picked up the tray.

"Thanks, Ellie," Agent Randolph said. "Could you please send in our two guests, and make sure they have coffee?"

"Already done, Sir. They each got a mug when I put them in the conference room. I'll get them now."

"Thanks, Ellie."

Josh took a sip of the coffee. It was good. "Great coffee, Sir. Back when I was in the Coast Guard, we would always buy the local stuff during port calls in the Caribbean. Never could figure out why the coffee in the local supermarket there tasted much better than the stuff we buy back in the States."

"They must export the seconds to us." Agent Randolph took a sip of coffee. "This is good. Ellie does a great job on the brewing."

Another knock on the door and Ellie walked in trailed by two guests carrying mugs of coffee. Both Josh and Agent Randolph got out of their chairs.

Agent Li came in first. Her black hair was pulled back tight in a ponytail. She had minimal makeup, but it couldn't hide her classic Chinese beauty. She wore the standard agent official uniform, a dark navy pantsuit with white button-down shirt, and black low heel shoes. She was trailed by

Agent Britt, who wore an ill-fitted blue suit fresh from the rack at Kohl's, a wrinkled white shirt, and a red tie. His long brown hair was also pulled back in a ponytail. They both came to a dead stop when they spotted Josh.

"What the fuck is he doing here?" Agent Britt said.

"You gotta be kidding me." Agent Li stared daggers at Josh.

They both set their coffee and meeting materials on the conference table and stepped back like they were getting ready to arrest someone.

"Please sit down, and I'll explain," Agent Randolph said. He gestured to the seats. "Thanks, Ellie." Ellie nodded and closed the door on her way out. Both Li and Britt pulled out chairs at the end of the table and sat down. They both continued the death stares, which Josh thought was humorous since he could put them both down in about two minutes. Well, the Army hobo for sure. The Chinese lady may take a while since she looked like she could kick some ass. Both Randolph and Josh sat back in their seats and took another sip of the fine coffee.

"This," Agent Randolph pointed at Josh, "is Special Agent Josh Martin of the FBI."

"You're shitting me." Agent Britt looked like someone spit in his coffee.

Josh took his FBI credentials out of his left breast pocket and tossed them down the table to Britt, who caught them with his right hand. He flipped them open.

"Son of a bitch." Britt passed the credentials to Agent Li.

"Aww, crap." Agent Li tossed the credentials back down the table to Josh. They both relaxed into their seats.

"Aww, crap is correct. Two years of undercover work disappeared." Agent Randolph stared at both Britt and Li with a perturbed look on his face.

"Wait a minute…we didn't know." Agent Li sat forward and put her hands on the edge of the conference table to challenge Randolph. "We were chasing the ghost of the Cash Man."

"Which leads to the second question, how did you find out about the buy?" Agent Randolph took a sip of coffee to ease the tension.

"Benny," Agent Li sat back in her seat.

"Thought so," Josh shook his head in resignation.

"We picked him up on a possession charge two weeks ago. It was his third strike. He gave you up in about 10 minutes." Agent Li nodded at Josh.

"What about Casas?" Josh turned to face Li.

"We know the La Libertad Cartel rotates their rep about every 90 days. We always get an airport alert when someone on our watch list shows up. Casas came through Logan on Tuesday. Benny said the cartel rep is always at a large buy, so we figured he would be there." Agent Li took a sip of coffee.

"No idea about me?" Josh looked at Li to gauge her response.

"No. We thought you were a war hero turned drug dealer. Whoever did your backstory, did a helluva job. Eh, sorry, Sir, but I gotta ask…"

"Why didn't we include the DEA in a narcotics investigation?" Agent Randolph offered.

"Yes, Sir."

Agent Randolph looked hard at both Agent Britt and Li. "What I'm about to tell you can go no farther than this room. Your SAC knows about it, but he's it. Understand?"

"Yes, Sir," both Li and Britt replied in unison.

"You've got a mole in your Boston office at a pretty senior level."

"Fuck, I knew it." Agent Britt hit the table with his hand. "Sorry, Sir. It's just we've had several investigations blown for no apparent reason with the La Libertad Cartel. We show up to do a raid, and the house is empty when our CI said there was a large quantity of dope. A couple of CIs disappeared without a trace. Things got weird. We chalked it up to shit happens."

"What do you want from us?" Agent Li looked from Randolph to Josh.

"Did you file reports on your investigation of the Cash Man and the incident on Saturday?" Agent Randolph opened a folder in front of him.

"Yes, Sir. We did." Agent Li's shoulders slumped because she knew the ramifications of her answer.

Agent Randolph turned to Josh. "Well, I guess you're out of play."

"I would second that." Agent Li ran her finger around the lip of her coffee mug. "No way you can show up as the Cash Man now. You'd get made as a cop."

There was a knock on the door, and Ellie stuck her head in. "Sir, you have the director on line one."

"Thanks, Ellie." Agent Randolph stood along with Agent Li, Agent Britt, and Josh.

"Well, if you'll excuse me, I must take this call. Agent Li, Agent Britt, thank you for coming by. I'll be in touch with you on a game plan to go forward. We need some time to sort this stuff out. Ellie will show you out. Josh, could you hang back a bit?"

"Yes, Sir." Josh closed his portfolio.

Everyone shook hands, and Ellie held the door open for Agent Li and Britt, who followed her out of the office. She closed the door behind her.

Agent Randolph sat back down in his chair.

"What about the director, Sir?"

"No phone call, Josh. Just a quick way to end the meeting. I don't think they were going to provide any more information."

"Ah, the magic buzzer. I bet you've received quite a few phone calls during meetings." He sat back in his chair.

"More than my share."

"We also have another problem." Josh reached into his backpack and pulled out the Enzo check and slid it across the table to Agent Randolph. "Enzo knows."

Agent Randolph looked at the check and gave it back. "A lot of zeros. How did he find out?"

"No idea. He approached me after the game yesterday in my casino office. The money is for my share of the club."

"He wants you out?"

"No, he gave me an option. Resign from the FBI and keep the club, or take the money, and I'm out."

"How much time did he give you?"

"A week."

"Well, I guess that makes the decision for us."

"Yeah, I'm afraid so."

"Any idea on what you're going to do?"

"Not a clue, but then, it's not my decision."

"Yeah, I hear that. Chris Anthony's got your firearms. They were cleared, so you can have them back. Why don't you take a week of leave and figure things out with your bride? Come back and see me next Monday."

Josh rose out of his chair. "Thank you, Sir. See you in a week." Josh picked up his backpack and walked out of the office.

28

Quinn Christy was back at his usual table at O'Toole's. He arrived before the lunch crowd so that he could get his favorite spot. He put a tablet and two folders on the restaurant table set for four near the back wall. Alyssa came by to grab his order.

"Good morning, Alyssa. I'll have the corned beef sandwich, a side of French fries, and a Guinness. There will also be one more for lunch."

"Okay, Mr. Christy. Do you want me to put your order in now, or wait for your friend?"

"Put the order in now. I'm not sure my friend will be eating."

"Yes, Sir, Mr. Christy." Alyssa walked away to place the order, and Quinn watched her go. Brooks Brothers douche bag was right; it was nice to watch her walk away. Too bad he couldn't get the fucking cartel to walk away. *I gotta figure this out, or I'm going to get fucked either way,* he thought. He tapped the laptop with his fingers. Alyssa brought the Guinness back and set the glass in front of Quinn. He took a drink and wiped the foam away from his mouth with the back of his left hand. He took another drink and saw the Brooks Brothers douche bag walk through the front door. He spotted Quinn and headed through the crowd to his table. Still wearing a gray suit. Must be laundry day.

Mr. Smith pushed across the green leather bench in front of Agent Christy. "Good morning, Quinn. Do you have something for me?"

"Do you want lunch first? I already ordered, not knowing if you were going to eat."

"Is the pretty waitress on duty?"

"She is. In fact, she took my order."

"Then I think I'll eat. What did you order?"

"Corned beef sandwich, fries, and a Guinness." Quinn waved to Alyssa. She walked over. "My friend here is going to order."

"Okay, what can I get ya?"

"I'll have the same thing as my friend here, but I'd like some of your excellent coffee instead of the Guinness."

"Yes, Sir. Corned beef sandwich, fries, and coffee coming right up. Do you want the coffee now?"

"That would be splendid, thank you."

Alyssa walked back to the bar and came back with a mug of coffee. She set it on a coaster in front of Mr. Smith. They both watched her make the transit.

"I can see why you eat here. So, what do you have for me?"

"I have something huge, but I need some assurances before I pass it over."

"You think you're in a position to negotiate?"

"I do. I need to disappear."

"Disappear? I can arrange that now. No trouble."

"Not like that. I need to retire. They'll come looking for me; once I turn this over."

"Now, you do pique my interest," Mr. Smith said.

Alyssa brought the food over, and they both fell silent.

"Here you go. Two corned beef sandwiches with fries, and a cup of coffee for the well-dressed gentlemen. Can I get you guys anything else?"

"No, I think we're good." Quinn reached for a French fry.

"Okay, you enjoy."

The sandwiches were piled high with corned beef, sauerkraut, and slathered in German hot mustard, and the fries were hand-cut, lightly salted, and hot from the oven. They both attacked the sandwiches with gusto, forgetting all about the discussion. When they were done, Mr. Smith wiped his mouth with his napkin.

"Now that was a good sandwich," Mr. Smith said. "So, back to business, what kind of retirement plan are you talking about?"

"I want to retire and walk away."

"You want out? You're asking a lot. Our employer has a lot invested in you."

"I know, but this is worth it. I need to leave before they trace it back to me." Quinn took another swig of the Guinness.

"If this is as big as you say it is, we may be able to work something out."

Quinn handed him two, plain, green folders.

Mr. Smith took the folders and scanned each one. They were the personnel files for Agent Chen Li and Chase Britt complete with service records, home addresses, phone numbers, bank account information, and assignment history. They also contained official DEA head shots of each agent standing next to a U.S. flag.

"So far, nothing worth an early retirement," Mr. Smith said.

Quinn picked up the tablet and turned it on. The screen showed a city map of Boston with a green dot in the center. He showed it to Mr. Smith.

"So, what is that?"

"This is the latest in agency GPS tracking. Since I oversee administration and personnel, I can't access active investigations. I can't get information on the Cash Man. But, I am responsible for issuing equipment. Agent Li checked out a GPS tracking tablet, and one tracker, last Thursday. She returned the tablet on Sunday, but not the tracker."

"So, this dot represents the current location of the Cash Man?" Mr. Smith asked.

"I think so. And, it gets better." Quinn touched the tablet with his finger, and a menu appeared. He tapped current location, and One Center Plaza, Boston, Mass, appeared on the screen. "Do you know what is at One Center Plaza in Boston?"

"No idea." Smith shook his head no.

"Boston office of the FBI." Quinn watched for the expression on Mr. Smith's face. He was not disappointed.

"Son of a bitch. Cash Man is a fed."

29

Josh found Chris Anthony's office after he left the meeting with Agent Randolph. He knocked twice on the door and walked in.

"You know watching porn at work is a federal crime?"

Chris looked up from his desk to see Josh standing in the doorway. "Yo, it's the felon. Come on into my humble abode."

Chris's office was a small cubicle with a window. It had your standard government gray desk, with a computer screen on the right, wraparound bookcase and hutch, and a credenza file cabinet behind his desk, below the window. Two gray padded chairs were in front of his desk. Josh took the one closest to the door.

"So, I hear you have something for me?" Josh pretended to shoot Chris with his finger.

"Oh, yeah, your shooting irons." Chris turned around and opened one of the file drawers in his credenza, took out the Glock and the P938 Sig Sauer, and set them on his desk. He went back and got the clips for each gun and put them next to the pistols.

Josh stood, picked up the Glock, inserted the clip, and smacked it with the palm of his left hand to ram it home. He turned left, pointed the gun at the floor, and jacked a round into the chamber with his left hand. He put the gun into his shoulder holster and closed the catch. He did the same thing with the P938 and inserted it in the carry holster in the small of his back.

"There, now I feel like a real G-man again." Josh sat back down in the chair.

"So, is your undercover gig as a club playboy over?"

"Yes, now I have to go back to a real job."

"What are you going to do? Hostage rescue team?"

"Get some lunch. I'm buying. You in?"

"Hell yeah. I never turn down a free lunch. Want me to get Owen?" Chris got out from behind his desk and grabbed his jacket.

"Absolutely, Josh said. "Must be 'take an agent to lunch day.'"

Mr. Smith stood, reached into his pocket for his money clip, and peeled off a hundred. He dropped it next to his coffee mug and scooped up the tablet and the two personnel folders. "I gotta address this shit now. We can talk about your retirement later. If this pans out, you get a pass."

Smith walked out of the bar, and a dark blue Chevy Tahoe pulled to the curb. Another ex-military type got out of the rear and held the door for Mr. Smith. Smith leaned in and whispered in his ear. Smith got into the Tahoe and pulled the door shut. The military guy walked into the crowd.

"Head to the jerk chicken place and make it quick," Mr. Smith said. The driver pulled away from the curb and hit the gas. The Tahoe surged into traffic. Mr. Smith pulled out his phone and hit dial. The call was answered on the first ring.

"Yeah?"

"Bring 'em to the jerk chicken place."

"Now?"

"Yes, now, you fucking idiot." Smith ended the call and punched up another number.

"Hello."

"I'm coming to you."

"Who the fuck is this?"

"Your well-dressed friend."

"Oh, shit. Sorry, man."

"Clear your restaurant and round up your crew. We have a mutual problem. I'll be there in 30 minutes." Smith ended the call.

Quinn finished his lunch and ordered another Guinness. *This is going to work out well,* he mused. *I'll put in my retirement letter, take a post-career vacation to Taiwan, and I won't come back. All my money is already out of the country, with half of it sitting in a safety deposit box in Taipei, as gold Krugerrands. Nothing like physical gold for security in uncertain times.*

These qualified as uncertain times. There's still a couple of grand in a checking account, and I can just withdraw that at an ATM when I'm on the move. Jenny will be pissed, when she finds out I'm gone. Oh well, nothing like young Chinese pussy to help with my grief. He got hard, just thinking about it. One final toast to his new life, and he drained the remaining Guinness.

Quinn picked up Mr. Smith's hundred and put it in his pocket. He dropped two twenties and a ten to cover the $46.50 tab. *No sense over-tipping, since I won't be coming back.* He smiled, waved at Alyssa, and headed to the door, pushed through it, and turned right. His car was parked in a garage around the corner. The air was crisp and clean, and he breathed deep. Nothing like fall in New England. He would miss the four seasons. Well, maybe not winter. Fuck winter. He walked up three steps into the elevator waiting area for the parking garage and punched the up button. The elevator dinged, and the door opened. He got on and hit 3. The door closed, and the elevator jerked up. He watched the numbers blink 2, then 3, and the elevator stopped. The doors opened, and he stepped out. He scanned the garage. Place was empty. He pulled out his key fob and hit the unlock button. A blue Toyota Camry, four cars up on the left, flashed its lights, and beeped the horn twice. He edged between the parked cars and got into the Camry, being careful not to hit his door on the car next to his. He put on his seatbelt and lowered the driver side visor mirror to check his teeth for any remains of lunch. Clean, and pearly white. He admired himself in the mirror. "You are one lucky son of a bitch." He flipped the visor back up and reached for the ignition button.

There was some movement by his driver side window. A military type guy tapped on his window. Quinn hit the window down button. "Can I help you?" Recognition hit Quinn, as the bullet entered his left eye, exited the back of his skull, and sprayed blood, brains, and bone throughout the interior of the car like someone threw a balloon filled with red paint into the front seat. A dark blue Chevy Tahoe pulled up behind the Camry, and the military type guy got in.

"Thanks for lunch, Josh," Chris said.

"I second that," Owen added, as they all stepped out of the Emperor Japanese Grill and Sushi Bar into the bright sunshine. They turned right and headed up Bowdoin Street to get back to the office.

"You're both welcome. You know, I haven't felt this free in a long time. No looking over your shoulder in case you run into someone you know. Always wondering, if this is the day it all goes south." Josh watched the flow of pedestrians go past.

"What are you going to do?" Owen put his hands in his pockets.

"Take a long vacation to somewhere warm. Maybe Hawaii. Depends on what my wife wants to do."

"Now that sounds good," Chris agreed.

They continued up the next few blocks, enjoyed the fall weather, and walked back into the One Center Plaza building. They flashed their badges and walked around the security check lane.

"I can't remember the last time I did that." Josh stopped in the lobby. "Hey, I need to head up to the sixth floor to handle all my administrative crap to rejoin the ranks of the FBI. I'll check with you guys later."

"Roger that." Chris shook Josh's hand, along with Owen. "See you later." They both walked to the elevator.

Josh walked over to the stairwell to take the stairs to the sixth floor. Time to get back in fighting shape.

30

The dark blue Tahoe pulled into an empty slot in front of Marley's Jerk Chicken Restaurant. *They reserved it just for me,* thought Mr. Smith. He got out of the Tahoe with the tablet and the two folders and walked towards the restaurant. His driver also got out of the car and hustled ahead. He pulled the door open for him, and then followed him in. The place was empty of customers. Jason Brown and an even bigger black dude were seated at a table with two other empty chairs. Jason had a knee brace on his right knee. His bat was next to his right hand. Eight other bangers were spread out in tables around the edges.

Mr. Smith walked over and sat in one of the empty chairs. Anger and fear were evident on both Jason and the big black dude. He put the tablet and personnel folders in front of Big Papi. The driver stayed by the door

"Jason, could I please get a Diet Pepsi with ice?" Mr. Smith asked.

Big Papi snapped his fingers. One of the edgers scurried behind the counter and came back with a can of Diet Pepsi and a glass of ice. He put them in front of Mr. Smith, who popped the top and poured the Diet Pepsi over the ice. He stopped it before it overflowed and took a sip.

"Thank you, Jason," Mr. Smith said. "Now, *we,*" he pointed his finger at both Big Papi and himself, "have a problem. A big fucking problem." He slammed his hand on the personnel folders. The anger disappeared from Big Papi's face, but the fear remained.

"What are you talking about, boss?" Big Papi tried to control the fear in his voice.

"Your Mr. Cash Man is a fucking fed!" Mr. Smith screamed.

"No fucking way, boss. We checked him out, and we've been dealing with him for years. He's our best customer."

"Yes, fucking way, Jason," Mr. Smith said. He flipped open the tablet and powered it on. The screen lit up with the same green dot parked in the center of the screen. "The DEA tagged the Cash Man's car with a GPS tracker, before the buy on Saturday. It's still active. That is the green dot in the center of the screen. Guess where the green dot has been parked, since 1000 this morning?"

"No idea, boss." Big Papi shook his head no.

"Well, let me give you a hint. One Center Plaza. Do you know what is at One Center Plaza?"

"No, boss." Big Papi still looked clueless.

"The motherfucking FBI, that who's at One Center Plaza!" Mr. Smith screamed.

"Oh shit." Recognition filled Big Papi's face.

"You got that right, oh shit." Mr. Smith sat back and took another drink of Diet Pepsi.

"Hey, boss, they're here." The driver by the door nodded at Mr. Smith.

"Who's here?" Big Papi craned his neck to see out of the door.

"Your family, Jason," Mr. Smith said. "I'm returning your family."

Big Papi struggled out of his chair and limped towards the door, as his daughter Nichole came flying through.

"Daddy!" Nichole ran to Big Papi and jumped into his arms.

Big Papi scooped her up and gave her a big hug. "Are you okay, baby?"

"Yes, Daddy. We got ice cream. I got a new dolly, and we got to stay in a fancy hotel. You could order any kind of food you wanted over the phone. They even had a pool inside."

"Where's Mommy?" Big Papi looked over at the door.

"She's outside in the car. The nice man will take us home. I just wanted to say hi, before we go."

"Okay, baby girl. You go back with Mommy, and I'll see you tonight for dinner." He put Nichole back on the ground. She ran back through the door.

"Bye, Daddy! Love you," and the door closed behind her.

"You know, we took care of Chino." Big Papi turned back to Mr. Smith.

"Yes, I knew that. We have a few guards at Concord."

"Why did you return my family?"

"Because, Jason, I do not want you to have any distractions, and you no longer need motivation for your tasks, if you want to stay out of jail for a very long time."

"You got that right. How does that tablet work?"

31

Josh signed the last document, 90 minutes after he first stepped through the door into the FBI personnel office. They created all Josh's employment files from scratch since he went straight to undercover after graduating from the FBI Academy. New hires were always the best for undercover work, if they came with Josh's skill set because there was no FBI paper trail to track the agents, as they didn't exist in the system. Even if the system got hacked, there was nothing to find, because he didn't exist. This was particularly important when dealing with cartels because they always hired the best cyber security experts money could buy. Josh's FBI salary was routed through the Champions Club under residual profits.

Josh went to the sixth-floor stairwell, walked two floors down to the parking garage, and pushed through the door with a large green four painted on it. He unlocked the truck, climbed in, and tossed his backpack into the rear seat. He wound through the parking garage, with the tires squealing on the corners, and approached the exit. The yellow arm lifted on his approach. He did a quick look left and accelerated into traffic. Traffic was slow but moving, which was a plus in downtown Boston. He turned right on Sudbury Street, crawled through a couple of lights to I93, and turned right on the entrance ramp to I93 south.

Josh picked up the gold Charger as soon as he exited the garage. Not only was it an ugly color, but it was obvious when it pulled into traffic behind Josh when he passed. It also was the signature car of the Centre Street Kings. They all drove gold Chargers to match their gold tooth. *Just a coincidence,* thought Josh. *No way they know me. I only dealt with Chino, and he was a stain on the floor in Concord.*

Josh checked his rearview mirror when he accelerated to get on the highway. The gold Charger was six cars back in the right lane. Josh kept to the far-right lane and stayed with the flow of traffic. From the far-right lane, he could see anyone coming up the breakdown lane, so he would only have to worry about the left lanes. When he crossed the State Street exit, another gold Charger pulled in behind the first. One is a coincidence; two is a problem. A problem that needed to be worked out.

Big Dog and Runner picked up the blue F150 when it exited the parking garage. They had a warning when the green spot moved, and the tablet announced, "Moving." Runner eased the Charger behind the truck a few cars back. No sense drawing attention; they would always know where the truck was going. The initial plan was to box the truck on four sides, and then hose it down with AK47s. *Nowhere to hide, motherfucker,* thought Runner.

Big Dog was handling the tablet. "Turn right to I93 South," reported the tablet's electronic voice. Runner followed the truck on the highway. Runner checked the rearview mirror after they crossed State Street, and another gold Charger fell in behind them with Double Down and Dime Bag.

"Yo, Runner, we on your six," Double Down reported over the radio. "This shit is cool." They were using a Harris; a voice activated, encrypted, voice communication system provided by Mr. Smith.

"I see you, DD." Runner accelerated to close the distance with the F150.

"Why don't we just hose the bitch now?" came over the radio.

"No, man, stick with the plan." Runner shook his head.

"What does that fool want?" Big Dog glared at Runner.

"He wants to hose him now." Runner checked his mirror. DD was close. He couldn't see the license plate.

"Tell that motherfucker to get with the plan, before I hose him." Big Dog turned around and stared out the back window at DD to convey his message.

"I did, Big Dog. We good." Runner gripped the wheel, hoping he didn't wind up like Chino.

Josh kept an eye on the pair of Chargers. They were hanging back. They chose their option well. No place to go on an interstate in heavy traffic. They could just close anytime and start shooting. They wouldn't worry about civilian casualties. Josh was not afforded that luxury.

He could call 911. And say what? *Two gold Chargers with possible gang members are following me in traffic. I wouldn't bet on that response time.* Josh continued to follow traffic, and two more gold Chargers joined the parade at the South Station exit. If anything were going to happen, it would happen soon. They couldn't risk traffic opening up and giving him room to maneuver. Josh watched for any movement on the part of the gold convoy. They were content on keeping pace. He could exit and find a police station, but there weren't any close by, and they would close the gap and hose the truck if he tried to exit. The sign for the E Berkeley Street exit passed down the right side of the truck. The exit loomed on the right, just ahead.

Josh jerked the wheel to the right and stepped on the gas. The big Ford leaped forward, hitting 60 mph in 4.5 seconds, and he rocketed down the E Berkeley St. exit, slammed on the brakes at the end of the exit ramp to avoid flipping the truck, and turned the wheel hard to the right, fish-tailing through the corner. When the truck straightened after the turn, he stomped on the gas again and accelerated like a bullet weaving through traffic. Horns blaring, the 700 HP engine roaring, he didn't have time to check his rearview mirror. He closed on the Warren Avenue/E Berkeley intersection, praying the light would be green. The luck of the drunken sailor was with him, as he hit the intersection on the green, and fishtailed through another power turn to the left and down Warren Avenue. He slammed on the brakes, made a hard-left turn, and drove into the Paul Revere Parking Garage without taking a ticket. *I'll pay on the way out.* Josh drove to the top of the garage and backed into a spot on the roof. He drew his Glock out of his holster and waited.

Runner kept a close watch on the F150. His hands were tense on the wheel. The truck suddenly jerked right and took off. Gravel flying, tires smoking, down the exit.

"Son of a bitch." Runner jerked the wheel right and stepped on the gas.

"Go, go, go." Big Dog pounded on the dash with his hands.

Runner just got to the top of the exit in time to see the truck fishtailing right at the end of the exit ramp, and then screaming down the street. Runner hit the bottom of the exit with the other three Chargers in pursuit and accelerated into a right turn and slammed on the brakes. He skidded to a stop six inches from the back bumper of a U-Haul truck stopped at a light.

"Fuck me." Runner braced his hands on the steering wheel as the Charger skidded to a stop. "That truck can fly."

"Nah, it's all good." Big Dog held up the tablet, so Runner could see it. "Look here." He showed Runner the tablet screen. "Our boy has stopped up ahead on the left. Nowhere to hide, motherfucker. Let the boys know. Party time."

___

32

Josh waited for 30 minutes. No sign of a gold Charger. He put his Glock back in his holster and pushed the call button on the steering wheel. "Call Cory Randolph."

"Afternoon, Josh, what can I do for you? Miss me already?"

"Yes, Sir, dearly. I'm sitting on top of a Paul Revere garage in Back Bay. The Centre Street Kings just tried to throw me a going away party."

"Are you okay?"

"Yeah, I'm fine. I'm going to need some new tires on the truck."

"How did the Centre Street Kings find out about you? I thought you only dealt with Chino."

"No idea. I always dealt with Chino. No exceptions."

"Well, somebody knows. What are you going to do now?"

"I'm going home. No one knows about that place. It will give us some time to figure some things out. Maybe go pay Big Papi a visit."

"Okay, I'll put the tact team on standby. In the meantime, I'll check things on my end. Maybe a good time to take the bride on an extended vacation."

"I was thinking the same thing. I'll call you when I'm home."

"All right, be safe." Agent Randolph ended the call.

Josh started the truck and eased out of the parking space and headed down the ramp to the exit. He descended to the third level and was coming around a cement pillar to a small straightaway, when he hit the brakes. "Fuck me." Two gold Dodge Chargers blocked the ramp, end to end, with four bangers on the other side with AK47s pointed at him.

"Time to go." He shifted into reverse and scanned his rearview camera for the best avenue of escape. Two more gold Dodge Chargers came in behind him, blocking the exit. Four more bangers hopped out of the rides.

Toting AK47s, they took position behind the cars. "Okay, time to fight, motherfuckers."

Josh released his seat belt and dove into the rear of the truck on the floor, just as hell opened up. 7.62 cal. rounds from 8 AK47s with 30 round clips rained on the truck like hail on the tin roof. The sharp, distinct sounds of AK47 fire echoed off the concrete garage walls, creating a deafening roar.

Becka Kendall finished the tuna fish sandwich, wrapped the paper and plate into a tight ball, and lofted a perfect three-pointer into the waste-basket at the end of the desk. "Score." She raised her arms over her head to signal touchdown. The red alert light flashed on top of her monitor, followed by Local (Boston) blinking on her screen. She moved the mouse cursor over and clicked on Local. Assistant Special Agent in Charge DEA Boston office found shot in downtown Boston parking garage. Quinn Christy was found shot in the head at close range by Boston PD at 1335 local. Circumstances are suspicious. More to follow. Becka copied the report. Pasted it into a secure email and sent it to the director.

"Jimmy?" Becka called.

"Yes, Ma'am."

"Local alert from Boston. Follow up and get what information you can."

"Yes, Ma'am. On it."

Becka hit clear on her alert screen, and the screen went back to the prompt. *Another fun day in Beantown,* she thought. *I wonder how old White 55 is doing.*

Josh rolled on the floor, tight to the rear bench seat with a single thought—*good thing I got the upgrade package. If you're going to spend 100 grand on a truck, what is an extra 250K?* Because the Shelby is a modified Ford F150, he had it further upgraded with ballistic protection. DeFender Automotive removed all the components from the truck's body (interior trim, wiring, carpet, seats, etc.). Then the doors and all other cavities (such as the pillars) were cut open so various materials could be stuffed or welded into those voids. The doors and pillars were bolstered with steel plates, a combination of ballistic nylon and Kevlar. The doors were all fitted with a third hinge to support the additional weight. The firewall and rear bulk-head were steel plated, and the floor and ceiling lined with ballistic fab-rics. The stock bumpers, designed to crumple and absorb energy during major impacts, were reinforced so the truck could bash through an impro-vised roadblock without damaging the radiator. The vehicle's glass was all replaced with "transparent armor." It's not a thicker version of the safety glass found in the side windows of standard cars, but rather a sandwich of polycarbonate (a type of plastic) and leaded glass. They were rated to stop rounds up to an AK47, but transparent armor is not "bullet proof." It will fail after the impact of five rounds, which was quickly achieved with 8 AK47s hammering away.

The front and back glass failed, almost immediately caving in. Shards of glass rained on Josh's head, and rounds whizzed overhead and slammed into the body of the truck. *Feels like Fallujah minus the SEAL team.* The firing stopped. The silence was surreal with the smell and smoke of gunfire drifting through the garage. Must be mag change-out time. Poor fire dis-cipline. These douche bags are spray and pray. *They could have fucked me by rushing the truck. I could get two or three, but eight professional shooters with automatic weapons, in a confined space, would have no problem taking me out, which means these guys are not professionals.*

"Yo, motherfucker? Why don't you just come on out? We'll kill you quick. Promise," came a voice from the front of the truck.

"Give me a minute. I need some time to think," Josh yelled.

"Think quick, motherfucker. We ain't got all day," came the voice from the front.

Josh hit a circular, 3-inch, steel button, on the front of the rear seat. The bench popped up on two hinges to reveal an armory. Never leave home without it. Josh reached in and pulled out a Benelli M1014 automatic shot-gun equipped with a grip-activated Streamlight TLR-4 laser and flashlight combo mounted on a Picatinny sight rail. He loaded the shotgun with eight rounds of Winchester PDX1 rifled slug and three buck pellet ammunition, which is three pellets of Grex® buffered 00 plated buckshot nested on top of a 1 oz rifled [non-segmenting] slug. The 1 oz PDX1 12 Defender slug exits the barrel of a standard shotgun at an estimated 1350 feet per second, generating 1700 foot-pounds of muzzle energy. You need about 10 foot-pounds of muzzle energy to enter a human skull. When you absolutely must put the scumbag down with one shot.

He reached in again and pulled out a bandolier of backup shotgun ammunition, draped it around his neck, and got his go bag, which contained spare magazines for his Glock, zip ties, and 6 MK84 stun grenades. It would be nice to have some MK67 frags, but politicians outlawed them for use by law enforcement, too much chance of civilian casualties, and no possibility of a trial by your peers. *Too fucking bad, by my book.* He also took out his smoke bag, which contained 10 Mod 308-1 smoke grenades and an FRM-40 gas mask. Josh rolled over flat on his back and yelled out, "Okay, I'm coming out. Make it quick." He put earplugs in each ear, reached up, and unlatched the door on the passenger side, and pushed it open with his hand, and did the same thing with the driver side rear door and kicked it open.

Big Dog sighted down the barrel of his AK47, as he saw both rear doors fly open. "Everybody get ready. The minute that pendejo is clear of the truck, waste him." Big Dog held the AK47 firm to his shoulder and put the front sight just to the left of the right rear door. *This is fucking awesome. Imagine the look on that motherfucker's face, when he sees us all stacked up, waiting on his ass. Big Papi is going to love this shit. That truck is a tank; I gotta get one of those. Maybe next time don't set up in a crossfire. I think the Charger took a couple of hits. All right, get some.* Two objects came flying out the front window, followed by another object out each side, and two out the back.

"What the fuck?" Big Dog lifted his head to get a better look.

The objects thrown from the F150 emitted sparks, started rolling around on the concrete floor, and spewed a dense cloud of white smoke, which quickly filled the parking garage and totally obscured the truck from view.

"Shoot, shoot!" Big Dog pulled the trigger on the AK and sent a string of eight rounds into the cloud of billowing white smoke, where he thought the truck was located. The rifle recoiled into his shoulder, his eyes stung, and he started coughing on the smoke.

33

Once the doors were open, Josh put on the gas mask and pulled the bottom straps for a snug fit. He pulled the tab on a smoke grenade and tossed it out the front of the truck through the blown-out window. It hit the hood and bounced to the floor. He pulled the tab on the second grenade and tossed it out the front window. It cleared the hood in the air and skidded across the concrete floor. He continued to throw 308-1 grenades, one out each side, and two out the back window. The smoke cans popped like opening a beer that was shaken, and a thick white smoke started to fill the garage.

Josh rolled out of the truck through the right rear door and crouched between a white Ford Escape and a green Toyota Prius. He pulled his go bag and shotgun with him. Bullets hit both cars, which broke the windshields and tore up the hoods. Both sides now fired indiscriminately into the smoke, and bullets whizzed around the garage, ricocheting off the walls. On the plus side, the bangers stood just as much a chance of getting hit by a ricochet as Josh. The open ballistic rear doors provided some protection from the assholes firing from the front, which is why step one was to attack the rear.

Josh reached into his bag and pulled out two MK84 flash bangs. Almost on cue, the firing stopped. Mag change-out, right on time. Josh pulled the tab on an MK84 and tossed it into the smoke. He aimed high to hit the wall behind the Chargers and into the line of shooters. He followed up the first MK84 with a second, then he ducked down between the cars, covered his ears, and shut his eyes.

The first MK84 hit the side of a Charger and rolled to the left. The second MK84 cleared the Chargers, hit the back wall, and dropped, rolling to the feet of the shooters, who didn't know what the fuck was going on. Each MK84 fired within 2 seconds of each other when the magnesium-based pyrotechnic charge ignited, sending a 180-decibel sound wave and 8 million candelas flashing through the smoke screen and reverberating through the garage.

At the crack of the detonation, Josh sprinted from between the parked cars to the rear Chargers. The wind through the garage started to vent the smoke. When he cleared the end of the truck, he could see the Chargers in a small cloud of haze. He pointed the shotgun in front of him and squeezed the laser grip. A red laser flashed through the smoke, and a red dot danced on the rear of the left Charger. A head popped up over the Charger waving an AK47 still trying to orient itself. The banger ripped off a string of rounds, which hit the ceiling, sending cement chips flying. He started swinging the muzzle towards Josh. The red dot centered on the banger's head, and Josh squeezed the trigger. The shotgun slammed into his shoulder, and the report resounded off the walls. The head disappeared. Brains and blood sprayed the back wall.

Josh continued to the rear of the Charger and crouched by the rear fender. He did a quick peek around the corner of the car and saw three more bangers staggering around still holding their AKs.

"Drop your weapons," Josh ordered, which came out muffled through the gas mask. The closest banger looked at Josh in disbelief and raised his gun. Josh placed the red dot in the center of his chest and squeezed the trigger. The shotgun slammed into his shoulder, and the banger rocketed backward like he got kicked by a mule. He caught the 1 oz slug and 3 00 buckshot pellets square in the chest, which blew a fist-sized hole clean through him. The banger flopped down on the shoes of the other two shooters, who dropped their guns and puked all over the hood of the Charger.

Josh took off the gas mask and looked at the other Chargers, but they were still shrouded in smoke, but he could see his truck all shot to shit. Josh slung the shotgun over his shoulder and moved on the other two shooters. He grabbed the backs of their shirts and threw them on the hood of the Charger face down in the fresh puke.

"Don't move, assholes." Josh unslung the shotgun, slammed the butt into the passenger side window, and shattered the glass all over the front seat. He reached in and pulled the door open, got his handcuffs out of his back belt, and cuffed the two remaining bangers together through the open window, and then he tossed all the AKs away from the car. He reloaded the shotgun from his bandolier. Four down and four to go.

"Dime Bag, Dime Bag, can you hear me?" Big Dog called on the radio.

Josh heard the voice coming from the floor and saw the wireless headset by the rear wheel of the Charger. He picked it up and put it on.

"Dime Bag, Jesus, what the fuck's going on?"

Josh peered across the roof of the Charger. The smoke was just about clear out of the garage. He sprinted around the Charger to the tailgate of the truck, laid down prone, and sighted the shotgun under the truck. So much for the Zegna suit. *Kat's going to kill me unless these mutts beat her to it.*

"Yo, dickhead?" Josh spoke into the headset. "Why don't you pussies come back here, so I can fuck you up the ass."

"You're a dead man. My name is Big Dog, and my face is going to be the last thing you see on earth, motherfucker."

All the bangers started running around the Chargers to approach the truck. Josh sighted at one shin and pulled the trigger. The shotgun slammed into his shoulder, and the lower leg disappeared, followed by a banger dropping to the ground, and he fired again into the flopping figure. Fire till they drop or stop.

Josh rolled right, got to his feet, and sprinted to the right front fender of the truck. The other three bangers tried to register what happened to Double Down when Josh centered his red dot on Big Dog and squeezed the trigger. The shotgun slammed his shoulder and knocked the Nigerian nightmare off his feet, flopping on the hood of a silver Beamer. The other two bangers stared at Josh in disbelief and dropped their guns.

"Right decision, boys. On your face, hands behind your head, interlock your fingers, cross your legs." They both assumed the position. "Anyone moves, and you can join your friend over there." Josh pointed at the silver Beamer with the barrel of the shotgun. A parade of sirens wailed in the distance. *I guess a couple of flash bangs, a few hundred rounds from an AK47, and some shotgun blasts gets a little attention in Boston.* Josh leaned back on the remains of his truck. All the headlights, tires, windows, license plate,

Ford emblem, and hood were shot out like these fools were at a shooting gallery, and the truck was the target. Josh patted the hood.

"I owe you, old girl, but it doesn't look like I can get you back."

He walked over to the truck and pulled his suit jacket and backpack off the rear seat. Josh wedged them between the backseat and the raised lid of his installed armory when he opened it. He put on the jacket, which matched nicely with his torn, blood-smeared, white shirt and the dirt stains on his pants from crawling on the floor. He retrieved his FBI credentials and inserted them in his jacket pocket so they faced out, and then pulled out his phone. He scrolled through his contacts and hit the button for Agent Randolph.

"Hey, Josh, did you make it home?"

"No, I'm still in the Back Bay. Somehow, and I don't know how, the Centre Street Kings were waiting for me, as I was driving out of the garage."

"Are you okay?"

"I'm okay; the truck's not. I got the entire Boston Police Department headed my way. You had better roll our whole squad, forensics, shooting team, and some support agents. I got four down, and four in custody."

"Are you sure you're okay?"

"For now. When Kat finds out, maybe not."

"Roger that. Where are you?"

"Parking garage, third deck, at the corner of Warren Avenue and E Berkeley Street."

"I'll call the Boston PD and let them know we have an agent on the scene."

"Thanks, boss."

"Hold tight, see you soon." The call cut off.

Josh put the phone back in his pocket and set the shotgun on the hood. The wail of sirens stopped, which meant that Boston SWAT must be making an entry. A few minutes later, two SWAT guys in full gear poked their heads around the rear of the Chargers. Two more guys were coming up fast from behind; their boots crunched along the concrete.

"Let's see some hands," ordered the first SWAT officer by the Charger.

Josh got off the truck and put his hands behind his head. "Easy, guys. FBI."

The two SWAT guys from behind grabbed his shoulders, spun him around, and pushed his face down on the hood of the truck.

"ID is in my left jacket pocket." Josh remained frozen. Cops hate quick, sudden movements.

One of the officers patted his pocket, felt the ID, and pulled it out. "We're clear. It's him." The officers helped him off the truck and handed back his ID.

"Sorry about that, we just needed to confirm it was you." The SWAT officer put his M4 carbine on safe.

"No problem, officers. Did you guys set a perimeter?"

"Yes, Sir. We were told to establish a perimeter and find you. Is this it?" The officer pointed at the two bangers on the ground. The officers by the front of the Chargers kneeled over the Centre Street Kings, handcuffed them, and patted them down for weapons.

"Two more are cuffed in the door of one of the Chargers behind us." Josh cocked his thumb in the direction of the rear Chargers.

"Yeah, we got them." The SWAT officer extended his hand. "Jim Dwyer, and this is my partner, Bernard Tan."

Josh shook both their hands. "Josh Martin, thanks for helping me out."

Both officers looked around at the scene with the stench of gun smoke, smoke grenades, and blood swirling around. Dead bodies on cars, on the floor, and every car on both sides of the garage full of holes with windows and tires shot out.

"I don't think you needed much help. If you ever want a career change, we're hiring." Officer Dwyer leaned on the truck.

"Thanks for the offer, but I think I'll stick with my day job." Josh relaxed.

Officer Dwyer touched his ear. "Roger. I'll tell him. Your crew just rolled up. They want you out front."

"All right, let's go." Josh stepped past the bangers and started out of the garage.

34

A Parson's Bakery truck, a family tradition since 1958, backed into the slot in front of Marley's Jerk Chicken restaurant. The driver got out, walked to the back of the truck, and pulled up the back door. He unstrapped the dolly and lifted it to the ground. He pulled three boxes of dinner rolls from the back, stacked them on the ground, and slid the dolly underneath. He tilted the dolly back and walked it to the front door. A customer leaving the store held the door open for him, and he walked in.

Aunt Clarice was behind the counter taking orders. She put the phone to her chest. "Put them in the back storeroom," pointing to the rear door. Four couples were eating dinner, and one loner read the paper in the corner. They all sweated through the spicy jerk chicken dinner special. The driver rolled over to the storeroom door, opened it, and pushed the dolly through. A big, black dude in a Big Papi Red Sox jersey sat in a chair bent over an old desk. He munched on some chicken and stared at a cell phone and bat on the desktop. A black brace wrapped around his right knee.

"Where do you want these?" The driver put the front of the dolly on the ground.

"Put them anywhere and get the fuck out." The big black dude never moved.

The driver wheeled the rolls over to a stack of canned tomatoes, set them down, and pulled the dolly out. He took the invoice clipboard off the stack of rolls.

"Are you going to sign for these, or is the lady behind the counter?" The delivery guy held up the clipboard.

The black dude motioned him with his left hand, never looking up from his food.

The delivery guy came over and set the clipboard on the desk with a pen chained to the top. The black dude reached over for the pen and started to scrawl his name on the X line.

The delivery guy pulled a black Ruger SR22 with a fitted silencer from a holster strapped to the small of his back. In one fluid motion, he put the barrel at the base of the big black dude's head and squeezed the trigger, which made a metallic click. A muffled PFFFFT sent a 22LR, Winchester, Subsonic, 42gr bullet crashing into the big black dude's brain. The black dude's face flopped into the plate of chicken and rice, and chicken pieces sprayed across the desk. The delivery guy froze and counted to ten for any sound of an alarm. It was unlikely, as the subsonic round didn't work the automatic's action.

The delivery guy put the pistol back in the holster and covered it with his work shirt. He picked up the clipboard, grabbed the dolly, wheeled it out of the office, and closed the door. He waved to Aunt Clarice. "The Big Guy signed for it."

"Okay, thank you." Aunt Clarence watched the delivery guy from behind the counter. "Where's Ronnie?"

"Ronnie called in sick." The delivery guy wheeled the dolly over to the door. "He'll be back next week. Enjoy the rest of your day."

"Thank you." Aunt Clarice went back to taking orders.

The delivery guy pushed the dolly out of the restaurant to the back of the truck. Pulled open the back door and tossed the dolly inside. The dolly landed on Ronnie. The delivery guy got into the truck, drove about a half mile down the road, and pulled into an alley behind a strip mall. He parked the truck and walked to a dark blue Chevy Tahoe and got in.

Mr. Smith pulled the vibrating phone from his pocket and pressed the green phone button. "Yeah?"

"It's done."

"Any problems?"

"No."

"Are the packages in place?"

"Yes."

"How are we going to do it?"

"Eyes on."

"Okay, good," Mr. Smith hung up. He put his phone back in his pocket, opened the right top drawer of his desk, retrieved his cellcrpyt phone, and called the only number in the contact list.

"Yes?" came the response, after the call bounced off three satellites, and routed through cell towers in Hong Kong, Uzbekistan, and Venezuela.

"I need to speak to the boss," Mr. Smith said.

"Wait one," came the response.

"Good afternoon, Mr. Smith. How are things in America?" El Jefe inquired.

"They are good, Sir. We've taken care of our partnership and retirement problem, and our three packages are in place," Mr. Smith said.

"Excellent. Call me again when the mission is complete."

"Yes, El Jefe," Mr. Smith said, and the line went dead.

35

Josh walked through the garage with the Boston Shooting Incident Review Group and outlined his actions during, and after, the shootout. They secured his shotgun for testing as part of their investigation. The preliminary investigation cleared Josh, pending review by the Headquarters review team, but it was a definitive case of self-defense, and there were no civilian casualties.

Josh leaned on the back of the FBI forensic response truck and took a couple of drinks on a water bottle when Agent Randolph walked up.

"You need something stronger than that." Agent Randolph stopped in front of Josh to get a look at his face.

"You got that right." Josh took another hit on the water bottle. "Smoke always dries out your throat."

"The SAC cleared you for duty. Might be time to take that vacation we talked about. Boston PD just got a report of a dead black male in Jamaica Plain, with a gunshot to the back of the head."

"Any suspects?"

"No. No one heard or saw anything. With Big Papi, Chino, and Big Dog dead, and seven more gang members dead or looking at hard time, I'd bet the Centre Street Kings are going to have a hard time holding on to their turf. Oh, they also found Quinn Christy with a bullet hole in his head in a parking garage downtown."

"Who's Quinn Christy?" Josh splashed some water into his eyes and blinked a couple of times.

"He's the DEA ASAC for administration and personnel."

"Oh shit, I guess we found our DEA leak." Josh took another sip of water.

"Yeah, someone is cleaning up some loose ends."

"Cartel?"

"Best guess, but we got no identified members in New England, and you took care of the guy we knew about."

"They must have contracted out."

"We can worry about that tomorrow." Agent Randolph put his hand on Josh's shoulder. "You look and smell like you need a shower and a stiff drink. Hey, Lester?"

Lester Johnson ran over in his FBI raid jacket. "Yeah, boss."

"You doing anything?" Agent Randolph squeezed Josh's shoulder.

"No, Sir, we've completed our initial review. Photo guys and evidence collection are going through it now. When they finish, we gotta haul all the vehicles down to the impound lot so that we can go through them."

"All right, that sounds good. How about you give our Special Agent here a ride home, and then come back and get me?" Agent Randolph handed him the keys to his black Lexus.

"Sure thing, boss." Lester took the keys and smiled.

"And Lester, keep it under 60."

"Always, Sir. You ready Josh?"

"Yeah, let's go." Lester and Josh walked over to Agent Randolph's Black GS F turbo and got in.

"You know, this baby is track rated for 143 mph." Lester started the car and revved the engine.

The timer on Becka Kendall's desk registered 15:19:19, only 3 hours and some change to Monday Night Football. The Jets and Cardinals would kick off. Becka grew up in Westchester, New York, so she came from a long line of suffering Jets fans. She still enjoyed Jets games with her dad, but the Jets also provided their unique brand of misery like the butt fumble that ruined Thanksgiving. *Mark Sanchez still sucks*, she thought.

Boston Correlated Event flashed on her screen. She moved the cursor over and clicked on Boston. There is a 75% chance of an event in Boston, Mass, within the next 72 hours. White 55 was involved in a shootout with eight Centre Street Gang members in a parking garage in Back Bay. Four gang members killed, four in custody. White 55 uninjured. ASAC Boston DEA Quinn Christy killed by a gunshot to head in parking garage downtown Boston. The leader of Centre Street Kings murdered in a restaurant in Jamaica Plain. Gunshot to head. Communication intercept between an encrypted phone in Boston and Juan Pablo Rodriguez in Colombia indicates three packages are in play, no further information.

"Son of a bitch." No game tonight. Becka picked up the phone and called the director.

Lester turned into the South Weymouth Naval Air Station and stepped on the gas. The Lexus went from 0 to 60 in about 5 seconds, blowing past the CDR Shea Memorial.

"You know there are kids in here." Josh gripped the armrests.

"Nah, Coast Guard housing is on the other side of the reservation." He eased off the accelerator and tapped the brakes after the two-mile entrance stretch. Lester took a left on Glendenning Terrace, coasted by the General's house at 25 mph, and turned into Josh's driveway. "Not too bad. Still not like the truck, even with all the extra weight. Are you going to replace it?"

"I'm thinking about it, or it may be time for a sports car."

"Now you're talking." Lester changed the music from Country to Rap.

"Yeah, don't get your hopes up. I may let you wash it, ain't no way you're gonna drive it. Do you know why candy is like music?" Josh looked at Lester.

"No, why?" Lester turned up some P. Diddy. "*Roll with me.*"

"Because first, before you can enjoy it, you gotta get rid of the wrapper." Josh smiled.

"Oh, man, not cool." Lester laughed. "You can't disrespect the Diddy."

Josh got out of the car and leaned in. "Thanks for the ride."

"No problem. Best to the wife, and I drove like a saint. Right?"

"It was like riding with Saint Michael." Josh pushed the door shut and walked to the back entrance. *Now, the fun really starts.*

Lester backed out of the driveway. Josh waved and got a two-honk response. He walked around the Explorer, through the back door, and received the best greeting in the world, unless you got kids.

Syrin waited for him. She did her best "Daddy's home" dance, with her tail banging off the wall, and her entire body doing the booty shake. "Who's a good girl?" Josh squatted down to her level, and Syrin licked his face. "Where's the ball? Syrin, fetch," and she raced into the house.

"Hey, babe, I'm in the kitchen," Kat said. "We're having lasagna. Why don't you go up and change and get us some wine and sparkling apple juice? It's just about ready."

Josh walked into the kitchen.

"Holy crap, what happened to you?" Kat was cutting garlic bread. She put the knife on the cutting board and walked over to give him a hug. She stopped about three feet away. "Man, you stink. You guys play football at the office again?"

"How about I take a shower, change, and I'll tell you all about it."

"Don't touch, or sit, on anything."

Josh leaned in for a kiss and got the hand on the chest.

"Momma don't kiss the bum. Now go get cleaned up." Syrin tore into the kitchen with her ball. "You can kiss Syrin. She likes stinky."

Josh took the ball from Syrin and tossed it through the dining room and into the living room. It bounced off the back of the couch with Syrin in hot pursuit. "So, I guess a joint shower is not an option?"

"Pretty smart for an FBI guy. Now go." Kat pointed in the direction of the staircase.

Josh headed for the shower with Syrin bringing up the rear, carrying her ball.

"Don't stop quick; you'll get a dog up the ass." Kat went back to cutting garlic bread.

36

"Thanks, Becka," Vincent P. Santiago said as he hung up the phone. Vince was Hispanic with black hair cut military short, dark brown eyes, and a scar over his right eye courtesy of a skinny's bullet in Mogadishu. A former Delta operator, and CIA paramilitary officer, at 42 years of age, he could still pass the Army's physical fitness test at 5'10" and 180 lbs.

Bad news never stops. Vincent stared at the small oil lamp that sat on the front of his desk. The light of freedom, "Let it forever shine on the cause of democracy," or something like that according to legend. FDR was the original owner, and it sat on his oval office desk during WWII. Now, it has rested on the desk of every director of the Black and White Club, since Colonel Ned Buxton. It didn't travel very far. Colonel Buxton had it in Providence, Rhode Island, until his death in 1949. It then spent 20 years in the Old Executive Office Building, now called the Eisenhower Executive Office Building, after Clinton signed legislation in 1999, naming it for our 34th president. It moved to its current location, on the third floor of the New Executive Office Building in 1969, when the building opened. Now, it sits on Santiago's desk.

Director Santiago picked up the phone, and the caller answered on the second ring.

"Hello."

"Good evening, Mr. President, this is Director Santiago. We have a situation in Boston. I would like to schedule a meeting for tomorrow at 1400."

"Okay, Vince, I'll contact the others. Have a good night."

"Thank you, Mr. President," and the call ended. He hung the phone up, and a chill went up his spine. Not bad for a poor Hispanic kid from Houston. It got him every time.

Josh showered with his guard dog on duty outside the door. He put on jeans, a blue Coast Guard Academy T-shirt, a gray fleece jacket, and slipped on a pair of brown boat shoes. When he stepped out of the bathroom, Syrin greeted him with her ball in her mouth. Josh took the ball and threw it across the room with Syrin in hot pursuit. He walked into the hallway, got a trash bag out of the closet, and headed back to the bathroom to retrieve his discarded clothes, which smelled like they were in a house fire for a week. He slung the bag over his shoulder and padded down the stairs.

"Where's your guard dog, and where's your truck?" Kat called out of the kitchen.

"Syrin's upstairs trying to find her ball. I think it rolled behind the bed. The truck's a long story." Josh walked outside and threw the bag of trash into a can on the side of the house.

"What was in the trash bag?"

"What was left of a $5,000 suit." Josh came back into the house.

"So, what about the truck?" She carried a pan of lasagna into the dining room. "Also, get some wine, if you want it. I already got Chateau Concord, not sure of the year, but I hear it's pretty good."

Josh ambled into the dining room and stood behind his chair. He reached over and took Kat's hand. "Bless us, Oh Lord, and these thy gifts which we are about to receive from thy bounty, through Christ, Our Lord. Amen." They both made the sign of the cross and sat down. Josh cut two big pieces of lasagna from the pan with cheese dripping down the side. He put a big piece on Kat's plate and one on his own. He took a couple of bites with some garlic bread. "This is fantastic, babe, and I'm hungry."

"Are you going to tell me about the truck, or am I nagging you all night?" Kat took a bite of lasagna. "This is good."

"First. I'm done."

"What do you mean done?"

"Done. I'll submit my resignation to the FBI. We sell our share of the Club to Enzo and head back home to New Hampshire. What do you think?"

"Wow. What the hell happened today?"

"Have you seen the news?" Josh took another bite of lasagna, which burned his tongue, but was worth it.

"Oh, baby, that, was you?" Kat reached out and grabbed his hand. "It's been all over the news."

"Yeah, that was me. Randolph told me to take a vacation for a while. I think we need to take a permanent vacation away from all this. Take the dog, the baby, and head to the mountains. I'm finally tired of chasing ghosts. The guys are gone, and nothing I do will bring them back." He squeezed her hand.

"Are you sure?"

"Yes, you get a moment of clarity, when you could lose everything in a blink of the eye." He leaned over and kissed her on the cheek. "What's your news?"

"What news?"

"You don't make lasagna like this unless you got news." Josh stuck a piece of lasagna with his fork.

"I saw Enzo today at work, and I submitted my resignation." She took a sip of Chateau Concord.

"So, you're good with the plan?"

"Yes, I'm good with the plan. Maybe not New Hampshire…I'm thinking of some warmer locale…but I'm in on a slower pace of life. Now, what about the truck?"

"The truck didn't make it, sweetie." Josh took a sip of wine, swirled the delicious liquid in his mouth, and swallowed.

"Bad?"

"Oh, yeah, awful, like crush it, and forget it, bad." Josh wiped his plate clean with a piece of garlic bread.

"Are you going to replace it?"

"No. They only made 500, so I don't think I can get another Shelby. I'm thinking something more exotic like a Maserati."

"You can't fit a car seat in a Maserati, so you better think minivan, stud." Kat got out of the chair. "I cooked…you get to clean up. I'll feed the dog. Speaking of which, where's Syrin?"

"Still chasing the ball." Josh stood to get the dishes.

"Syrin? Where are you, baby?" Kat headed towards the stairs.

Josh cleared the table, rinsed all the plates and pans, and put them in the dishwasher. He never understood why you had to wash the dishes before you put them in the dishwasher, other than the Gospel according to Kat. Halfway through the cleanup, Syrin paraded through the kitchen with her ball.

"So, you finally got it." Josh watched Syrin walk through the kitchen with her prize. She did the dance of the seven veils displaying her ball. Syrin ignored him and walked over to the food bin to wait for mommy.

"The ball was stuck behind the headboard. Your princess was laying on the floor staring at it." Kat walked into the kitchen and got the dog bowl.

Kat prepared Syrin's food, set down the dog dish, and headed into the living room to assume the position. *Wheel of Fortune* was on. Josh finished the dishes and wiped down the counters in the kitchen. He headed to his office to check his email and looked at the TV as he passed through the living room.

"White Sandy Beaches in Paradise. Let me know what trip I won." He went in and shut the double French doors to his office.

He turned on the computer and checked his email. Nothing from his special friend and nothing else of interest. He signed off the computer and touched the picture of his boys in Aruba. "Sorry, guys, time to move on." His phone vibrated in his pocket. He looked at the screen. Detective Hollis. He swiped the green accept button. "Ryan, how are you? Take any bribes lately?"

"Out, fucking, standing, General, and no. Guess where I'm standing?"

"No clue."

"I'm standing in front of 178 Broad Street."

"So, you got old Leroy?"

"Yes, Sir. We found him hiding behind some boxes of old clothes in his aunt's attic. It smelled like mothballs, old lady, and it was hot as fuck. I think old Leroy was happy to see us. Looked like he'd been living up there for a week. We found the proceeds from the robbery in a paper bag, so I think he's going to be the guest of the State for the rest of his life."

"That is good news."

"Are you, and your bride, doing anything on Saturday? I'd like to have you guys over to the house to thank you for helping us out."

"Sounds good to me, Ryan. Let me check with the boss, and I'll get back to you."

"Okay, General, thanks again, and you have a good night."

"Thanks, Ryan, you too." Josh pressed the red cancel button and put the phone back in his pocket.

Josh walked through the double doors into the living room. "What trip did I win?"

"We're going to Portugal."

"Sweet. I've never been. Are we doing anything on Saturday night?"

"No plans yet. Why?" Kat looked back over the sofa.

"I just got a call from Ryan Hollis. He invited us over to his house for dinner on Saturday."

"That sounds good. Do we need to bring something?"

"I'll bring some wine. I'm going up to read for a while, and then I'm turning in. It's been a long day."

"Okay, sweetie, I'll be up in a while. I want to watch *Jeopardy*."

37

The watcher saw the light turn on in Chase Britt's second-floor bedroom. Britt lived in a small, 1500 square foot home at the end of a dead-end street in Scituate, Mass. His gray Ford Fusion beater sat in the gravel driveway in front of a one-car garage. He told everyone the car was for work, but in reality, it was all he could afford. The garage was full of boxes without a home, after the divorce.

"Target one is up," the watcher spoke into a burner phone.

"Roger," Mr. Smith said.

"Target two is also up," came another reply.

"Roger," Mr. Smith said. "Execute as planned."

Mr. Smith picked up a pair of binoculars and focused on the front of the house. The target opened his front door and stepped out on his porch with a dog. It was still dark, so he couldn't discern any features. The target set out on the run with his dog. It looked like the location memory feature in the tracking tablet was correct. This was the address of the Cash Man.

"Do you want us to take him now?" came a request in his earpiece.

"No, stick with the plan," Mr. Smith said. He leaned back on the tree. Nothing to do but wait.

Josh raced Syrin back to the porch, and as usual, he lost. "Good girl." Josh wrapped his arm around her head at the top of the steps and gave her a big hug. He pushed on the front door and went in. Syrin panted down the hallway in search of her water bowl. Josh headed up the stairs for a shower. Kat walked out of the bathroom, as he headed in. She was in a pink bathrobe with a towel on her head.

"You're up early." Josh leaned in for a kiss.

Kat leaned back and pushed him off with her hand. "Not until you've had a shower, stinky."

"Your loss, baby. You should have waited on the shower. Where ya going?"

"I'm taking the Explorer to the casino. The girls at work are throwing me a going-away breakfast. We're meeting at the Surfside Diner." She walked over to her dressing table and started putting on makeup. "What are you going to do?"

"Syrin and I are going to do some car shopping online after breakfast." He walked into the bathroom.

Chase Britt rinsed the coffee mug and set it in the sink. He looked at the backyard through the kitchen window. A layer of leaves covered the brown grass. *Maybe the wind will blow them next door, if I leave them long enough,* he thought. He walked out of the kitchen through a tiny dining room and living room to the front door. He grabbed his Army jacket off the coat tree by the door and slipped it on. He checked the Glock 17 in his holster and the two extra clips on his belt. He walked through the front door, stopped to lock it, and walked over to his car. Several turkeys walked down the street, as he approached his car. Hmm, maybe a cheap Thanksgiving dinner. He put the key in the car door, unlocked it, and slid into the driver seat. He put the key into the ignition, and the watcher pressed the button.

The 1.25 lb block of C4 under his seat detonated in an explosive shockwave at 8090 meters per second. It blasted through the bottom of the Ford, shredded the car and Britt, and sent a fireball of dirt, debris, and flying metal soaring into the air. The shockwave resounded throughout the sleepy neighborhood, shattered every window in Britt's house, and sent the flock of turkeys squawking in every direction, except a single tom that took a piece of shrapnel to the head.

The watcher walked back through the woods to his extraction point. "Target one down." The watcher tossed the phone into a creek that ran around the back side of Britt's house. He walked up to the road and waited in a small cluster of oak trees. A dark blue Chevy Tahoe pulled up, and he got in.

Agent Li bounded down the steps of her condominium in Boston's Eagle Hill neighborhood and hit the unlock button on her fob. The lights blinked on a red Camry, parked curbside, in front of her house. She walked behind the rusty green Ford Ranger parked in front of her car and opened the driver's side door. She tossed her lunch into the rear seat, slid behind the wheel, and pulled the door closed.

The red Camry disintegrated in a fireball. The force of the blast lifted the back end of the Ranger off the ground and ignited its gas tank, which also exploded in a fireball and sent steel flying in all directions. The force of the dual blasts shattered every window in a two-block radius and set off every car alarm throughout Eagle Hill. A black plume of smoke rapidly spread throughout the neighborhood, and expanded hundreds of feet into the air, as the dark blue Chevy Tahoe drove down Condor Street and headed into the city.

Mr. Smith put the phone back in his pocket and looked into the binoculars focused on the green Ford Explorer parked in the driveway. "Come on, asshole, time to go to work," muttered Mr. Smith. If he didn't move soon, they would have to think of another option. The black back screen door opened, and a woman with short black hair, and painted-on jeans, walked out of the house and around the front of the Explorer.

Max Lindy was on his second cup of coffee and reading the morning intercepts when the alert blared throughout the op center. Everyone in the center looked at their screens. *White 55 in immediate danger of car bomb. Notify now* flashed on the screen. The computer automatically dialed every contact number for White 55. Max picked up the phone on his desk and listened to the ringing phone. The audible alarm stopped when he picked up the phone. All the analysts stared at him, willing White 55 to answer.

Josh scrolled through pictures of the Maserati Levante online. Who knew they made an SUV? You could put a car seat in the back of that. Of course, why are you paying $80K for an SUV? *The Gran Turismo convertible in ruby red looks a little more my style, but $145K for a two-seater is* *not going to get by the budget committee.* "What do you think, Syrin? Do you think mommy would okay a two-seat convertible?" Syrin didn't get a chance to answer. Both the house phone and his cell phone started ringing. Josh looked at his cell phone ringing and vibrating on his desk. *What are the odds of that happening?* he wondered. The call screen indicated, "White 55."

"Holy shit." Josh picked up the cell phone and hit the green phone button. The house phone stopped ringing. "Hello?"

"White 55, there is a car bomb in your vehicle. Do not drive any of your vehicles. Call your field office bomb response unit immediately."

"Wait. What? Kat? No. Oh God, please no."

Mr. Smith watched the babe get into the Ford Explorer and the vehicle backed out of the driveway. He couldn't see the babe anymore due to the heavy window tinting. It was not the Cash Man, so he aborted the attack. Something caught his attention on the left. An older lady in a white overcoat walked out of her house and down the front steps. She headed to the one-car garage on the left of the house. The front door of the Cash Man's house banged open, and a male tore out of the house. He chased the Explorer down the street, screaming something, with a dog in close pursuit. The older lady saw the man running down the street. She held up her hand to stop the Explorer, walked in the direction of the car, and pointed at the man in pursuit. She pushed her garage door opener, and the Explorer exploded.

38

Director Santiago looked around at one of the most exclusive, and secure, conference rooms in the world. It was a little nondescript for its purpose. It was a square, concrete box, located 200' beneath the New Executive Office Building. It was only accessible by an elevator with two access points outside the director's office, and one stop on the Leadership Subway. There were no buttons on the elevator. You only gained access via a biometric hand scanner and voice recognition.

The Eisenhower Administration built the Leadership Subway. It connected the White House, the Pentagon, Congress, the State Department, and the Supreme Court via a private subway system. It allowed the country's leadership to meet at various locations without any prying eyes, including the press. It also provided security to move leaders around the city in times of war or unrest. Access to the Leadership Subway was granted only to the President, Vice President, Speaker of the House, President Pro Tem of the Senate, Chief Justice of the Supreme Court, the Secretary of State, the Secretary of Defense, and the Chairman of the Joint Chiefs.

The Black and White Club conference room was even more exclusive than the subway system with only six members. Director Santiago placed name placards around a circular conference room, since every member in this chamber was equal: President, Vice President, Speaker of the House, President Pro Tem of the Senate, and the Chief Justice of the Supreme Court. Director Santiago was a member, but he didn't get a vote. He placed the placards at random during meetings, so no one got the impression of a personal seat. Large video screens surrounded the table on each of the four walls, so one could get an unobstructed view no matter where the chair was. A refrigerator in the corner contained each of the members' favorite non-alcoholic drinks. A modular bar sat next to the fridge in the shape of a wine barrel. It opened into a bar and held each of the member's favorite alcoholic drink. Ike donated the bar when he built the conference room. A coffee cart with two Keurigs plumbed into the wall was located on the opposite wall with a carousel of coffee pods next to them offering a variety of flavors. A basket of flavored creamers and sugar was next to the pods. Paper towels and stirring straws were in bins on a shelf below the cart.

The elevator door chimed, and a green light lit over the doors. The doors opened. The Speaker of the House and the President Pro Temp of the Senate walked in.

"Good afternoon, Vince." Katherine F. Rich was the Speaker of the House from California's 12th District in San Francisco. She wore a green, flowered-print, knee-length dress. She had short brown hair parted to the right with gold hoop earrings and a matching gold necklace with the name SAM on a gold chain.

"Good afternoon, Madam Speaker. Can I get you anything?"

"No thanks, Vince. I'm just going to get some coffee." She walked over to the coffee cart.

Donna Ruiz Alonzo, the senior senator from Florida, and the top Republican in the Senate, located her placard and sat down. Her long brown hair fell loose below her shoulders. She was the only daughter and heir to a sugar fortune in Florida. She wore a gray and black sweater dress with black pumps. She had an intense white smile, brown eyes, and a small mole on her right cheek.

"Vince, is everyone going to make it?" Senator Alonzo looked at Vince.

"Yes, Senator, we should have a quorum."

"Is this about Boston?"

"Yes, Senator."

The elevator chimed again, and the doors opened. President Brian C. Byrne and his Vice President Amelia Evelina walked through the doors. The president carried a large, black, leather briefcase. Inside was an aluminum case that contained the nuclear launch codes for all U.S. nuclear forces. The military aide on duty usually carried the "football." This was the one place that was off limits to the Mil Aides and all Secret Service personnel. The Coast Guard Presidential Mil Aide and the Vice President's

Navy Mil Aide were topside on the subway platform along with Secret Service details.

"Ladies, how is everyone doing?" President Byrne scanned the room with a smile.

"We're fine, Mr. President." Speaker Rich poured a cup of coffee and added some cream and sugar. "Good to see you again."

"Same here, Katherine." The president walked over to Vince, and the vice president walked over to get coffee.

President Byrne was an athletic, 45-year-old, former Republican Governor of Iowa dressed in a tailored, dark blue, power suit, solid maroon tie, crisp, white shirt, and shined black classic shoes. He had piercing blue eyes with a short military haircut cut close on the side of his head to hide his gray hair. He exuded power and money.

"Anything new on Boston?" President Byrne shook hands with Vince.

"Yes, Mr. President. We identified the victims. I'll cover it in the brief."

"Okay, Vince, thanks." He looked at his watch. "Anyone seen Carlo?"

"He was wrapping up some oral arguments when I talked to him this morning," Vice President Evelina said. She walked over to the table carrying her coffee. Vice President Amelia Evelina, the former Republican Senator from Georgia, was the first African American female elected Vice President of the United States. She was the perfect partner to President Byrne with her long black hair pulled back and piled in a tight bun on the back of her head. She wore a black-and-white, horizontal-striped dress off the shoulder with matching black-and-white striped shoes with a flat heel. She always had a ready smile and would hold her own in any beauty pageant in the country. She took her seat at the table, stirring her coffee and watching Vince.

The elevator chimed again. "That is probably Carlo." President Byrne turned towards the elevator doors.

The doors opened and in walked Carlo Virgilio, the Chief Justice of the Supreme Court. He looked like a college professor, and he fit the job description. He had been nominated to the Supreme Court while he was a law professor at Harvard. Carlo was pushing 70 with a gray receding hairline, gray beard, and mustache. He walked with a slight limp from a

mountain biking accident last summer in Colorado. He took off his wrinkled blue sports coat and draped it over his seat.

"Sorry I'm a little late, folks. The lawyers wouldn't shut up." Carlo
pulled out his chair and sat down.

"Lawyers are long winded? Say it isn't so." Katherine walked over from
the coffee cart and sat down.

"Mr. President, I believe we have a quorum, would you please call the
meeting to order." Vince nodded at the president.

"All right, Vince." President Byrne opened a black binder in front of
him and started reading:

> Under the purview of Executive Order 9513, Addendum A, this
> meeting of the Black and White Club is called to order. All actions
> taken by this committee must be by unanimous decision and based
> on the best judgment of each member without consideration to posi-
> tion, political affiliation, or current United States law. The only guid-
> ing principle is the preservation of the democratic institution which
> is the United States of America and the defense of our Constitution
> against all enemies foreign and domestic. All the proceedings, and
> decisions, made during this meeting shall never be divulged beyond
> these founding members. Does everyone agree?

Brian looked around the table. They ignored official titles and positions once the meeting started. It was one person, one vote. Everyone nodded in agreement. "Okay, Vince, the floor is yours."

"Thank you, Brian." Vince pressed a button on a video remote. A map
of the United States appeared on the screens with a star over Boston.

"This morning, at approximately 0700, three separate car bombs
exploded simultaneously in Boston, Situate, and at the old Naval Air Station
in South Weymouth, Mass." He clicked through a series of three pictures,
which showed the blast area at each site. "The bomb in Boston claimed the
life of DEA Special Agent Chen Li." Vince brought up pictures showing the
smoking remains of a red Toyota Camry and the service picture of Chen Li
smiling next to an American flag.

"The bomb in Situate claimed the life of DEA Special Agent Chase Britt." Two more pictures flashed on the screen of Chase Britt and his smoking gray Fusion.

"We believe the third bomb in South Weymouth was intended for FBI Special Agent Joshua Martin. As an aside, Special Agent Martin is one of ours, White 55."

"Any correlation to us?" Amelia looked at Vince.

"We don't believe so." Vince scanned the group. They were pissed. He could always tell. He continued.

"The bomb in Weymouth killed Josh's wife Katherine, and a neighbor, Ellen Page. Ellen is the wife of Brigadier General Robert Page, U.S. Army. They are neighbors of the Martins. We think Ellen was collateral damage. The Pages were not the target. Also, Katherine Martin was three months pregnant." Vince stepped through pictures of Josh and Katherine posing with Syrin and a shot of the Explorer wreckage.

"Son of a bitch," muttered Katherine. "What about Agent Martin?"

"Agent Martin was airlifted to Mass General Hospital in Boston, where he is in stable condition and under 24-hr protection from both the FBI and the U.S. Marshals Service."

"What about the dog?" Donna stared at Vince like the answer better be she had a personal veterinarian.

"FBI agents brought the dog to the hospital to stay with Agent Martin." Vince switched to the next slide.

"Good on them," Brian chimed in.

"In addition to the targeted attacks this morning, there were additional homicides over the weekend related to this case." Vince clicked to a picture of Quinn Christy slumped back in the driver seat with a black hole in place of his left eye.

"This is DEA Assistant Special Agent in Charge Quinn Christy. He was shot yesterday afternoon by unknown assailants in a downtown Boston parking garage." Vince put up another picture of Chino lying on a shiny tile floor in a pool of blood.

"This is Chino. He was the number two for the Centre Street Kings. He was killed in the Concord Correctional Institution on Sunday watching the Patriots game on TV.

"And this is a picture of Big Papi in his David Ortiz Jersey face-down in a plate of chicken with a dime-sized hole in the back of his head. Big Papi is Jason Brown and the leader of the Centre Street Kings."

"Any of this related to the shootout in the Back Bay parking garage?" Carlo stroked his beard.

"Yes, thanks for the lead-in. The Back Bay event was an ambush of Agent Martin by the Centre Street Kings." Vince moved through a series of pictures showing the dead bodies behind the Chargers, Big Dog sprawled on the Beamer, and Double Down lying on the concrete floor in a pool of blood with a missing lower leg. "The gentleman flopped on the silver BMW is Tyler Lanier, also known as the Nigerian Nightmare, and Big Dog. He was the number 3 in the Centre Street Kings."

"What happened to Agent Martin?" Brian's face turned a brighter shade of red with each picture.

"Ruined suit and his truck looks like this." Vince brought up a picture of Josh's truck covered in bullet holes, blown-out windows, tires, and all the lights shot out.

"Holy crap." Brian shook his head in amazement.

"Yeah, he wasn't too happy with that. The truck was a Shelby F150 and one of only 500 made in the United States."

"Does his insurance cover that?" Carlo took a small notebook out of his pocket and made a note.

"I don't think his personal insurance will cover it, but the FBI will as it was in the line of duty," Vince replied. "But I don't think he is too worried about it. His net worth is over 30 million."

"30 million?" Donna's brow creased with the question. "How is that possible on a government salary?"

"Inheritance. His grandfather was one of the founders of the Bank of Boston and his family owns the largest dairy operation in New Hampshire."

"So, he's not doing this for the money?"

"No, Amelia. If you ever want to meet a real patriot, this is it." Vince pushed a picture of Josh in his SEAL uniform into the center of the table.

"I've got to ask." Katherine folded her hands in front of her. "This looks like a gang war. What does it have to do with us?"

"This," Vince flashed a picture of Vincent Casas on the screen, "this is Vincent Casas. He's the son-in-law of one Juan Pablo Rodriguez."

"The drug lord?" Donna was interested now.

"The one," Vince confirmed. "Agent Martin was part of an FBI under-cover operation targeting the La Libertad Cartel, the Centre Street Kings, and a possible mole in the Boston DEA."

"Agent Christy?" Carlo made another notation in his book.

"Yes. We found a DEA GPS tracking tablet in one of the gold Chargers in the Back Bay ambush. We also found a DEA tracker on Agent Martin's F150." Vince flashed to pictures of the tracker on the underside of the truck and the DEA tracking tablet.

"The fingerprints on the laptop belonged to Agent Christy. Our finan-cial forensics team also found a safety deposit box in Thailand, and an off-shore bank account in the Cayman Islands, which belonged to Agent Christy. We're working with State to access both accounts."

"On Saturday, Agent Martin conducted an undercover buy for a kilo of heroin with the Centre Street Kings. The Centre Street Kings are the distribution arm of the La Libertad Cartel in New England. Vincent Casas was present in the hotel room when the buy went down. The DEA raided the hotel room, not knowing an undercover buy was in progress. During the takedown, Casas and Agent Martin's CI were killed." Vince flashed to pictures of Benny lying on a carpet between two hotel beds with most of his head gone, and a picture of Vincent Casas wedged between the TV and the wall.

"Who killed who?" Amelia looked at Vince.

"Benny, the CI, was shot by Vincent Casas. Agent Martin shot Casas in self-defense."

"The raiding DEA agents were Agents Li and Britt. Chino was also present in the hotel room." Vince checked his notes to make sure he got the sequence right.

"So, someone is cleaning house?" Brian sat back in his chair. "The cartel?"

"That is our theory." Vince put the remote on the conference table. "But they are using a third party, and we have no information on their identity. There are no known La Libertad Cartel members in New England at this time."

"So, that is why you involved us?" Katherine also took out a small notepad. None of the principals put anything related to the Black and White Club into an electronic format. You can't hack a piece of paper, and distribution is limited to one person at a time.

"Yes. In the span of 72 hours, the La Libertad Cartel is responsible for the deaths of three DEA agents, the attempted murder of an FBI agent, and the killing of eight other Americans on U.S. soil."

Vince opened a folder in front of him, then passed out a single sheet of paper to each member. "This is a direct-action request against the Libertad Cartel, and any person, persons, or companies employed by the cartel for the furtherance of their criminal enterprise," Vince said.

Everyone around the table reviewed the document. Everyone knew that direct-action meant *to remove, kill, or prosecute anyone connected to the La Libertad Cartel in the U.S., or foreign soil, without the benefit of a trial by their peers.* Sometimes the best solution is the 38-cent solution, a bullet to the back of the head.

"We have a motion before the committee for direct action," Brian said. "All those in favor?" Everyone raised their hand. "The motion carries. Please sign the document."

Everyone signed the document and handed it back to Vince, who collected them and slipped them back into the folder.

"Any other business?" Brian looked around the table.

"Just one," Vince said. "I recommend we recruit Agent Joshua Martin into our Black Operations Directorate."

"Do you think he's qualified?"

"Yes, I do, Donna. He's a graduate of the U.S. Coast Guard Academy, a decorated Navy SEAL, a trained FBI undercover agent, and he killed four and arrested four of the gang members who ambushed him with AK47s and walked away with a shot-up truck and a ruined suit. Also, based on recent events, I believe he's very motivated," Vince said.

"Any objections?" Brian looked at everyone around the table, and they all nodded in agreement. "Okay, Vince, approved." The President slapped the table with his hand. "Adjourned."

"Thank you, Mr. President," Vince said.

Everyone stood, gathered their things to leave, and walked over to the elevator. President Byrne remained behind. "Amelia, please tell my detail I'll be right up," President Byrne said.

"Will do, Mr. President," Vice President Evelina said. She got on the elevator with the others, and the doors closed.

"Vince," President Byrne said. "I'd like to personally meet Special Agent Martin if he accepts our invitation, and he passes the initiation."

"Yes, of course, Mr. President."

The president walked over to the elevator and picked up the football. "I know you guys are selective in deciding who stays and goes, but in this case, I think you should err on the side of go. Bombing two innocent women, one three months pregnant, on a street in America. That just can't happen without consequences. Certain folks in the world need to know that's bad for business." The elevator doors opened, and the president stepped inside. He gave Vince a wave of his hand as the doors closed.

39

"Cutter YEATON, this is Sierra Tango, actual, in the red," Josh said, as he keyed the mike on the secure radio. "We are on the beach and making our approach."

"Roger," came the reply.

Josh gave the advance signal, and the SEALs moved out. Chief Dormann and Petty Officer Phillips moved right. Petty Officer Boye and Carter moved left. Josh went straight ahead with Banana as his swim buddy with Miller and Sneeds right behind. The Sea Island Security sisters, McDonald and Lacava, trailed everyone.

They moved quickly through the beach sand and the vegetation to get on target before everyone took off. No need for stealth. Everyone knew they were coming.

"Contact," Chief Dormann said. "Two Tangos down. Eyes on the prize. No runners."

"Roger," Josh said. "We're moving now." Josh and his team doubled time along the edge of a well-worn path to the clearing. A gray fiberglass submarine sat in a cradle about 5 feet off the ground surrounded by all types of construction equipment. Dormann and Phillips were standing next to the sub. Boye and Carter came in from the left. Josh turned back from the sub and walked over to a palm tree to take a leak. The clearing erupted in a giant fireball, as the narco sub exploded. Josh pitched forward, pushed by the hot hand of the devil. He flew 10' in the air and impacted face first into the sand. Being dragged through sand. Hot sand. Up his nose, in his eyes. Down his throat. *I can't breathe, I can't breathe. Kat. I can't breathe, help me, Kat....I—*

Josh jerked awake and opened his eyes. Owen Quinn and Chris Anthony were sitting in a pair of chairs watching *The Price Is Right* on the wall-mounted TV. He moved his head a little, and the room started spinning. He opened his eyes wider to clear the fog. The blood pressure cuff tightened on his arm and then released. The heart monitor beeped above his head, and a dead weight pressed against his left leg. He moved the leg a little to free it up, and Syrin popped her head over his hip and whimpered.

Owen looked over at the sound of Syrin. "Hey, look who's back." Owen walked over to Josh. He got Syrin off the bed. She sat down next to him. Chris walked out of the room, and he came back trailed by an entourage.

A middle-aged Korean woman in a white lab coat led the pack. "Mr. Martin, my name is Lilly Kang. I'm your doctor. Can you hear me?" She waved a small flashlight in each of Josh's eyes.

Josh blinked at the brightness of the flashlight and tried to speak, but something was in his throat. He nodded up and down.

"Okay," Dr. Kang said. "You have a breathing tube. We're going to take it out. Lean your head back." Josh tilted his head back, and the doctor pulled the tube out of his throat. "There you go, better?"

"Yes," Josh whispered. His throat burned. Someone handed him a glass of water, and he took a few sips, which helped clear his throat.

"You took quite a blow to your system," Doctor Kang said. "We ran a lot of tests while you were out. Everything is negative. You'll have a headache for a couple of days, but you should be fine. Let me know if you need anything." She turned to leave and looked at Syrin.

"What is that dog still doing here? This is a hospital, you know."

"Doc, we've been over this before. The dog stays. Call your hospital administrator. She gave the approval," Owen said.

Doctor Kang turned and marched out of the room with her entourage on her heels.

Owen turned back to Josh. "She's the best neurologist on staff, but she's a bitch. Also, doesn't like dogs. Come on, Syrin. You can get back up. The mean lady is gone." Syrin hopped back in and gave Josh a few licks on his face.

Josh scratched Syrin on the head, and tears welled up in his eyes. He gave her a big hug, holding her close, feeling her chest rise and fall. "Sorry, girl, I tried to save Mommy." Syrin whimpered at the word "Mommy." The

THE BLACK AND WHITE CLUB: GENESIS 195

tears rolled down Josh's cheek, as he held Syrin close. Owen and Chris walked back to their chairs to give Josh some space.

Josh cried with Syrin. His body trembled with each sob. Feeling the emptiness and sense of futility. So much lost…over what? He played over the explosion in his mind. The Explorer going up in a fireball, Ellen disappearing, the force of the blast hitting his body, the blackness, no Kat. Josh held Syrin for over an hour until he had no more tears to shed. Deep in the recesses of his conscience, he flipped the switch from grieving husband to warrior. Time to make things right.

Mr. Smith retrieved the cellcrpyt SAT phone from his right desk drawer and punched up the only number in the contact list.

"Is it done?" came the voice on the other end of the call.

"Almost, El Jefe, but we have a problem."

"What does almost mean?"

"We missed on the Cash Man. We wired his Explorer, but the wife took the car. I aborted the op. A next-door neighbor walked out of her house and used her garage door opener. The signal detonated the device. But we got bigger problems."

"Get to the problem; I got things to do."

"The Cash Man is LT Josh Martin," Mr. Smith said.

"Are you sure?"

"Yes, Sir. He chased the SUV down the street before the bomb went off. I had a clear view until the explosion knocked him on his ass."

"No chance to finish him?"

"No, El Jefe. It was on an old Navy base. Military types run towards an explosion, not away from it. We had to pull out fast."

"Where is LT Martin now?"

"They took him to Mass General Hospital. He's got a massive security detail both in and out of the hospital."

"Well, get it done, Mr. Smith. Our favorite Navy SEAL does not get another chance. Do whatever you have to do, but make sure he disappears," El Jefe said.

"Yes, boss." The line went dead.

40

They kept Josh overnight and released him in the morning. A five-car security escort took him over to the Cape Sands Resort. A casino with its own private security force and 24-hr monitored video surveillance was the safest place in Boston, especially with a U.S. Marshal security detail camped outside his office. Owen and Chris walked him and Syrin to his office apartment and then left to get some sleep.

Josh walked over to his bar and got Syrin's bowl out of one of the cabinets. He filled it with water and set it on the floor. Syrin slurped for about 20 seconds, and then climbed on the couch for a nap. Josh got a glass, filled it with ice, and retrieved a 12 oz can of ginger ale from the fridge, and poured it over the ice. He set the can on the counter and walked over to Syrin and sat next to her on the couch. She put her head on his lap, and Josh stroked the top of her head and looked out the windows at the Boston skyline. It was a bright clear day, the sun was shining, and a few white puffy clouds dotted a blue sky. Kat and the baby were dead. His world shattered, but the sun still came up, and the world moved on like nothing happened, just like losing his SEAL team so many years ago, like nothing, fucking, happened. Josh got to his feet and threw the glass of ginger ale at the desk, which broke on impact, sending glass, ice cubes, and ginger ale cascading on the floor.

"Why the fuck did this happen? Why does this always happen to me?" Josh clenched his fists and entire body. "Why did you take her, God? She never did anything to anyone. Why do you always leave me?" Josh paced around his office wanting to strike something, anything. A knock on the door snapped him back into reality.

"Josh, its Enzo."

Josh felt the calm return to his body. He put the anger and rage back in the box like he had done so many times before and walked over to his office door and opened it.

Enzo walked in looking like a billion bucks in a dark, custom-tailored, navy suit, white shirt, and red power tie. He gave Josh a big hug.

"Josh, I'm so sorry," Enzo said, releasing the bear hug. "If there's anything you need?"

"Thanks, Mr. Bosco. Can I get you anything?"

"No, I'm good, Josh." Enzo walked over and sat down at the conference table, ignoring the glass and ice crunching underfoot. Josh pulled up a chair across from him.

"So how are you doing? Physically?" Enzo studied Josh to gauge his response.

"Everything checked out fine. They gave me some 800 mg Motrin for headaches and no booze for a while."

"So, you didn't waste any good bourbon?" Enzo gestured at the floor covered in melting ice and glass.

"No, Sir, its ginger ale. I deposited the check."

"I know, son."

"I was also going to resign from the FBI. We were going to raise kids away from all this. I wanted to go back to New Hampshire, but Kat wanted to go somewhere warm."

"Any idea on who is responsible?"

"Gotta be the La Libertad Cartel. Who else has the balls to kill two federal agents and try to get a third?"

"What's the plan?"

"I'm taking Kat back to New Hampshire. Her parents were killed in a car accident a few years back, and she was an only child. There will be a small memorial service in Lancaster, and then I plan to spread her ashes in Martin Meadow Pond. I asked her to marry me in a boat in the middle of that pond, just as the sun was starting to set." Josh shook his head a little, as he could feel the tears welling up. "For us, it was heaven on Earth, at least in the summer."

Enzo stood and put his hand on Josh's shoulder. "Why don't you get some rest? You can stay here as long as you want. We can talk about your future when you get everything settled."

"Thanks, boss."

Enzo walked out of the office and pulled the door shut behind him. Josh looked over at Syrin. "Ready for a car ride?" Syrin jumped off the couch and bounded over to Josh, wagging her tail.

41

Jim Palmer got out of his chair, reached both arms over his head, and stretched his 6'1" frame. He was clean-shaven with blond hair and a short military haircut dressed in tan khakis, an LL Bean buttoned-down, light blue shirt, and a maroon cardigan. He picked up a mug of coffee off his desk, took a sip, and looked out his office window at the overcast, dreary day, which shrouded the city of Montreal. It would be like this until spring. *How the hell did I get stuck here? I need to get some sunshine on the next assignment. They owe me.* His phone vibrated in his pocket and started playing "Flight of the Valkyries." He pulled it out and looked at the screen. Unknown number. He pressed the green accept button.

"Yeah?"

"You got an assignment. We just sent the details to your account."

"When?"

"Now."

"On it." The phone went dead.

Becka Kendall answered the director's call on the first ring.

"Yes, Sir."

"Good morning Becka, what is the status of White 55?"

"Let me check, Sir." She punched up her screen and clicked on White 55. "Released from the hospital yesterday. Spent the night at the Cape Sands, and he's now traveling north to his hometown of Lancaster, New Hampshire."

"Any security?"

"No, Sir. He refused it."

"Okay, thanks. Have a good watch."

Josh set the cruise at 65 mph on the rented white Ford Flex and headed north on I93 out of the city. Syrin was in the passenger seat enjoying the smells wafting through the car vent from the outside circulated air. Y2K country played on the sound system, and Toby Keith wished he was a cowboy. The ride from Boston to Lancaster was 168 miles, which took a little over three hours depending on traffic. The traffic was light heading north in the morning, so it didn't take long to cross the border into New Hampshire. He followed the highway north, watching the faded colors of fall drop to the ground in piles of yellow, orange, and red the further he got into the North Country. He remembered his dad saying that fall moves south at about 26 miles a day. No idea if it's true, but it made a good memory, just like this ride. He envisioned this trip before, driving the Shelby north, Kat laughing in the front seat, Syrin in the back, music playing, leaving the city behind to raise a family in God's country. *Now*, he thought, *Kat is riding in a box in the back of a piece of shit rental car, and Syrin is riding in the front, realizing no more mommy.* Josh wiped the tears from his eyes and scratched Syrin behind the ears. She rubbed against his hand. *Just you and me girl. I hope we get it right.*

Jim Palmer looked over at his driver, Greg Bennett. Greg was a former Army Ranger from Albany, New York, entirely bald with the look of George the Animal Steel from the Professional Wrestling Hall of Fame, about 6'0, and 270 lbs of muscle going to fat. He wouldn't win a beauty contest, but he would slit your throat and wipe the blood on your shirt.

"Everything set?" Jim turned to look at Greg.

"Let me check," Greg said. "Bravo team. Ops check?"

"Bravo team, locked and loaded," came the reply from Car 2.

"Roger. Charlie team. Ops check?"

"We are ready to kick ass and take names," came the reply from Car 3.

"Standard comms," Greg said.

"Qui. Charlie team. Locked and loaded, ready to kick ass and take names," came the reply from Car 3.

"Roger," Greg said. "Fucking French, why did we have to take these guys?"

"Short notice request," Jim said. "Besides, French Foreign Legion is not bad in a firefight, provided you can put up with the bullshit."

"Seems like overkill to me," Greg said. "For one fucking squid."

Jim turned in his seat and looked back at Cameron "Cam" Cooper and Aaron Mitchell. They were both dressed in woodland camouflage uniforms with short military haircuts and intense looks on their faces.

"You guys ready?"

"Yeah, boss," Cam said. "Rangers lead the way. I also think this is over-kill for one guy, but I'm not paying the bill. Did we really need the Joint Force 2 guys? Aaron and I could just pop across the border, put two in the back of the target's head, and be back in time for evening chow."

"Boss wants to make sure this guy is deader than a roadkill skimmer," Jim said. "So, we go in heavy. Like the Frenchies, the Joint Force 2 guys were available, plus we want to see them in action on the other side of the gray line."

"If they don't add up?" Greg started the SUV.

"They don't make the return trip," Jim said. "All right, let's roll."

The three-car convoy of dark blue Chevy Tahoes pulled away from the curb and headed south.

42

Josh wound through the White Mountains of New Hampshire on I93 and turned into the parking lot of what was left of the Old Man of the Mountain. He hopped out of the Flex and opened the back door to get a jacket. He closed the door, walked around the front, and opened Syrin's door. She bounded out of the car and ran over to a patch of grass near the parking lot to use the facilities. The lot was empty, except for an old gray Chevy pickup and a red Nissan. They must work at the gift shop. Syrin ran back, looking to play. A cold wind blew some leaves across the pavement. Josh zipped up his jacket and started down the path to Profile Lake. Syrin took off to the trees on the side of the walkway to look for squirrels or anything else of interest. Josh's mind wandered to a different time.

Every summer Josh, his sister Jess, his brother from another mother "Little Jim," and Mom and Dad would take a trip down through the mountains and hit all the tourist spots: The Old Man of the Mountain, the Flume, the Gorge, and the journey would end at Clark's Trained Bears. The sound of laughter from long ago drifted through the trees, along with the sound of Kat asking a million questions about the fate of the Old Man of the Mountain, when they walked this path to Profile Lake tracing Josh's childhood memories. One of Josh's favorite photos of Kat was taken with her posing in front of the historic Old Man sign: "*Men hang out their signs indicative of their respective trades; shoemakers hang out a gigantic shoe; jewelers a monster watch, and the dentist hangs out a gold tooth; but up in the Mountains of New Hampshire, God Almighty has hung out a sign to show that there, He makes men.*"

Josh watched Syrin crisscross the asphalt path running from one tree line to another and checking on Josh's progress. She didn't want to lose anyone else. Profile Lake loomed in the distance just beyond Profile Plaza.

Kat never got to see the Old Man of the Mountain. He fell off the mountain on May 3, 2003. Some hikers heard a rumble at night but had no way of knowing what they heard. Two Park Rangers saw the aftermath the next day. Josh remembered getting the call from his mom telling him about the event. He was a Third Classman at the Academy studying for finals. They said it was like losing a family member, but it wasn't. He could still feel the intense pain of finding out his dad died of a heart attack as a freshman in high school. He and little Jim were walking up the driveway from the bus stop when he saw his younger sister crying on the front steps. "Daddy died." He could still hear the words and see the anguished look on her face. Daddy died. Almost as bad as your wife and child are dead. A bunch of rocks falling off the mountain didn't come close.

The path to Profile Lake ended at the Old Man Profile Plaza, which included seven steel "Profilers" that recreate the visage of the Old Man looking over Franconia Notch. The Plaza also included hundreds of paver stones purchased by friends of the Old Man from throughout the Granite State and far beyond and engraved with personal messages. A mosaic of gray stones of various sizes engraved with family names, conservation groups like the Appalachian Mountain Club, and personal remembrances. Josh walked over to the edge of the Plaza and knelt next to a stone and ran his hand across the gray surface, feeling the roughness against his fingers. His tears stained the stone, as they ran down his cheek and fell to the ground. He traced the engraving with his finger. "Josh and Kat Martin. So others will remember."

Josh got up and wiped away the tears from his face with the back of his left arm and looked across Profile Lake with patches of white wave crests running away from the wind. "It wasn't supposed to be this way. We were going to grow old together, and I would die one minute after the Good Lord took you to heaven. I guess he had a different plan."

Syrin was getting a drink in the lake and checking to see if there was anything worth chasing in the water. "Come on, Syrin, let's go." Syrin splashed out of the water and shook off, which sent water flying in all directions. She did a little shimmy shake and ran over to Josh. "You better hope you air dry before we get back to the car, or you're riding in the back." She sprinted down the path back to the car, barking in the wind.

Mr. Smith punched the number on his cryptcell.

"Yes?"

"Everything is in motion. We have a team coming across the border. There's a memorial service in his hometown. Some place called Lancaster in New Hampshire. He's going to dump his wife's ashes in a pond outside of town. We'll take him there, away from any witnesses."

"Okay. Remember—no witnesses."

"Yes, Sir," Mr. Smith said, and he clicked off.

LCDR Becka Kendall picked up the phone and hit the director's call button.

"Director Santiago."

"Afternoon, Sir," Becka said. "We got you a Pave Hawk out of Andrews. It's waiting for you now. It will bounce once at Coast Guard Air Station Cape Cod for fuel, en route to your final destination at the Mount Washington Regional Airport. The airport is located just outside Whitefield, New Hampshire, about 17 miles south of Lancaster. A team out of Boston will meet you upon arrival."

"Thanks, Becka. Sounds good."

43

Josh pulled out of the Old Man parking lot and headed back north on I93. He cleared the notches and took Exit 41 into the thriving metropolis of Littleton, New Hampshire, about 6,000 souls. Not a metropolis by urban standards, but it was to a farm kid from Lancaster. The town of Littleton straddled the Ammonoosuc River. "North of the Notch" is how it's described by the locals, meaning Franconia Notch, but it's north of Crawford Notch too, and almost parallel with Jefferson Notch. It was also a town of firsts for Josh. First McDonald's, first real movie theater, and the first taste of penny candy at Chutters, the longest candy counter in the world according to the sign on the door and the Guinness Book of World Records. Josh passed it on the right, as he bumped along with traffic down Main Street, headed to Route 3, and north to Lancaster. At the end of Main Street, he hung a left on Route 3, past the Jax Theater on the left. Syrin turned doughnuts in the front seat because she knew what came next. Ice cream. Josh pulled into the parking lot of the Martin Dairy about ½ mile down on the right and parked between a blue KIA and a white Corolla.

The Martin Dairy was a white building with blue trim and a string of multi-color Christmas lights strung around the edges. A blue neon sign with Martin Dairy and a red blinking arrow pointing at the building was mounted on the roof. There were six parking spots in front with a lot in the back for about eight more. There were two walk-up windows in front facing Route 3. Six brown picnic tables were set up to the left of the building. A young mother with a stroller was sitting at one, trading licks on an ice cream cone with a toddler in the stroller. Two more women were eating ice cream sundaes, in a deep conversation about something.

Josh opened his door and got out, and Syrin jumped across the seat and followed him right out the door. "So, what do you think you're going to get?" Syrin wagged her tail and did the ice cream dance around Josh's legs as he stepped up to the order window on the right. A sign on the left window said, "Pick up."

The window slid open, and a young girl behind the counter in a pretty pink dress with printed flowers, and her blond hair pulled back in a pony-tail greeted them with a smile. "Can I help you, please?"

"Yes. I'd like two large vanilla cones, one with chocolate jimmies, and could you put a little extra on the cone without jimmies for my friend here?" And just like that, Syrin put her front legs on the counter and put her head in the window.

"Of course, I can. What a pretty dog," said the ice cream girl, patting Syrin's muzzle.

"Syrin, sit," Josh said. Syrin dropped into a sitting position next to Josh.

"Wow, she minds well too. I wish my dog did that," the ice cream girl said. "That will be $8.57."

Josh handed her a $10 bill and put the dollar and change in a plastic tip cup on the counter.

"Thank you. You can pick up your order at the next window."

The girl turned to make the ice cream cones, and Josh caught the profile of a mother-to-be. The tears started to well in his eyes, but he willed them away. He reached into his pocket and pulled out his money clip, peeled off three hundred-dollar bills, and stuffed them into the tip cup.

The window opened on the pickup side, and an extra, extra-large vanilla cone emerged from inside wrapped in a napkin.

"This is for the pretty dog," the ice cream girl said.

Josh took the cone.

"And this is for you," the girl said, as she reached out with another cone with chocolate jimmies.

Josh took the second cone, walked over to the picnic tables, and sat on the one that was set back the farthest from the road. Syrin followed him over on high alert in case someone decided to attack Josh before he got to the picnic table with the cones. Josh sat on a bench and started eating his cone. He licked the jimmies off, careful that none of the ice cream dripped on his hand. He held out the second cone for Syrin, who had no such worry about drips. She licked the ice cream, and ice cream dripped all over Josh's hand. Syrin made quick work of the ice cream and then munched the entire cone in two bites. She then cleaned up Josh's hand.

Josh finished the jimmies off the cone and started on the ice cream, when a man, about Josh's age, walked out of the side door of the dairy. He had curly black hair with a scar over his right eye that ran the length of his eyebrow. He wore white pants, a white shirt, with a white apron covered in chocolate stains. He approached Josh, holding the three hundred-dollar bills in his trembling hands.

"Excuse me, Sir. My wife said you left these in the tip jar. Did you mean to do it, or was it a mistake?"

"No, I intended to do it," Josh said. "I noticed you guys were expecting, and I thought you could use the extra money, and your wife?"

"Audrey, and my name's David," said the man, extending his hand.

Josh shook his hand. "My name's Josh. And your wife Audrey was kind to my dog, Syrin."

"Well, thank you, Sir. You don't know how much we need the money," David said. "Baby stuff is expensive."

"You're welcome, David. Boy or girl?"

"It's a boy."

"I don't mean to pry, David, but does this place offer health insurance?"

"Yes, Sir. The Martin family is very generous. Working for the Martins is the best job in the North Country, especially with the downturn in the economy. I'll let you get back to your ice cream. Thank you again, Josh. Audrey and I really appreciate it." David walked back inside.

Josh finished the ice cream down to the cone and gave it to Syrin, who finished it in one bite. "You better be careful. You're going to get fat eating all that ice cream." He grabbed Syrin on both sides of her head and scratched behind her ears. She wagged her tail and leaned into Josh's knees. "Okay, girl, let's get going. Time to get home." Josh slid off the bench and looked at the top of the weathered picnic table. Someone had scratched Kat loves Josh into the wood. He tapped it twice with his left hand. "Time to get home." Josh walked back to the car. The window slid open on the order side.

"Thank you so much," Audrey said, waving out the window.

"You're welcome." Josh opened the driver door, and Syrin hopped through, assuming the shotgun position. Josh got in and said, "Who do you want to listen to?"

Syrin barked.

"AC/DC it is. IPOD, play song, *'You shook me all night long.'*" Josh started singing to the music. He backed the Flex out to Route 3, shifted to drive, and headed north; 20 miles to home.

44

U.S. Customs and Border Protection Officer Joe Twydell took a sip of coffee and set the mug down on his copy of the *USA Today*, which was spread out on his desk. He was three hours into his eight-hour watch at the Pittsburg/ Chartierville border crossing in New Hampshire. Officer Twydell was almost 58, and he felt every year. He had black hair going gray on the sides with a prominent nose, blue eyes, and a slight paunch. Three more years and he could retire at 40 years of service. His desk faced the roadway and the security area to inspect incoming vehicles. The Canadian Entry building was also visible out his window to the left. He had coffee with Rudy, the Canadian inspector, before coming on duty.

Joe saw the three-car convoy of dark SUVs rolling down Quebec Route 253 on the early warning camera three miles out, so the inspector would get advance notice of approaching vehicles. New Hampshire shared a 58-mile (93 kilometers) border with the Province of Quebec, but the only Canadian border crossing was located at the northern end of the town of Pittsburg at the terminus of U.S. Route 3. The road carried vacation travelers and locals. Roughly 7,400 passenger cars and 1,150 commercial vehicles go through the U.S. port at Pittsburg each year. Most of the traffic through this port comes in the summer vacation months of July and August; not so much in late fall, especially a three-car convoy.

Joe keyed his radio. "Rudy, do you see these guys?"

"Yeah, I see 'em, Joe," Rudy said.

"You get any info on VIP crossings today?"

"Nope, nothing."

"Yeah, me neither. Watch my back, will ya?"

"You got it, Joe."

Joe took another sip of his coffee. He zipped up his uniform jacket and walked outside. The cold air filled his nostrils. The three-car convoy of dark blue Chevy Tahoes pulled up to the inspection line and stopped. Joe walked around the front and approached the driver side window. A Sea Island Security advertising magnet was stuck on the driver side door. The driver side window went down.

"Good morning. Where are you folks headed?" Joe gave the occupants of the vehicle a quick look to make sure there were no visible weapons.

"Good morning, Officer," said a big bald guy in military woodland camouflage. "We're on official government business." He passed four brown U.S. passports out of the window.

Joe took the passports and flipped open the first one to a picture of the ugly, bald, driver, Greg Bennett. He flipped the next and saw a picture of Jim Palmer, preppy asshole. He flipped the next two and saw pictures of Aaron Mitchell and Cameron Cooper. Joe looked in the rear seat and saw Aaron and Cameron.

"Are the other two vehicles with you?" Joe looked back at the other vehicles.

"Yes, Sir, they are," Greg said.

Joe handed the passports back to Greg. "Let me check the guys in the other vehicles, and you can be on your way."

"Thank you, officer."

Joe walked back to the other two vehicles and conducted ID checks. Satisfied, he walked back to the lead vehicle.

"Okay, gentlemen, you're cleared. Have a great day." Joe stood back and waved them through. The driver closed his window, and the SUVs drove through the checkpoint.

Joe walked back into the inspection building and sat back down at his desk.

"So, who was that?" Rudy asked over the radio.

"Some military contractors on official business. Some outfit called Sea Island Security. Ever heard of them?"

"Nope."

"Yeah, me neither."

"What do ya think they're doing?"

"No idea, but I don't think it's deer hunting," Joe said. "Just glad they're not after me."

"You got that right."

Greg pulled into the parking lot of the Third Connecticut Lake about 1 mile south of the Border crossing. It wasn't much of a parking lot; just a speck of dirt turn-off with a boat launch ramp and a single green porta-potty. Aaron and Cam climbed out of the rear seat and walked over to the shoreline. Villa and Zerbino got in.

Jim turned to the new rear seat passengers. "Everyone set with the plan?" They all nodded in agreement. "All right, let's leave here on a staggered departure every 30 minutes. There's only one highway into Lancaster, and a three-car convoy may cause some unwanted attention. Also, take the magnets off your doors and put them in the back. Any questions? Okay, let's go."

Aaron and Cam got back in the truck, and Greg pulled out on the highway. "Maybe we'll see a moose in the next 13 miles," Greg said.

"Director Santiago, we're about 30 clicks out from our refueling stop," came the pilot's voice on the radio. "Do want to do a hot refuel and go, or do you want us to shut down?"

"You guys need a break?" Director Santiago looked at the pilots in the front.

"Yes, Sir. We could use a head break and pick up a little chow."

"Sounds good to me. Shut her down. We'll do two hours on deck."

"Roger, Sir. Thank you," came the reply over the radio.

45

Josh followed Route 3 north out of Littleton and cruised along the Ammonoosuc River. "Probably some leftover brook trout in there, Syrin." Syrin didn't say a thing. She was racked out in the front seat. *Must be an ice cream coma,* thought Josh. *She had better conserve her energy for the boys. They'll be ready to play.* The boys were his mom's dogs, Bob and Brady, and the farm cat Bill. Bob was a tan and white American Bulldog, who his mom rescued from the Lancaster Humane Society, and Brady was a Brittany Spaniel she bought from a local breeder for hunting. Bill was a gray short hair cat, who did whatever the hell he wanted. Josh's mom was a huge Patriots fan, so she named them after Bob Kraft, Tom Brady, and Bill Belichick.

The next town up from Littleton was Whitefield, which had a town common with a green-and-white bandstand. Josh drove around the rotary that surrounded the Common, passed another Martin Dairy on the right, and headed up the hill following Route 3. He remembered kissing Jenny Swanson while sitting in the grass on the Common listening to a summer band concert. The music sucked, but Jenny Swanson was hot. Further up, he passed by his old high school on the left. White Mountain Regional High School spelled out in white letters on a brick entrance. A few more hills and turns and he passed the turn off to Martin Meadow Pond. He didn't stop, just went right by. The first time, he didn't stop at the pond on the way home. So many good memories of long-ago summers, fishing, camping, swimming, shooting, hunting, with great friends and family. He couldn't bear to look at it now. Knowing what he had to do tomorrow.

Josh topped Corrigan Hill, and now it was a long descent into the village of Lancaster. He slowed to 20 mph when he hit the main drag. No sense getting pulled over by the locals. There was another Martin Dairy on the right, as you first started down Main Street. Josh looked over at the ice cream queen, but she was still cutting the zzzzz's. Just past the tourist information booth, a blue Lancaster police cruiser pulled in behind Josh and hit its lights. Josh saw it in his rearview mirror, pulled into the Rite Aid parking lot, and put the Flex in park. The cruiser circled Josh and pulled up to his car with driver side windows facing each other. Both the windows went down.

"Hey, Josh," Sergeant Brad Watson said. Brad had a short buzz cut with blue eyes, a weightlifter's face, a square jaw, and a ready smile. He could have been a Marine recruit poster. Both Brad, and Josh's brother Jim, enlisted in the Marine Corp together out of high school. They both did eight years.

"Hey, Brad, how did you know I was coming and driving this beautiful ride?" Josh spread his arms to show off all the features of the Ford Flex.

"Chief got a call from the State Police, who got a call from the FBI. They gave us an ETA and a description of your excellent ride. Rental?"

"Yeah, only one left."

"I've been sitting over there waiting on you for about 45 minutes."

"Someone wanted ice cream." Josh nodded at Syrin.

"Hi, Syrin," Brad said, waving through the window. Syrin pranced in her seat and barked at the sound of her name. "Josh, man, we're all really sorry to hear about Kat. If you need anything, let me know. We're going to have a cruiser parked in your driveway, as long as you are here, and the whole department will be on duty tomorrow."

"Thanks, Brad, I appreciate it. I better get going, or my mom will come looking for me."

"Won't be the first time, will it? Tell your mom, the chief sends his respects."

"Will do. You take care."

Brad waved and put up his window. The cruiser pulled out of the parking lot and turned left, back down Main Street. Josh left his window down and circled through the parking lot to an exit and turned right. Further down Main Street, Josh passed the All Saints Catholic Church on the right, and Josh looked away as he drove past. Tomorrow is going to suck.

At the end of Main Street, the road became a fork. Route 3 continued to the right to the Canadian border in Pittsburgh, and Route 2 started, going across the Connecticut River to Saint Johnsbury, Vermont. Josh turned left to Route 2, also called Bridge Street, and just past Ice Pond Road on the right was the family welcome sign, "Welcome to the Martin Family Farm," in big gold letters on a pale blue sign. Josh's family owned everything on both sides of the road from this sign to the Connecticut River, and a good deal north and south on the New Hampshire side of the river.

Like magic, Syrin popped her head up when they passed the sign, and looked around with an air of anticipation. "So, who's waiting for you?" Syrin danced in the seat, bounced on her front legs, and barked. Josh always liked the view from the entrance sign.

Like a Norman Rockwell painting, the Martin Farm spread out on a canvas of fields, cows, and farm buildings with a couple of tractors turning the stumps of corn back into the ground for the winter. Josh's great grandfather Dan Martin started the farm in 1899, with a mule, a wife, 30 head of cattle, and 40 acres. At least, that was the family story.

Now the farm had 2,600 dairy cows, with a majority of them Holsteins, 2,300 of which are milked three times a day, producing about 10 gallons of milk each. Most of them were spread out across the fields on both sides of the road. Josh laughed at the sight of cows and the remembrance of his favorite T-shirt growing up, the picture of a cow's ass with the words, "How do you like my dairy air?" Those words carried a special meaning in the spring when they treated the crop fields with fertilizer. The entire area would smell like cow shit for weeks. No one complained—the Martin Corporation was the largest employer in the North Country. To the locals, it was the smell of money. The Martins also ran a herd of 300 Brangus cattle along the Connecticut River. They used most of the meat for personal consumption or sold it to employees at cost. The Martins donated anything left over to the All Saints Catholic Church food pantry.

All those cows needed to eat often and a lot—roughly 100 pounds of feed per cow a day—and to meet that demand the Martin Farm cultivated 2,400 acres of corn silage, in which the entire plant, including the stalk, was turned into cow food. The farm also grew 2,400 acres of grass, which was combined with the corn silage as well as other nutrients, such as soybeans, grains, and bakery yeast, which provided the cows with an optimal energy supply. Most of the milk products were turned into ice cream and sold through 61 Martin Dairy stores throughout the state as well as grocery stores. There was also a line of Martin Farms Premium Milk, which commanded a top price since the Martin Farm was always named a Dairy Farm of Distinction by the New Hampshire Department of Agriculture.

Further down on the right, Josh noticed the new calf and heifer barns, which they added last summer. The new heating system kept calves and workers warm in the cold New Hampshire winter. Two additions to the barns and the new feed storage facilities increased accommodations to 376 stalls for the heifers and 540 stalls for the milking cows as well as two bunk silos. The farm employees did all the concrete and the carpentry work to keep costs down.

Josh thought back to all the seasons taking care of cows, harvesting fields, mending fences, working in the dairy store, or hundreds of other jobs. The day started at 0330, and lasted most days, until sundown and beyond. He couldn't wait to leave it when he graduated from high school, and now he wanted to come back. Back with Kat and a new baby. But now, back with Kat and the baby in a box.

Josh wiped the tears from his eyes and smiled at the sight of the Martin Sugar House. It was set back from the highway with a dirt parking lot in front of a red wooden building with a large veranda porch with 10 rocking chairs spread out along the length of it. Kat's favorite activity was sitting in one of the rocking chairs eating fresh Martin's vanilla ice cream with Martin's maple syrup poured over the top, watching the world pass by.

Martin's Sugar House was another part of the Martin legacy. Josh's dad started the maple business in 1982. He wanted something of his own. To pass down something that he created and did not inherit. The red wooden sugar house was just a storefront for the tourists. The real action was in the state-of-the-art sugarhouse in the back, where all maple production, packaging, and wholesale shipments occurred. The Martin Maple Sugar Company tapped maple trees in eight "sugar bushes" or "maple groves" in the Lancaster area and north to Berlin. A plastic tubing system collected sap from the trees and transported it to the sugarhouse, where they boiled it into golden smooth syrup. Each spring, 21,000 maple trees were tapped for 348,000 gallons of maple sap to produce more than 8,000 gallons of pure maple syrup from their NH maple syrup farms. The retail store sold the syrup, maple candy, and tourist stuff direct to the public and online. They sold any leftover syrup to the Maple Grove Corporation in Saint Johnsbury, Vermont.

Thoughts of maple syrup production cleared from his head, as he saw the Martin mailbox perched on a single wood post on the left side of the road, and a Lancaster cruiser blocking the driveway. *No idea why we still have a mailbox.* The mailman would drive down the road, every day, to deliver mail to the house, since Josh's dad died back in 1998. A mailman's way of paying respect. He never stopped at the box. So, the mailbox sat there like a security guard with nothing to do. Josh signaled left, and the cruiser backed up to let him pass. Brad must have radioed ahead. Josh gave the patrolman a wave as he drove by.

Jim Palmer answered the phone on the first ring.

"Yeah?"

"Tango just turned down the driveway. He's driving a white Ford Flex. Plates and car match. Wait one. Target just got out of the car. It's him. Do you want us to take him now?"

"Negative. Stick with the plan," Jim said. "We just finished checking out the church. Only two ways out of town, and only one way across the border, so we gotta be smart. Stick with the plan."

"Roger, boss, out." The phone went dead. "Fucking Frenchies," Jim said. He turned back to Greg. "Let's get back to the hotel. We can check in with our Canadian contingent."

46

The White Mountain Regional Airport had a single newly repaved runway that was 4,001 feet long, 75 feet wide, at an average altitude of 1,074 feet, beneath the Yankee One Military Operations Area (MOA). It was about three miles east of Whitefield, New Hampshire. The Pave Hawk landed at the start of Runway 10 and taxied over to the airplane tarmac, before shutting down the rotors.

Director Santiago stepped out of the Blackhawk when the rotors stopped turning. He walked over to a green SUV with NH State Police marking. A trooper in full uniform with a dark green uniform shirt, tan pants, and a forest green Smokey the Bear hat worn low over his eyes walked up and reached out his hand.

"Director Santiago, Paul Ferguson, it's good to meet you."

Director Santiago shook his hand. "Call me Vince. Thanks for helping out."

"No problem, Sir. Colonel Barton said to give you anything you need. First time I got a personal call from the colonel."

"The colonel is a good man," Vince said. "Can you take me over to the Mountain View?"

"Yes, Sir. Do you have any luggage?"

"The air crew will bring it over to the hotel when they check in. I want to get there early to make some calls. Cell service out here sucks."

"Okay, hop in." They both climbed into the SUV, and Trooper Ferguson headed off the tarmac.

The Martin driveway was about a mile from Route 2 along a smooth gravel road. For the first half mile, the entrance followed a fence line on both sides, with cows looking at Josh and Syrin as they drove past. For the last half, the driveway entered a tree line with a mixed growth forest on both sides, except for the final 50 yards, which were fir trees. The fir trees formed a circular perimeter around the cluster of buildings that made up the family compound. The compound sat in a clearing of about 1.5 acres of grass, which Josh had mowed many times. The fir trees provided a wind and snow break in the winter.

Josh drove into the clearing, and the main house appeared against a backdrop of trees. It was a gray with white trim, colonial-style home, built in 1999, called the Caleb Nickerson House. Josh's mom bulldozed the old farmhouse, just after his dad died. She didn't want to live in a house where everything reminded her of Lee. The new Caleb house was about 3,200 square feet, plus an additional 450 square feet when they added the work-shop to the back of the garage in 2004. A two-door garage with a porch on the left fronted the driveway. The main house flowed away from the driveway. A patio with a barbecue and a screened eating area was set to the left of the house and just off the main entrance. Two Brookfield guest barns sat to the right of the house. Each barn was 1,800 square feet with two stall doors on the ground floor facing the gravel parking lot in front of the house. They each had a complete 900 square feet apartment on the second floor. Big Jim Johnson lived in one, and his son little Jim Johnson lived in the other. Both barns were painted New England red with a cupola on top, complete with a brass rooster weathervane. Josh pulled in front of the left garage stall and put the car in park. He got out and walked around the back of the car to let out Syrin, who was now in full breakdance mode.

Bertrand Picard, a former member of the French Foreign Legion, put the crosshairs of his Schmidt & Bender 3-12x50 mm Police Marksman II LP scope right behind Josh's ear and said, "*Bang!* We could end this now, you know. No muss, no fuss." He was prone in a bed of leaves about 400 yards out, sighting his M40A5 sniper rifle through a break in the fir trees.

"Observe only," Arno Raymond said, also a former member of the French Foreign Legion. Arno saw Josh clearly in his Swift Pathfinder spot-ting scope. Josh opened a door and let out Syrin. "Dog," Arno said. "Time to go." They both got up off the ground and started walking back to their car, which was parked in a turn-off, about two miles back. Another pair of hunters walking in the woods.

Syrin jumped out of the car and went tearing to the front porch. She was just about to the steps when the side door of the house burst open, and a 100-pound American Bulldog and a Brittany Spaniel came running off the porch, howling and scuffling, trying to get traction on the wood porch. All three met at the top step in a ball of dogs and tumbled out into the parking lot, where they took off in a race, barking and taking turns chasing each other around the car and over to the barns. The dogs were followed by a gray cat, which walked out and took a perch on the top step to survey his domain and watch the three idiots running around the yard.

"Who's making all the racket out here?" Sarah Beatrice Martin walked out and stood next to the cat. She was wearing a USCG sweatshirt over a purple checked flannel shirt, jeans, and LL Bean low-cut boots. She was fifty-something with strawberry blond hair pulled back in a ponytail with wire-framed, square glasses, an Irish complexion with freckles on her cheek, and a perfect smile. She was still in dancing shape and tough as nails from years of farming.

Josh saw his mom on the top step, and tears started to fill his eyes. He walked over and gave her a big hug. She smelled of flowers and lavender soap. She smelled of home. "Hi, Mom, it's good to be home."

"Oh, Josh, baby," Sarah said, seeing the tears in her son's eyes. I'm so sorry." She held him in a big hug. After she finally let him go, she said, "Come in, baby. Are you hungry? I just made some corn chowder with homemade biscuits."

"That would be great, Mom." He started to follow his mom into the house.

"Josh, man...I'm sorry, bro." A Denzel Washington look-alike walked around Sarah to give Josh a hug.

Josh could feel the strong arms of his brother giving him a squeeze. "JJ, you look good," Josh said, stepping back to look at his brother.

Little Jim Johnson was four days older than Josh, and he looked like a movie star, but he was farmer strong with thick wrists, a firm grip, and calloused hands. He came to the Martin farm back in 1988, with his father, Big Jim, from Arizona. There were too many J's in Jim Johnson Junior, so everyone called him JJ. Big Jim was hired to run the farming portion of the Martin Company. JJ came along as a package deal. Josh and JJ had been brothers since the day the little kid with the curly black hair and different color skin walked around the side of the house. Racism had to be taught. Josh never learned.

"Thanks, bro. Did I hear a troublemaker in the yard?" JJ looked at the dogs chasing each other around the yard.

"Yes, you did," Josh said. "She couldn't wait to see her boyfriends."

"Well, come on inside. Your mom made some outstanding chowder as usual, and I'm hungry. She wouldn't let me eat any until you showed up." JJ walked toward the kitchen entrance to the house with Josh bringing up the rear.

"Where's Pops?" Josh looked at the paint on the side of the house. It was holding up well.

"You know him. He's out driving a tractor turning over the fields for the winter." JJ opened the door.

"He does know we hire people to do that, right?" Josh caught the door from JJ.

"He still likes to get his hands dirty, every day. He says it reminds him of an honest day's work. I think he just enjoys playing with the tractor." JJ laughed.

Josh pulled the door shut behind him and walked through the mud room into the kitchen and took a deep breath. The smell of fresh baked biscuits filled his nostrils. He did a quick scan of the house, and everything was the same. Some new flowers were on the windowsill over the kitchen sink. The kitchen was set up in a U pattern, with Colonial blue wooden cabinets against white cream walls and a center island with a marble top. The old, black, school clock was still over the three windows on the right above the sink. Josh walked by the basement door on the left, which led to the media room, pool table, wine cellar, and gym, and into the combination breakfast nook and dining room. His mom had converted both rooms into the dining room with a single cherry dining table running the length of the space with two end captains' chairs and four additional chairs on either side. His mom sat at the head of the table, ladling chowder into blue ceramic bowls. The steam arose over the rim. Josh took a seat to his mom's right, and JJ sat across from him.

"Let's say grace," his mom said.

They all joined hands around the table. Josh could feel the familiar warmth and touch of his mom and the strength of his brother.

"Bless us, oh Lord, and these your gifts which we are about to receive from your bounty. Through Christ our Lord we pray, Amen," his mom said.

They all said "Amen" and made the sign of the cross.

His mom passed bowls of chowder to both Josh and JJ, along with a plate of biscuits. Josh took two and passed them over to JJ, who took two and set the rest on the dining room table. Josh took a tentative sip because it was hot.

"This is great, Mom. Just like I remember it. It's been awhile since I've had good corn chowder." He finished two bowls of chowder and two more biscuits, before pushing away from the table.

"Are you sure you don't want us to come with you after the service?" His mom gave him the look. "That should be a time for family."

"I know, Mom, but this is something I got to do by myself. Now, if you'll excuse me, I gotta get my stuff, and check on Syrin." Josh rose out of his seat, bent over, and gave his mom a kiss on the cheek. "I love you."

His mom reached and grabbed his hand. "I love you too, sweetie. JJ, give your brother a hand."

"Sure, Mom." JJ pushed away from the table and turned out of his chair. "He definitely needs my help with the heavy lifting."

"I got your heavy lifting right here." Josh stood, turned his back to his mom, and grabbed his crotch.

"No, bro, I said heavy lifting, not a light workout." JJ laughed.

Josh put his arm around his brother, as they walked through the kitchen to the front door. "Let's get outside, and I will show you some heavy lifting."

"You boys behave." Sarah Martin started clearing the dishes off the table and smiled at the sight of her sons together.

"Always, Mom," Josh said. They both waved their hands over their heads.

47

Jim Palmer put the keycard in the slot of Room 227 at the Littleton Motor Inn. The light turned green, and he pushed through the door, followed by Greg. The Canadian contingent was seated around a round wooden table, looking over a bunch of photos. They were all dressed in woodland camouflage pants with green T-shirts. They piled their jackets, orange fluorescent vests, and orange hats on the bed. The hotel room had one king-size bed that faced a credenza with a TV, an ice bucket full of Canadian Molson beer, a small microwave, and a coffeemaker.

Jim addressed the group. "So, gentlemen, what do we got?" Both Jim and Greg walked over to the table to look at the pictures.

"Do you want a beer? They've been icing for a while," Lawrence Villalobos "Villa" said. Villa was the leader of the Canadian contingent, which consisted of Torai Takemura, Juri Reimink, and Bojan Jovic, all former members of Canadian Joint Forces 2. Joint Forces 2 were Canada's version of Tier 1 Special Operators. Villa had the look of a Canadian with a dark complexion, brown eyes set too close together, and short black hair, but he was all business, which Jim appreciated.

"No, I'm good," Jim said.

"I think I'll get one," Greg said. He walked over and pulled one out of the ice bucket, popped the top with a bottle opener he grabbed from the credenza, and took a long pull. "That's good. Canadians know how to make beer."

"We drove out to the pond," Villa said. "It's pretty quiet. All the camps are closed for the winter. We did see one green pickup truck pulled off to the side of the road. There was a box of .308 shells on the front seat, so they were deer hunting, but we didn't see anyone."

"What's the best way to do it without leaving any trace?" Jim looked at Villa.

"Depends on whether he's alone or has company. Company will be a problem. We can make one disappear, but two, or more, will be an issue, but here's what I think," Villa said.

Trooper Ferguson pulled the SUV in front of the Mountain View Grand Resort and Spa and parked near a staircase with a black iron railing.

"Thanks for the lift, Paul," Director Santiago said.

"No problem, Sir. Pick you up tomorrow at 1000? The ceremony starts at 1100," Trooper Ferguson said.

"That would be great." Director Santiago climbed out of the SUV and swung the door closed. He tapped the hood twice and walked up the cement stairs to an enormous white veranda porch. The porch stretched the length of the resort and fronted the large Central Hotel, which was painted a light yellow with white trim. He looked back to see the rear of the SUV headed down the road. He stood on the porch and looked up at the façade of a forgone era of grand resorts, where the rich took summer vacations in the mountains and played croquet on the front lawn. The porch was empty as there was a chill in the air, but it was packed in July. *I need to bring the family back here.* He walked back to the edge of the main building and sat in one of the wicker chairs that were spread out across the porch and pulled out his cell phone. Full bars. Nice. He figured a resort must have good phone reception. He punched up a number.

"Good afternoon, Director," Max Lindy said. "What can I do for you, Sir?"

"Hi, Max, just checking in. I made it to the hotel. Anything going on?"

"No, Sir. All quiet. No chatter on White 55."

"Okay, thanks, Max. I'm going to check in and take a nap. I've got good cell service so that you can reach me."

"Roger, Sir."

Director Santiago hit the red end button and put the phone back in his pocket. He looked at the view of the White Mountains, which stretched beyond the 18-hole golf course. Most of the leaves were off the trees, but it still was a beautiful sight with the mountains framed against a blue sky. He stood and walked into the lobby.

Josh and JJ walked out to the front porch and saw Syrin, Bob, and Brady sprawled out, panting with their tongues hanging out of their mouths, and Bill the cat still thinking they were idiots. All the tails started smacking the porch when they walked out, except for Brady, who didn't have a tail, but his little nubbin was twitching like a hummingbird's wing.

"Looks like someone is going to sleep good tonight," Josh said.

Syrin scrambled to her feet and ran over to JJ, who gave her a big hug. "How's my girl? These boys bothering you?" Syrin gave JJ a big lick. "Oh, thanks for that." He stood and wiped his sleeve across his mouth. "Now, I got dog cooties." JJ held her head in his hands and gave her a kiss between the eyes, and she went back to the boys and laid down.

"Now that is one sweet ride," JJ said, motioning at the Flex. "What happened to the truck?" JJ walked over and put his hand on the Flex. "And frosty white to complete the ensemble."

"The truck didn't make it," Josh said. He walked over, opened the rear door, and pulled his bag out of the back.

"What do you mean 'didn't make it'? Mom's got you in the guest suite."

"Not a word to Mom."

"No, course not." They both started walking back to the house.

"I got jumped by eight bangers with AK47s. They shot the shit out of the truck."

"That was you in Boston? They only said undercover FBI agent on the news."

"Yeah, that was me." Josh walked to the porch and through the door. He took a right in the mud room, through the laundry room, and into the garage.

"Fuck me, bro, that was crazy. Is that what started all this shit with Kat?"

"I don't know. Car bombs are a little sophisticated for your average street gang. They just drive by and hose the neighborhood with automatic weapons. Three simultaneous car bombs required a little more sophistication." Josh took a slight left after entering the garage and walked up the stairs to the guest suite. He walked over and heaved his suitcase on the bed. JJ hung his garment bag on the back of the bathroom door.

The guest suite was comfortable with a king-size bed centered under a window that overlooked the front parking area and gave a bird's-eye view of anyone approaching the house from the front, including the driveway. There were matching oak nightstands on either side of the bed, and a four-drawer oak dresser against the wall to the right of the bed. An 80-inch 4K TV was mounted on the wall in the corner closest to the staircase, and two brown leather recliners were set back from the TV with a small oval table in between. On the left side of the bed against the wall was a small refrigerator with a table next to it with a Keurig coffee unit hard plumbed into the water system. There was also a green-and-tan dog bed on the floor at the foot of the bed. A plastic trash can full of dog food was next to the dresser with a dog bowl on top. Fresh towels, a face cloth, and a white robe were neatly laid out on the bed.

Josh brushed his hand on the towel. "You gotta love Mom."

JJ walked over to the fridge and pulled out two bottles of DOS XX Amber and tossed one to Josh. "Yup, gotta love Mom." They both walked over to the recliners and sat down. They flipped the caps on the beer with an opener on the coffee table.

"To Mom," Josh said. They clinked bottles together in a toast. He sat back in the recliner and kicked out the footrest.

"What are you going to do now?" JJ took another sip of beer, set the bottle on the side table, and kicked out his footrest.

"Kill the motherfuckers who killed my wife and kid," Josh said. "These chairs are comfortable. I could sleep for a week."

"Roger that. Wait, what kid?" JJ kicked the footrest back, sat up in the chair, and looked at his brother.

"Kat was pregnant. We weren't telling anyone until we got past the first trimester." Josh took another sip of beer.

"Shit, Bro. I'm so sorry. Mom know?"

"No, and I want to keep it that way,"

"Okay, no problem. Any idea on who wants to whack you?" JJ reclined back in the chair and took another sip of beer. "You got great taste in beer."

"I'm thinking cartel, but I'm not sure. This seems like something different. The cartels usually chalk shit like this up to the cost of doing business. Killing Federal agents is bad for business. You got your shit?"

"Semper Fi," JJ said. "What for? Ah, man, you're bringing them here. That's why you didn't want anyone with you tomorrow."

"Home field, brother. Home field," Josh said. He took a sip of beer.

"So, what's the plan?"

48

Jim Palmer walked out of the Littleton Motor Inn. The air was crisp with a hint of the forthcoming winter. He zipped his jacket all the way up, walked to the edge of Main Street, and watched the traffic creep along, and a few pedestrians walk past. The definition of a small New England town with a slow pace of life and a predictable future. Be born, work like a dog, die. *Shoot me now,* he thought. He reached into his coat pocket and pulled out his burner cell. Found the one contact number on the phone and hit the green phone symbol.

"Hello, my friend from the North," Mr. Smith said when the phone clicked on. "Is everything ready?"

"Yeah, we're all set. The only issue is exfil if something goes wrong. Only one road north and south. Only one border crossing, and the Canucks will honor any request to seal their border going north." Palmer stepped back from the street behind a red brick low retaining wall to get away from the wind. "It's also fucking cold here. I want a warm assignment after this."

"You were in the Caribbean for four years for your last gig, time for some payback, so put on your big girl panties and deal with it. Regarding exfil, if you can't go north, head south to I93. Once you make the highway, we can get you out. How are the Canadians doing?"

"Canadians are fine. It's the French guys who suck. They aren't much on following orders."

"Roger that, but they are stone cold killers when it comes to pulling the trigger."

"Tell me something I don't know. They were on a recon mission earlier today, and they wanted to smoke the target in his front yard. Subtlety is not their strong suit."

"Wow," Mr. Smith said. "Well, see how they do and make a decision when you get back. Call me for a final go tonight, and when you are back above the border. If something goes wrong, follow protocol. Stay warm."

"Fuck you," Mr. Palmer said, and the phone went dead. He pried the cover off the back of the phone and dumped the battery into a green trash can set behind the red wall. He took out the SIM card, snapped it between his fingers, and tossed it into the garbage with the battery along with the back cover of the phone. He threw the remainder of the phone into a large refuse container next to the Motor Inn lobby entrance, as he walked back inside.

Director Santiago sat on the sofa in the presidential suite and took a sip of Wild Horse 2014 Cabernet, set it on the small table next to the couch, and unfolded the *USA Today* to the front page. The headline banner read, "Insurance choices getting tougher." He finished the article and lowered the paper to see the view through the suite's double windows, which opened to a balcony. Mount Lafayette, Cannon Mountain, a partial view of the Kilkenny Range, and Percy Peaks were silhouetted against the blue sky with a dusting of snow on the peaks. *New Hampshire is beautiful. I'm surprised Josh wanted to leave, but then there was probably not much action on the mean streets of Lancaster and Whitefield. Some men are just drawn to something bigger. I wonder if he would have made the same choice if he knew it would cost him his wife.* He took another sip of wine, and his phone started playing, "The Navy Hymn." That would be Max Lindy's ringtone from the op center.

He stood and walked over to the king-sized bed and picked up the phone from the mattress. "Director Santiago."

"Good afternoon, Director, this is LCDR Lindy in the op center. We just got a hit on GNOSIS." The U.S. intelligence community was the finest collector of electronic communication information in the world. The problem was not the collection. It was analysis. How do you sift through all the information to find the one bit you need? GNOSIS solved that problem. The system provided keyword search and notification of all the collected information in real time.

"Where and when?"

"Littleton, NH, 5 minutes ago," LCDR Lindy said.

"What did it say?"

"Analysts are still working on it, but a quick synopsis, we got a Canadian and French team operating in the area. They talked about exfil routes, getting back across the border, smoking a target, and being cold."

"That sounds like White 55's welcome party," Director Santiago said. "Do we have any assets in the area?"

"Let me check, Sir. Not much. We got you and White 55 in the immediate vicinity, plus your State Police escort. Otherwise, we got a couple of assets at the NH State Police in Concord, a few in Manchester, and a couple on the coast in Portsmouth. We don't usually see much action in NH."

"Where's the closest Tact Team?"

"Boston, Sir," came the reply.

"Okay, get them headed north."

"Where to?"

"Send them to my hotel. Have them call me when they get here."

"Yes, Sir. Will do. Anything else?"

"Send White 55 an alert."

"Yes, Sir. Sending it now."

Director Santiago punched off the call. "Game on." He tossed the phone back on the bed and went back to his paper and wine. Not much to do now but wait.

49

Josh pushed up from the recliner, tossed the empty beer bottle in the trash, and walked over to look out the window. A light blue Chevy truck was headed towards the house, leaving a dust swirl in its wake.

"Looks like your dad's on final approach," Josh said. "Don't you think it's time for him to get a new truck?"

"You know him…he won't spend a dime unless he absolutely has to."

"How about you go out and buy Pops a brand-new Silverado with all the options for Christmas? It can be from the both of us. Send me the bill."

"Are you sure, Josh? That could run about 60K."

"Yeah, I'm sure. Also, while I'm thinking about it…you know the couple that runs the Littleton Dairy?" Josh turned from the window to look at JJ.

"Audrey and David. I think they're expecting their first child."

"Yeah, that's them. Syrin and I had an ice cream there. They are doing a great job, and they had nothing but good things to say about us."

"Did they know who you were?"

"Not a clue. I left Audrey a big tip in the tip jar. David came out to make sure it wasn't a mistake. Now, who does that nowadays?"

"They are good folk, and they are one of our top stores on a per capita basis."

"I want to give them a $25,000 Christmas bonus," Josh said.

"Man, I don't know, Josh." JJ shook his head. "We give out one 25K bonus to a store, we're going to have 60 other managers wanting to know 'where's mine?'"

"Now that I think about it, you're right. I'll give them a personal check on my way back through."

"Well, you know, since you're so flush with cash, I could use a new truck," JJ said with a laugh.

"Done. Get one when you pick out one for Pops, just don't take delivery until we give Pops his."

"Slow your roll, Josh; I was kidding."

"I'm not. You work hard, and I only got one brother from another mother, and you never know when your ride is over. Plus, you bring down the company reputation riding around in that piece of shit Chevy. If you're going to ride in a piece of shit Chevy, at least make sure it's a new piece of shit Chevy," Josh said.

"Wow. Look who's calling the kettle black. That white piece a shit Ford you got out front isn't exactly a chick magnet."

"It's a rental. Doesn't count."

"Hey, are you boys up there?" Pops called up from the garage.

"Yeah, Pops, we're up here," JJ said.

"Is Josh driving that Ford piece of shit, or do I need to call a tow truck?" Both Josh and JJ started laughing.

Josh bounded down the steps and gave Pops a big hug. He was still a strong man.

"Good to hear you laugh, son. I was so sorry to hear about Katherine. I'm glad you're home." Big Jim Johnson, "Pops," was about 6', heavy set, and around 220 lbs., with curly black hair on the sides, bald on top, and enormous hands. He could still toss a bale of hay on the truck with one hand. He was wearing brown Dickie work pants, Timberland boots, a red-and-black checkered flannel shirt, and a dark brown barn coat.

The phone buzzed in Josh's pocket. He walked a couple of feet away and looked at the screen.

Two groups of shooters, Canadian and French, in your AOR. NFI.

He slipped the phone back in his pocket.

"Anything important?" JJ tried to read his brother's response.

"No, just a text from my boss," Josh said.

"What do you say, we all go inside, and I buy you a beer?" Pops slapped both his sons on the back.

"Now that sounds like a very good idea," Josh said. They all headed to the porch door, when JJ said, "Ah, shit," looking back at the driveway. They all turned to look.

A dark blue Toyota Camry drove up the driveway to the house. One thing about living in a small town, everyone knew what kind of car you drove. The blue Camry belonged to the Foley Funeral Home.

"You guys go inside. I got this. I'll be right in," Josh said.

"No son, you're home now. We'll do this," Pops said.

All three men stepped off the porch and watched the Camry drive up. It stopped just in front of them, and Stewart Foley climbed out of the driver's seat. He was dressed in a tailored black suit, white shirt, black tie, and he looked like he was straight out of central casting for an undertaker. Foley's Funeral Home had buried folks in Lancaster for the last hundred years. Stewart was the fifth-generation Foley to run the business. He had red hair slicked straight back, a face full of freckles, and a bright shade of blue eyes. Of course, he had the nickname "The Undertaker" in school. Every Foley probably had the same nickname, since there were Foleys in Lancaster.

"Good afternoon, gentlemen," Stewart said. He walked up and shook hands with them.

"Thanks for driving over Stewart," Josh said.

"The least I could do, Josh. I'm sorry for your loss."

Syrin looked up from the porch at the gathering and walked over to the rear of the Flex and sat down. She looked at Josh as if to say, "Don't let them take Mommy." Josh wiped the tears from his eyes and walked over to her. He kneeled and patted her head.

"It's okay, girl. Stewart is going to watch out for her," Josh said.

He popped the latch on the Flex, and the rear gate popped open. He reached in and took out the cardboard box that contained the ashes of his wife and unborn child in a plastic bag. He tried to fight the tears, but it didn't work. They streamed down his face. He dropped to the ground sobbing with the box cradled in his arm. His body shook with emotion. Syrin started whining and licked his face.

Pops and JJ ran over. Pops sat next to Josh in the dirt, cradled his head in his lap, and put his other arm around Syrin, who licked his face to say thank you.

"It's okay, son. We got ya. JJ, why don't you take this?" Pops pulled the box from the crook of Josh's arm and handed it to JJ.

JJ took the box and walked over to Stewart and gave it to him.

"We'll take excellent care of her, JJ. Tell Josh everything is taken care of, just like he wanted. If you folks need anything else, just let me know. Please give my best to Mrs. Martin."

"Will do, Stewart," JJ said. JJ shook his hand, held on, and pulled him close. He nodded in the direction of Josh and Pops on the ground. "Nothing happened, correct?" JJ whispered.

"Yes, Sir. Nothing happened," Stewart said. JJ released his grip, and Stewart rubbed his hand. "Well, I need to get back. Again, if you require anything, please let me know." Stewart walked back to his car and put the box in the front seat. He didn't think it would be appropriate to put it in the trunk under the current circumstances. *God, I hope everything works out tomorrow.* He started the car, backed out into the gravel parking area, and headed back down the driveway.

Josh collected himself, eased off the ground, and brushed the dirt off his knees with his hands. He patted Syrin's head and sat down on the back of the Flex.

"Sorry, guys. It was the first time it felt like I was letting go. That they were actually gone," Josh said. He leaned forward and rested his hands on his knees.

"They?" Pops stepped back.

"Kat was pregnant," JJ said.

"Shit, don't tell Sarah," Pops said.

"No, Sir," JJ said. "That's the plan. Hey, Pops, can you give us a couple of minutes?"

"Sure, boys. I'll be inside getting the beers ready." He walked up the porch steps, across the porch, and into the house.

JJ went over and sat next to Josh. "So, who was on the phone?"

"We're in play. Two sets of scumbags are in our AOR. French and Canadian."

"I guess they don't think much of you. They send some Frogs and Canucks. How can you tell a French rifle?"

"Never been fired and only dropped once. Old joke. You still in?"

"Semper Fi, bro, Semper Fi. Let's go get that beer before Pops comes looking for us."

"Won't be the first time." He slapped JJ on the back, and they both stood. He closed the back of the Flex, and they headed to the house with Syrin in tow.

50

Director Santiago looked around at the 1865 wine cellar. Six thousand bottles of wine safely ensconced in oak trays and cubicles at the proper temperature, humidity, and angle of storage. The most romantic spot for fine dining per the hotel brochure. It was also the most private. He booked the entire space for two hours. He was dressed in a blue blazer, light blue shirt with a red tie, tan pants, and Italian loafers.

The maître d' approached the table with the sommelier trailing behind. They were both dressed in black tuxedos, and the sommelier had a silver tastevin around his neck on a silver chain.

"Good evening, Sir, my name is Scott. If there is anything you need to make your dinner more enjoyable, please ask for me, especially if you are not satisfied with anything. This is Jacob; he is our sommelier. He will help you with your wine selections for dinner this evening."

"Evening, gentlemen, my name is Vince. Pleased to meet you guys. I'm expecting four more for dinner, and possibly one more after dinner. If you could show them the way, that would be great. I told them the wine room, but they may get lost."

"Of course, Sir," Scott said. "I'll go find your dinner guests." He headed back up the stairs to the main dining room.

"And for wine this evening, Sir?" Jacob showed Vince the wine list.

"I think these guys will be a steak crowd, so let's go with a Cabernet. Any suggestions?"

"Domestic or foreign?"

"Always domestic in the States."

"Splendid, then I would suggest either a Honig Cabernet 2011, or a Stags Leap Cabernet 2014."

"Bring them both with dinner, Jacob, and make sure I get the check."

"Yes, Sir." He turned to leave just as Scott walked down the stairs with four men trailing behind.

"I think I found your dinner companions," Scott said. He stood aside as the aircrew and the State Trooper walked in.

"Gentlemen, welcome," Vince said.

They all approached the table and looked around at the wine cellar. The walls were lined with bottles of wine, and there were four tables for two complete with white linen tablecloths, fine china, and Swiss glassware. Single red roses in a bud vase adorned the center of each table. The staff created a table of six for Vince since he reserved the entire room.

"Did you guys all meet upstairs?" Vince looked at the group.

"No, Sir," Trooper Ferguson said.

"Okay, well this is State Trooper Paul Ferguson, and Paul, this is Lt Col. Dan Elmore, Major Paul Jackson, and Master Sergeant Dave Dixon of the finest Air Force in the world," Vince said.

They all shook hands around the table. The Air Force contingent was dressed almost identical in a business casual, dark blue sports coat, open-collar blue shirt, and matching tan khakis. Paul Ferguson was wearing a tan sports jacket with a yellow shirt and brown pants.

"Gentlemen, please be seated," Vince said. "And, everyone here is a club member. We have one more coming, but he'll probably not be here until after dinner. So, let's enjoy a nice meal, and then we can do business."

All twelve members of Sea Island Security were packed into Room 227 with pictures spread out on the bed. The remains of McDonald's for 12 overflowed from the single trash can.

"All right, gentlemen, let's go over it again," Jim Palmer said. "The ceremony is at 1000 at the All Saints Catholic Church on Main Street in Lancaster." He pulled a picture off the bed that showed the front of the church. "Greg, you will wait across the street, near the library here." He pointed to a concrete mausoleum-looking building across the street.

"When the service breaks, we expect the target will head to Martin Meadow Pond with the remains of his recently deceased wife to spread her ashes. There is only one way in, so Greg, call on secure comms to give us a heads-up he's coming. No more phones from now until we are across the border. Follow at a discreet distance and make sure he turns on Martin Meadow Pond Road."

"Aaron, you'll wait in the woods here." He pointed to a map of Martin Meadow Pond Road, which showed a right fork on the road from Martin Meadow Pond Road to Martin Road. "There's an old logging road on the left before you make the turn. We'll park our vehicles about a quarter mile in and make the approach on foot, so we don't tip him off on his ride in. It's an easy three-mile walk to the target area. Aaron, you will provide initial vehicle security, and check in when he makes the turn down Martin Road."

"Greg, you link up with Aaron and use your vehicle to block the Martin Road. No one in or out. I don't think you'll see anybody; the place is closed for the winter. The tourists are all gone, but remember, no witnesses. Once he makes the turn down Martin Road, the trap is set. It's just a matter of where we kill him."

Jim pulled another picture from the pile, which was blown up to poster size. "This is the target area. The main estate building runs east to west on top of this field." He pointed at a large building with brown shingles and olive-green trim. "Two more homes are to the right of the main estate, as you face the water with a tennis court in between. There's also an apple orchard above the main building. It gives you a good field of fire across the entire field all the way to the water." Jim put his finger on the grove of apple trees north of the main building. "There's a small boat house near the water that holds boating equipment. A single canoe is pulled up on the bank here." He touched the picture of a silver canoe turned over near the water. "There's also this small dock on the water."

"We expect the target to drive in and park here." He pointed at an open area near the main building. "He will follow this path from the parking lot to the water." Jim traced his finger along a well-worn path from the parking area to the dock on the water. "It's about 200 meters of open field. Once he gets to the water's edge, he's either going to dump her ashes from the dock or use the canoe to do it on the lake."

"Zerbino," Jim said.

"Yeah, boss," Zerbino said.

"You set up your Legionnaires here, along this stone wall. Use Ghillie suits." Jim pointed to a rock wall on the left side of the estate, as one faced the water. It ran the entire length of the field and was dotted with stands of fir trees every couple of meters. It was about a 100-meter shot from the wall to the boat house.

"Villa, you split your team into pairs," Jim said. "Put a team west of the main estate, between these two houses over here. Put two more in the woods farther west. Make sure one has a sniper rifle. It may be a long shot if somehow he moves west along the shoreline."

"Will do," Villa said.

"Cam, you and I will set up a sniper hide in the apple orchard. I'll spot for you. You take the kill shot. If he takes the canoe, shoot him when he just clears the dock. If he uses the dock, drop him at the end, so he falls into the water. I'll call the shot."

"Roger," Cam said.

"Gentlemen, the goal is one shot and get him in the water. It will take days, or weeks, to find him. We only need three hours to get back across the border. If Cam misses, or something else fucks up, everyone hoses him down, and we worry about what's left after."

"No way I miss at 200 to 300 meters," Cam said.

"I heard that's a little far for an Army Ranger," Zerbino said.

"Fuck you," Cam said. "Maybe I swing a little left and shoot a pile of leaves to get my zero down."

"All right, put your dicks back in your pants," Greg said. "I got a hundred bucks that Cam gets a headshot."

"It's a bet," Zerbino said.

"Now that we got that settled, any questions about the op?" Jim looked at his shooters. Everyone shook their head no around the room.

"Okay, remember, radio silence until we're back across the border and everyone back to their rooms for the night. We don't need anyone getting arrested for being stupid, and some deputy running a background check on your dumb ass."

Jim stuffed all the photos and maps in his black duffel bag, and everyone filed out of the room. Greg hung back.

"What do ya think?" Jim closed and latched the top of the duffel.

"I think if he makes it into that parking area near the house, there's one less killer squid in the world."

51

Josh, JJ, and Pops sat around the fireplace in the living room drinking Budweisers and talking business. A fire was going in the fireplace, and the sound of crackling wood filled the room. The light from the fire danced off the chimney stones and on the face of General Joshua Lawrence Chamberlain, whose portrait hung over the mantle; Sarah Martin's great something grandfather.

The living room flowed to the left out of the dining room/breakfast nook combo. A recliner couch faced the fireplace, and there were two black leather recliners on each side of the sofa angled to face the fire. A door on the back of the living room opened into the master suite. If you walked to the right of the fireplace, the main entrance was on the right with a hallway into the breakfast nook on the left. His mom's study was to the right as you came in the front door, and the staircase to the two bedrooms upstairs was slightly right as you entered the house. Josh's sister Jessica, who was an emergency room doc at Lancaster Memorial Hospital, occupied one of the bedrooms.

"So, Josh, we got a proposal we want you to think about," JJ said, taking a sip of beer. "As you know, we are maxed out on our maple syrup production. But, if I doubled our production, Maple Groves would buy everything we make. We also could start selling syrup out of our dairy stores, especially to summer tourists."

"That's going to take a lot of land to find eight more maple groves to support that increase in syrup volume. We also have to figure in transportation costs, since we already own all the maple woods in our immediate area," Josh said.

"Right on both counts," JJ said. "Here's the plan. The 23,000-acre Phillips Brook watershed is up for sale, and they have nine maple groves on the property that we know of. There's probably more."

"You can't make the numbers work on 23,000 acres by selling maple syrup," Josh said.

"You're right, but we can make the numbers work on selling lumber and electricity in addition to maple syrup," JJ said. "Plus, we could also sub-divide some of the land into 100-acre hunting and fishing camp lots. The area is loaded with deer, turkey, moose, partridge, and Phillips Brook has brook trout."

"How are you going to generate the electricity? The $200 million wind farm project was a bust."

"There's a company in North Carolina called Biomass Conversion Systems Inc. One of their 100 ton per day units can produce 4 megawatts of power per day when paired with two Caterpillar synthetic gas generators. We can sell the electricity to the power grid at .10c a kilowatt hour. It would give us a return of about 4 mil a year."

"How are we going to power the unit?" Josh asked.

"Sawdust, scrap wood, and green waste," JJ said. "We collect green waste from the public and the power company, who trim all the trees along their lines. We also need to build and staff a lumber mill. All the scrap wood and sawdust would feed the system."

"How much does this little slice of heaven cost?" Josh looked at JJ and Pops.

"35 million, all in," JJ said. "We need 7 million down, and we can finance the rest at 3%. We also should be able to get some money from environmental groups, the State, and the Feds for preserving land, provided we allow recreational use."

"Tell you what, JJ...you put everything into a project plan, and I'll look at it," Josh said. "If it pencils out, I'll loan the company the down payment at no interest."

"You got that kind of money laying around?" JJ questioned his brother.

"I do now. I sold the club. Kat and I were planning on moving back, before..."

Josh got out of the chair. "I need another beer. Anyone else?"

"I could use another one," Pops said.

"I'm good, Josh," JJ said, looking at the floor.

Josh walked by and rubbed the back of JJ's head. "No issues, bro, no issues."

Josh walked into the kitchen. His mom was bent over peering into the oven, checking the meat thermometer on a rib roast. She closed the oven when he walked into the kitchen. She was wearing an apron, which said, "Kiss the cook." Josh walked up and gave her a hug and a kiss. He hung on a little longer than usual, just holding on to the moment.

"It will get better, son," Sarah said. "I know it doesn't feel like it now, but it will get better. Trust me."

Josh let her go and kissed her on the forehead. "I know, Mom. I just wish everything was over."

"It doesn't work that way. Grief's a journey and not a moment, and you must make the trip. Just be glad you have family to lean on." Sarah gave Josh another hug.

"So, did the boys run the Phillips Brook project by you?"

"Yup. I told JJ to send me the project plan and the financials. If it pencils out, I think we should do it," Josh said. "What do you think?"

"I think it will mean a lot of jobs for a lot of people. If we don't lose any money, we should try it. I always wanted to be a land baroness. Dinner's ready. Get JJ and Pops. Your sister called. She's working late. She won't make it until tomorrow."

Josh walked back into the living room. "Mom says, 'Get your own damn beer,' and dinner is ready," Josh said.

"Joshua Chamberlain Martin, I said no such thing," Sarah said. "Quit causing trouble and get in here. Don't make me get my big wooden spoon."

"Ooooh," JJ said. "She used his middle name." Both JJ and Pops started laughing.

"Okay by me," Josh said. "You two hens keep squawking in here, and there won't be any rib roast left."

Pops and JJ moved pretty quick at the sound of rib roast.

52

Director Santiago took a sip of Colombian coffee and the final bite of the Mountain View snow globe, a flourless, chocolate cake and caramel mousse with chocolate cremeux. It was the fitting end to a fantastic three-course meal of a seared king, oyster mushroom Ravioli appetizer and grilled beef strip kohlrabi with a poached onion and sprouted wheat berries. The sprouted wheat berries sat untouched on the edge of the plate. They also polished off both bottles of wine.

"Well, gentlemen, that was an awesome meal, and I think I see our final guest, so time to talk about our operation," Director Santiago said.

David Tuley walked down the steps into the wine cellar and across to the table. He was dressed in a light green shirt with gray pants and an ill-fitting, dark green, Mountain View blazer, which was tight around the arms, shoulders, and chest. He was about six feet tall with short blond hair, blue eyes, a small scar on his chin, and the look of a heavyweight boxer. Director Santiago stood and shook his hand.

"Glad you could make it, David," Director Santiago said. "I see you dressed for the occasion."

"Yeah, the dining room host wouldn't let me down here, unless I was properly attired. I wouldn't want to ruin the appetite of such a fine-looking bunch of guys." He took off the coat and draped it over a chair.

"Can I get you something to eat or some coffee? The dessert was exquisite. I think they call it the 'snow globe,'" Director Santiago said.

"No, I'm good, Sir, thank you. We ate on the way up."

"Okay, well, let me introduce you around. This is Paul Ferguson, who's a trooper with the NH State Police, and Lt Col. Dan Elmore, Major Paul Jackson, and Master Sergeant Dave Dixon. They own the Air Force Pave Hawk parked at the local airport."

"Nice to meet you guys," Dave said. He went around the table and shook everyone's hands and sat down.

"Before we begin, everyone here's a club member so we can speak freely. You all already knew that by the vibrations on your wrist, but it's always good to say it," Director Santiago said. "We're here to help this guy." He pulled a 3x5 picture of Josh's official FBI photo out of his breast pocket and passed it around the table.

"His wife was killed in one of the three car bombs in Boston, a couple of days ago. Now, he's up here for her funeral service and to scatter her ashes, which is going to take place tomorrow. Intelligence indicates there are at least two hit teams—one Canadian, and one French—who are in the area to complete the mission that the car bomb assholes missed. We are not going to let that happen. Clear?"

Everyone nodded in agreement.

"Also, the president has authorized his recruitment as a black operative, so we need to protect our own. Dave, do you have a full team?" Director Santiago looked at Dave Tuley.

"Yes, Sir. Seven, plus me. They're checked in and doing weapon preps now. What are the rules of engagement?"

"We only need one," Director Santiago said. "Everyone else goes. Did you bring the other package?"

"Yes, Sir. It will be on target at 0800," Dave said.

Josh took the last bite of apple pie and pushed the plate away. "Mom, that was fantastic. I almost forgot how good a cook you are, since you've been running the business."

"Thank you, sweetie. I always have time to cook for one of my boys," Sarah said. She reached over and stroked the back of Josh's head.

"That was a wonderful meal," JJ and Pops said in unison.

"Well, I'm glad you boys liked it. You get clean up. I need to talk to Josh," Sarah said. "Let's go sit by the fire."

Both Sarah and Josh got up from the table and walked into the living room. JJ and Pops started clearing the table.

"Do you think she is going to tell him?" JJ whispered.

"I hope so," Pops said. "You clear the table. I'll load the dishwasher."

Jim Palmer walked through the lobby. The night clerk was hunched over the desk working on something, so she didn't look up when he went past. He pushed through the exit door and walked to the edge of Main Street. It was a dark and damp night. A couple of cars went by on the main drag, but no one was walking around. He turned left on Main Street and walked up a couple of blocks, looking for a cup of coffee to go with his phone call. No luck.

He stepped back under the overhang of the Minuteman Café, which was closed for the night. He pulled the burner phone out of his pocket and hit the send button. Mr. Smith picked up on the second ring.

"Good evening, my cold friend," Mr. Smith said.

"Fuck you comes to mind," Jim Palmer said. "Are you somewhere warm?"

"Yes, I am. They serve little drinks with umbrellas at the local cantina down here."

"Well, I hope you get dysentery. We're all set for the party tomorrow. Are we a go?"

"Yes, you're a go. Good luck."

"Roger that. Talk to you when it's done." Jim Palmer clicked off.

53

Mr. Smith put the phone back in his pocket and shivered under his over-coat. Jim was right. *It is cold up here.* He picked up the oversized bag at his feet. It was heavier than it looked since he packed it with a M183 demolition charge assembly consisting of 16 M112 C4 demolition blocks and four priming units. Each block weighed 1.25 lbs, so 20 lbs of C4, plus 25 lbs of 3 mm loose ball bearings packed into the case and another batch of ball bearings stitched into the outer fabric of the case.

He walked up the concrete walkway in front of the church and looked at the black porch lights mounted on either side of a set of simple glass doors. The lights reflected in the glass and off the white wood siding of the church. Two floodlights mounted farther up on the front of the church illuminated four life-sized stuffed cows, three brown, and one black grazing on fake grass on his right. He paused to read the inscription: "Holy Cows! In verdant pastures, he gives me repose . . . Until the cows come home."

Cows in front of a church...that must be a first, at least in New England. Probably all the rage in the Midwest. He scanned the surrounding area. A couple of cars moved along Main Street, but not a soul in sight, and no cameras. He walked the entire downtown in the afternoon and did an early recon of the church. No need to break in. It was open 24 hours a day to welcome God's children. *Who felt the urge to pray at 2:00 a.m.?*

He walked up the four concrete steps, opened the door, and walked in. The warmth of the church flooded over him, at least the heat of the church did. *I don't think the good Lord would welcome me with the warmth of his love on this particular visit,* he thought.

Through the doors was a small vestibule where the ushers hung out to avoid listening to the Mass. The priest could also bid adieu to his flock in the warmth of the church and not freeze his ass off outside. Mr. Smith walked through the vestibule and stood at the entrance to the church.

Wooden pews lined either side of a center aisle and faced an altar draped in green cloth with a large wooden cross of the crucified Jesus suspended from the ceiling. Three small, stained-glass windows were behind the altar, and larger stained-glass windows were on either side. A white marble lectern was on the left, and an outsized Thanksgiving display with flowers and pumpkins was in front of the altar. A large, poster-sized photograph of a young woman and her dog was mounted on a display easel on the right, and a silver urn was next to the photo on a small table.

Mr. Smith walked down the aisle and stopped in front of the Thanksgiving display. *I guess the good Lord is going to make this easy.* The display was a collection of pumpkins, gourds, and red, white, and yellow flowers exhibited on arranged boxes covered in a white cloth. He stepped up to the display and put his case down. He took a giant pumpkin off one of the boxes and put it on the ground. He pulled back the white cloth and slipped his case next to the box. He put the cloth back in place and arranged the pumpkin back on the box. He stepped back to look at his handiwork. Perfect.

He walked over to look at the photograph. *Boy, she was beautiful.* He ran his fingers over the picture. "Sorry, babe, wrong place, wrong time."

"Did you know her?" came a voice from the back.

Mr. Smith looked to the side of the picture and saw a priest walking through a door behind the picture. He was dressed in black pants, black shirt, with a white cleric collar. He had glasses, a full beard with brown hair, and a receding hairline. The weight of the Beretta 92F in the holster under his left armpit registered in his brain. *Kill the priest in his own church* went briefly through his mind. *Already going to hell, but they probably got a reserved room if you whack a priest in his own house.* The thought quickly passed. Only priest in a small parish. Kill the priest, no ceremony tomorrow. Plus, there won't be much of the priest left when his case goes off.

"No, Father, I did not," Mr. Smith said. "I'm just passing through on business. I always like to visit Catholic churches on my travels to say a prayer and see some of the local cultures. A church tells a lot about a community, like your herd of cows out front."

The priest laughed. "That is a first for me. They were a gift from the Martins. They own a large dairy farm in the area. In fact, this lovely lady was the wife of one of their members. A tragedy. Well, you take your time, my son, and may God be with you on your travels. I'll leave you to your prayers." The priest disappeared through the door in the back.

"I think God left me a while ago, Father."

Mr. Smith looked at his watch: 2000. Tomorrow at 1030, this holy place, and all the souls inside would cease to exist. The gasses in the initial detonation at 8,050 meters per second would apply an enormous amount of force to everything in the surrounding area. At this expansion rate, it is impossible to outrun the explosion like they do in dozens of action movies. So, anyone in the building is dead. To the observer, the explosion is nearly instantaneous—one second, everything's normal, and the next, destroyed. The effective lethal range of the ball bearings in a claymore mine is 100 yards. In addition to the explosive blast, the hundreds of ball bearings inside the case will shred anything within a 100-yard radius, including unlucky cars passing on the street or parked nearby.

Mr. Smith walked back to the front of the altar and down the aisle. He stopped at the back and turned around, looking at the Cross of Jesus suspended from the ceiling. *I wonder what you are going to look like at 1030,* he thought. *I could use a remote detonator and watch for myself, but a timed detonator is better. Once my package goes off, they will close all the roads, and there is only one way out each way. They will be looking for non-locals, who will stand out.* "So, goodbye, Jesus. See you in hell." He dipped his hand in the bowl of holy water at the back of the church and made the sign of the cross. *Well, I didn't burst into flames, so I must be good.* He pushed through the doors and walked out into the night.

Josh and his mom talked for hours about his dad, Katherine, and the business. The fire burned down to embers. JJ and Pops went off to their barn apartments, and Jessica called to say she would not be home until after midnight.

"When are you going to tell me what you've wanted to say all night?" Josh looked at his mom.

"That obvious?"

"Yes, Mom, that obvious. Are you okay?"

"Yes, I'm fine. You know I loved your father very much." She brushed some imaginary crumbs off her pants. "Pops asked me to marry him."

"About damn time."

"You're okay with it?"

"Of course, I'm okay with it. Pops has been a father to me since Dad died. If you're happy, I'm all for it. Life is too short. You never know when it will end. It could all be over tomorrow. So, when is the big day?"

"We were planning on New Year's Eve, until Katherine." Tears filled his mom's eyes.

Josh took her hand in his. "Mom, New Year's Eve is fine. Katherine would not want you to wait. She always liked a good party. At least Pops won't forget his anniversary."

They both laughed, and Josh hugged his mom, holding her tight.

"Where are those two?" Josh kissed the top of his mom's head.

"They're waiting in Pops' apartment. Pops isn't sure if he's sleeping in the barn or my room."

"I think you should make him sleep in the barn tonight since you're not married."

"Just like you and Katherine?"

"You knew about that?"

"Of course, I'm a mom."

They both climbed off the couch. "Please give my best to your fiancé. I'm heading up to bed. It's going to be a long day tomorrow," Josh said. "Come on, Syrin, time for bed." Syrin jumped up and headed for the bedroom over the garage. Josh followed behind, wondering if this was the last time he slept under this roof.

Mr. Smith crossed the Zakim Bridge into Boston just after midnight. The green Jaguar XJ held steady at 80 mph for most of the trip. The radar detector alerted a couple of times, but otherwise, it was a smooth trip. Traffic was light this late, so he made good time through the city. He took the South Station exit, right to Essex Street, and headed over to the Boston

Common. He took a left on Avery and pulled into the valet slot in front of the Ritz-Carlton Towers. He got out of the car and tossed the keys to the valet, who rounded the front of the car.

"I'm in for the night, Rico," Mr. Smith said.

"Very good, Mr. Adams," Rico said. "Do you want me to get the car washed?"

"That would be great, Rico. Thank you." Mr. Smith walked into the gleaming stainless steel and glass foyer of the Ritz.

He walked through the lobby to the bank of elevators and pushed the up button. The elevator door opened. He pushed the number 7, and the door closed. The elevator started to rise. Mr. Smith ran a checklist through his brain, contemplating the options. *If you prepare for the worst but expect the best, you will rarely be disappointed.* He laughed at the thought. It had been a long time ago at the Agency farm when he last heard that quote by one of his instructors. Time to prepare for the worst. Time to pack.

Josh's alarm clock jumped into bed and licked his face at 0630.

"Hey, hey, enough with the waterworks. I'm up, I'm up, Jesus." Josh rolled out of bed, stretched, and reached for the sky. Syrin danced around, brushing against his legs. He walked over to the table, between the two recliners, and put on his running clothes complete with FBI sweatpants and hooded sweatshirt. He also put on a fluorescent orange vest, and he put a vest on Syrin. No need to get mistaken for a deer. Survive a shootout with eight bangers in an enclosed garage and get killed by Elmer Fudd while jogging in the woods of NH. Some of the locals tended to shoot at movement and not necessarily a target.

Josh headed down the stairs and out the porch door. Daylight crept through the trees; the sun wouldn't be up for another 30 minutes. He headed off the porch and down the driveway with Syrin bounding ahead. Syrin's orange fluorescent vest flapped with every leap. She would definitely get mistaken for a deer without the vest. The air was crisp and cold on his face, and the leaves crunched under his feet. He headed down the driveway toward Route 2. He kept it comfortable for the first half mile through the fir trees, and then sprinted the last half mile to Route 2, touched the mailbox, and sprinted back to the house. Time would be tight this morning, so no time for a five-mile run. Syrin beat him to the porch again and headed back to greet Josh for the last quarter mile.

"Show off," Josh said. He ran into the clearing and stopped. He put his hands behind his head to catch his breath and walked to JJ's barn, just as JJ walked out.

"You let the dog beat you," JJ said. He scratched Syrin behind the ears, and she wagged her tail at the appreciation of her victory.

"You must have gotten up really early because I didn't see your fat ass out here running," Josh said.

JJ patted his trim midsection. "This is called functional fitness. I get it by working hard at farm work, not running around in gym shorts."

"How about gym shorts kicks your farmer ass?" Josh stepped up and grabbed JJ around the neck, and they started wrestling.

"Hey, if you girls are done dancing, breakfast is ready," Pops yelled from the front porch. JJ, Josh, and Syrin all ran for the front porch. Syrin beat them both.

"Fast dog," JJ said, as they topped the porch and walked through the door. The smell of pancakes, bacon, and coffee greeted them.

"Plates are on the table, boys. Dig in," Sarah said.

JJ headed to the dining room. Josh walked over to Pops. "I'd give you a hug, but I'm a little sweaty." He stuck out his hand. "Welcome to the family."

Pops took his hand and pulled him in for a hug. "Thanks, son. Your blessing means a lot to your mom and me. Now go get some food, before JJ eats it all."

"You got that right. I thought he looked a little pudgy this morning. Once a Marine, always a Marine," Josh said, walking into the dining room.

His sister Jessica was seated at one of the chairs, sipping on some coffee wrapped in a pink bathrobe with "What's up Doc" written on the back, a gift from Josh for last year's Christmas. Her blond hair was pulled back tight in a ponytail, but there were bags under her eyes from a long day and an early morning.

"Hey, beautiful," Josh said. He bent over to give Jessica a kiss.

"I'm so sorry, Josh," Jessica said.

"No, no tears, Jess. You know the rules. We celebrate her life, not cry at her death. Besides, you start crying, and JJ will start bawling like a baby."

Josh sat next to his sister. Grabbed five pancakes off the stack, five slices of bacon off the tray, and poured fresh Martin maple syrup over the stack and took a big bite of pancake.

"Now that is some fine maple syrup, brother. You still got the touch," Josh said. He took another bite and washed it down with hot coffee. "Coffee is good too. How was the night shift?"

"Pretty slow. One guy fell out of a tree stand and broke his leg, and we had two cases of the flu and one kidney stone."

"Oh, kidney stone," JJ said. "I had one during an exercise in Lejeune. Not fun. I cried like a Navy SEAL the whole time. It was embarrassing."

"Glad to see nothing has changed," Jess said.

They all finished breakfast, and the cleaning lady arrived for the weekly house cleaning. They had her come early, so she could do the dishes and clean the kitchen, while everyone else got ready for the ceremony at 1000.

"Well, that was good," Josh said. "Time for a shower. So, if you'll excuse me, I'll see you all in a bit. Come on, Syrin." Josh headed out of the dining room to the garage with Syrin bringing up the rear.

55

Director Santiago took a sip of coffee. He had just finished a ham and cheese omelet with some homemade wheat toast. He was seated at a small round table in his room, looking out the window at the Presidential Mountains in the distance. There was a knock at the door. He walked over and looked through the peephole. Dave Tuley.

He opened the door to let him in, and Dave walked past, carrying a touch screen tablet.

"Good morning, Dave. Can I get you some breakfast or coffee?" Director Santiago asked.

"Coffee would be great, Sir."

"Anything in it?"

"No, Sir. Black is good."

Director Santiago closed the door. "Well, have a seat."

Dave took a seat across from Director Santiago, who sat down and took a mug from his coffee tray. Turned it right side up, poured some coffee out of his carafe, and handed it to Dave.

"Thanks, Sir." He took a sip and set the cup down. He put the tablet on the table, touched the screen, and an aerial view of a pond with camps around it appeared on the screen.

"What am I looking at?" Director Santiago asked.

"This is an overhead look of Martin Meadow Pond from a Reaper drone."

"Ah, she got on scene."

"Yes, Sir. About 10 minutes ago."

"One of ours?"

"Yes, Sir. The pilot is Captain Dana Gordon, USAF. She's at Creech Air Force base outside Vegas. The aircraft is listed on the schedule for a recon run of the Canadian border for Customs and Border Protection. The aircraft is a Reaper MQ-9 drone with a thermographic camera, infrared, and a full spectrum communications intercept package. She has two AGM-114 Hellfire II air-to-ground missiles and two external fuel tank pods."

"On-scene endurance?"

"24 hours, Sir. On station time should not be an issue."

"Resolution?"

Dave touched the screen and a crosshair appeared. He moved the crosshair over to the large building on the north side of the pond and hit zoom. The screen zoomed to the top of the roof of the large building. He then slid the image over the front door and zoomed in again to see the doorknob.

"I see the resolution is good," Director Santiago said. "What about the helo?"

"Aircrew already left for the airport to do pre-flight checks. They'll be overhead the town of Lancaster at 0930. They'll have 4 hours of flight time before Bingo. They'll provide us air support for the trip from Lancaster to the pond. My crew is locked, loaded, and ready to roll. Departure in 30 minutes."

"Sounds like you got everything covered, Dave. Good job. I'll see you in the Lobby in 25 minutes." They both stood.

"Thanks, Director. See you downstairs." He walked over to the door and let himself out.

Jim Palmer climbed into the passenger seat next to Greg and pulled the door shut.

"Let's go." He turned back to look at Aaron and Cam. "You guys ready to rock?"

"Yeah, boss, let's get some," Cam said. He slammed the back of the seat with his hand.

"Hoo-ah, Rangers lead the way," Aaron said. "Crank some music and let's go."

Greg turned up the volume on the radio, and "Living on a Prayer" blared from the speakers. The three-car convoy pulled out of the Littleton Motor Inn parking lot and turned north on Route 3.

The trip from Littleton to the Martin Meadow Pond Road turnoff was about 15 miles. They made the trip in about 25 minutes following the speed limit the entire way. They turned left on Martin Meadow Pond Road and followed it about a mile to the fork in the road at the intersection with Martin Road. The pavement turned to gravel right at the intersection. They turned right at the intersection and followed the road. The wind blew leaves across the road, and the SUVs left a dust trail in their wake, but there was no sign of anyone. Halfway through, the scenery of hardwoods and brown leaves on the ground gave way to an open field on both sides of the road. There were homes on either side of the road bordering the field, but they were both shuttered for the winter. Another half mile of hardwoods, the road finally opened into the Martin estate.

Greg stopped the SUV, just after entering the grounds. The grove of apple trees was on the right, their limbs free of leaves, but a couple of apples still clung stubbornly to the branches. Cam and Aaron got out of the back. Cam walked around to the back of the SUV and pulled his rifle case out of the back, along with his shooting mat and his support pack. He headed right into the apple orchard to set up the sniper hide. Aaron headed back to the rear car.

Zerbino and the rest of the Legionnaires milled around the Tahoe, pulling out gear and zipping into Ghillie suits. They looked like walking leave piles.

"If you're not careful, some bear is going to piss on you," Aaron said.

"Then it will be the last piss he takes," Turner Carriere said, holding up his FN Special Operations Forces Combat Assault Rifle (SCAR) with an Aimpoint CompM4 red dot sight.

"Are you guys using the heavy or the light?" Aaron asked.

"The heavy," Turner said. "The 7.62 is a better round, especially for this open shooting." He gestured at the open field with his rifle.

The four leaf piles headed to the water along a stone wall which snaked from the road to the pond. Aaron shut all the SUV doors and hopped in the front seat. The three-car convoy continued another 100 meters into the estate and pulled into the parking area in front of the main house. The main house was shuttered with blue green shutters covering all the windows and doors. Everyone got out of the vehicles. The Canadians started prepping their C8 rifles, the Canadian version of the M16A1. They topped the C8s with AR-X Prism Scopes. Torai Takemura pulled an M40A5 sniper rifle out of the back of the Tahoe and slung it over his shoulder. Insurance, if they had to make a long-range shot. Everyone was dressed in woodland camouflage uniforms, just like Uncle Sam issued them.

Jim and Greg scanned the surrounding estate for signs of life. A hay barn was set back about 100 meters above the main house, and a small ranch house was to the right of the barn, probably the caretaker's house in the summer. Everything was closed up.

"Must be a bitch of winter, if they keep everything shut up," Greg said.

"Probably a lot of drifting snow. Tough to keep the road open," Jim said. "And for what? To sit around in your estate home and watch it snow? Money doesn't hang for the winter. I would be sunning myself in Hawaii."

"What do you think about parking one of the trucks behind the house over there behind the tennis courts?" Greg asked, pointing to the house on the far west side of the estate between the tennis courts and the woods. "It will be out of sight from the road in, and from the field if he's walking down to the water. It will save you a trek back."

"Good idea," Jim said. "Hey, Villa?"

"Yes, Sir," Villa said.

"Drive one of the SUVs on the other side of the house closest to the woods and park it there, before you get in position," Jim said.

"Will do," Villa replied. "Okay, boys, pile in." The Canadians climbed back into the SUV and headed to the far western side of the estate.

Greg and Jim got back in the Tahoe and headed back down the road to the apple orchard, with Aaron following in a trail vehicle. Greg stopped at the edge of the orchard, and Jim hopped out. He got his M4 carbine and a black case that contained an M151 Improved Spotting Scope and tactical aluminum tripod. The M151 has a 12-40x magnification with a 60 mm objective lens. The scope has a Leupold MilDot reticle for both range estimation and tactical collaboration with the shooter. The scope was weather resistant, and fog proof, not that weather would be a problem for this engagement. It was blue skies. Jim closed the hatch and tapped the back twice. Greg started down the road with Aaron in tow. Jim walked into the orchard. *I bet we could kill a couple of deer around here,* he thought, gazing at all the apples on the ground.

56

Josh looked in the mirror and pushed the Windsor knot on his black tie tight to the collar. He played with the dimple to make sure it had a perfect crease and adjusted the holster on his Glock 22 to position it under his arm- pit and not to bunch up the shirt. He walked over and picked up his black suit jacket from the bed and slipped it on. The suit was a custom-made Zegna, light wool, fall classic. He had the jacket let out to accommodate the extra bulk of a shoulder holster and extra mags pouch on the right side. He walked back to the mirror and turned a couple of times. No visible signs of a weapon. He walked back to the bed and picked up a black duffel bag that contained his tactical vest, extra magazines for his M4, and wood- land camo BDU. He had already put his boots and rifle case in the back of the Flex.

"Let's go, Syrin," Josh said. He opened the guest suite door, and Syrin bounded out and down the stairs. Josh came down the stairs and walked out through the garage since the door was already up. He walked to the back of the Flex, opened the back hatch, and tossed the bag in next to his boots and rifle case. He shut the hatch and turned at the sound of the garage door going up on JJ's barn behind him. JJ walked out of the barn dressed in an all-black suit with a crisp white shirt and black tie.

"You got your stuff?" Josh asked.

"Yeah, it's all in the truck."

Josh looked at his watch: 0940. "Time to get moving."

As if on cue, a black Lincoln stretch limousine came down the drive- way and pulled up to the house. The driver, in a black chauffeur's uniform, got out of the driver's seat and stood near the door. JJ and Josh walked up to the back of the limousine to wait for Mom.

Josh walked up to the driver and shook hands with him.

"Thanks for making the trip. Any traffic?"

"No, Sir, it was smooth sailing."

"Why don't you hop back in the car…we'll take care of loading everyone in," Josh said, motioning at JJ.

"Yes, Sir, no problem." The driver climbed back in the car.

The side porch door opened, and Jessica walked out. She was wearing a black overcoat, and her blond hair was pinned tight to the top of her head. Mom was next. She wore a matching coat and carried a black leather clutch. They both could have been stepping out on 5th Avenue in New York. Pops trailed the ladies dressed in an all-black suit to match the boys. Josh knew his Mom had to fly in a tailor from Boston to make Pops' suit. Josh opened the door, and JJ went to help Jessica down the stairs.

Sarah smiled as she walked down the stairs. "You both are such handsome young men."

"Thanks, Mom," Josh said. "Good genes. Not sure what happened to JJ."

"Hey now," Pops said, "He's the spitting image of his dad. Good looking."

"Yeah, come on, good looking, time to move out before we're late," Josh said.

Josh got everyone into the limousine and shut the door. He walked back to the Flex, opened the front door, and Syrin jumped in. He climbed in after her. JJ walked over to the barn and got in his Chevy truck, and the entire procession started down the driveway.

Two Lancaster police cruisers waited at the end of the road with their lights flashing to provide an escort. The first cruiser pulled out to lead the way, and the second cruiser blocked any oncoming traffic. The limousine fell in line behind the police escort, followed by Josh and JJ. The second cruiser fell in behind JJ. His mom must be loving this. Every once in a while, she liked to play New Hampshire royalty. She always portrayed the image of a simple farmer's wife, but sometimes she wanted to show what it meant to be a Martin. Josh looked in his rearview mirror at his brother's old Chevy truck, and today, the image was the Clampetts go to church. Josh laughed at the thought and pointed at the roof of Flex. "All for you, babe…all for you. What do you think, Syrin?"

Syrin barked at the sound of her name.

"Exactly."

Trooper Paul Ferguson pulled away from the Mountain View and followed Mountain View Road until he came to the resort entrance on Route 3. He took a right on Route 3 and headed to Lancaster. Director Santiago and Dave Tuley were in the back, watching the video feed from the Reaper drone.

"Well, you were right, Sir," Dave Tuley said. They watched the deployment of the assault team at the Martin estate on the drone tablet. The combination of thermal imaging and an instant camera feed allowed them to see the outline of men in various locations in real time, along with a couple of deer on the hillside on the north side of the main house. Four Tangos were along the edge of the field, evenly spaced on the east side. A two-man overwatch team was set up in what looked like an apple orchard, and two 2-man teams were set up on the western edge, one team on the side of a house, and the other in the tree line.

"Anyone who made it into that estate wouldn't make it out," Director Santiago said. "Are we still tracking the dark blue SUV?"

"Yes, Sir. He should pull out in front of us just over this hill. Paul, back off a bit. We want him in front of us," Dave said.

"Roger, Sir," Paul said.

"Delta Eight Foxtrot, this is Bravo Whiskey, is the target still moving?" Dave asked.

"Roger, Bravo Whiskey. Target is about a mile ahead of you turning left on Route 3 now."

"Roger, Delta Eight Foxtrot, please maintain high altitude surveillance. We're closing up now."

"Roger. Your folks are also in position."

"Okay, Paul, let's go." Paul hit the lights and the siren and stomped on the gas. The green State Police SUV Interceptor went from 60 mph to 100 mph, pushing both Director Santiago and Dave back into their seats.

57

Greg Bennett wound through Martin Road with Aaron following in the trail vehicle. He pulled up and stopped, just after entering Martin Meadow Pond Road. A logging road was visible on the right, and tire tracks in the mud led into the woods. Hunters used it to access the area. Bad luck, if Aaron found anyone down the road. They wouldn't be coming out. Aaron pulled the SUV past Greg and headed down the logging road. Greg gave him a wave and headed out to Route 3. Greg stopped at the intersection. No traffic. He turned left on Route 3 and headed into Lancaster. He just got to the crown of Corrigan Hill, when he caught sight of a police unit closing fast with lights and sirens. He glanced left as two tan SUVs pulled off and parked at the tourist view site on the left. He went further down the road, and the police unit continued to close fast. He pulled off to the side of the road to let him pass. The police unit hit the brakes and pulled in behind him.

"What the fuck?" Greg said, looking in the rearview mirror at the flashing lights of the police unit. It was a green State Police SUV. "What does this prick want with me?" He reached down with his right hand and picked up the Colt .45 that he had wedged between the seat and the center console. "Why is that fuck just sitting there?" He glanced at his side mirror. He could see the tan SUVs coming up the road. One of them pulled over and stopped with the front of the SUV even with his side mirror, about 6 inches away, trapping him in the vehicle. The other SUV cut 45 degrees in front of his car, cutting off his avenue of escape. Two operators in full combat gear piled out.

One stopped directly in front and pointed a M4 carbine at him. "Hands. Let me see your hands."

The other moved to the side passenger window and pointed his M4 carbine at his head. "You so much as twitch, and I'll end you, asshole. Toss the gun." Greg tossed the .45 into the passenger seat. "Now turn off your vehicle and toss the keys." Greg turned off the car, pulled out the key, and threw them on the seat next to the gun. "Now grab the steering wheel at 10 and 2. Don't even think about letting go." Greg grabbed the steering wheel at 10 and 2, and thought, *How the fuck did they know?* The operator at the passenger window waved his left hand.

"Looks like we're on, Sir," Dave said.

Both Director Santiago and Dave climbed out of the State Police SUV; the Director carried the drone tablet, and they walked over to the Tahoe. Director Santiago opened the passenger door. He picked up the keys and the .45 and handed them to the operator who put them on the hood, then he slid into the passenger seat. Dave Tuley got in the back and moved over, so he was directly behind Greg. He had a silenced Beretta 92F pointed at Greg's back through the seat.

"So, who the fuck are you guys?" Greg asked. "You're making a big mistake. I'm a government official on official government business."

"So, what's your name, Mr. Government Official?" Director Santiago asked.

"That's classified," Greg said.

Director Santiago held up the tablet and took a picture of Greg. "Did you get it?" Director Santiago asked.

"Yes, Sir," LCDR Kendall said, from Jacksonville. "We're running it now. Information should be coming to your screen."

"I got it, thanks," Director Santiago said.

"Mr. George Schneider, aka Greg Bennett. Nine years of service in the U.S. Army. Completed Ranger training. Bad conduct discharge for assault on a senior officer. Divorced. Ex-wife Colleen, and two daughters, Emily and Hannah. They live at 12 Colony Court in Keene, NH. Employed by Sea Island Security as an independent contractor, i.e. scumbag. Lives in Montreal, Canada, at 101 Avenue Tisserand. How am I doing so far?" Director Santiago asked.

"I've done nothing wrong. I'm just driving home after visiting my ex-wife and kids in Keene," Greg said. "So, unless you are going to arrest me, get the fuck out."

"How quaint," Director Santiago said. "You think we're law enforcement. We can be, but now, we're in the scumbag elimination business, and quite frankly, business is good. And here are today's first candidates." He tapped the tablet and the drone feed appeared on the screen. It showed the Martin estate and the thermal outlines of the 10 members of the Sea Island Security team spread throughout the area. "And then, we have this." He tapped the screen again.

A video of Greg talking to Jim Palmer appeared on the screen.

"What do you think about parking one of the trucks behind the house over there behind the tennis courts?" Greg asked, pointing to the house on the far west side of the estate between the tennis courts and the woods. *"It would be out of sight from the road in, and from the field, if he's walking down to the water. It will save you a walk back."*

"How nice. You're concerned about the health of your leader, Jim Palmer," Director Santiago said.

"Oh, fuck me," Greg said, sagging into his seat.

"Yes, fuck you, indeed, Mr. Bennett or Schneider," Director Santiago said. "Per my instructions, I only need one of you, the rest can go."

"What do you mean go?" Greg asked.

Director Santiago made a gun with his right hand and pointed it at Greg and said, *"Bang.* Like I said, today we're in the scumbag elimination business, so fortunately for you, you have some options. Unlike your other friends. You have three choices. Behind door number 1, you can help us out, in which case, I'll let my State Police escort arrest you. Behind door number 2, my associate here will shoot you twice in the back severing your spine, so you'll never walk again, or behind door number 3, my other friends in front of us, will take you into the woods and put two bullets in your brain. Your choice."

"What do you want me to do?" Greg asked.

"Good choice," Director Santiago said.

58

The Martin parade turned right on Main Street from Route 2 and headed up to the church. Josh thought of a comment from former President Clinton as he made the turn. Some reporter asked Clinton, what did he miss most about not being president? His reply, they no longer stop traffic for me. Well, they stopped traffic for Sarah Martin. The street was empty from the turn all the way to the front of the church. Cars lined both sides of the street, since parking in the church parking lot was limited. The curb was clear of cars in front of the church, so the motorcade pulled into the slot and stopped.

Josh put the Flex into park and got out, followed by Syrin. "Heel," Josh said, and she fell into position by his right hip. The officer in the lead car was already out and opening the door for the limousine. Officer Brad Watson exited the church, down the steps, and walked over to Josh. He was in his ceremonial uniform complete with 1930's style police hat.

"Everything's set, Josh," Brad said. "Everyone's already seated like you asked. The chief's in the front, on the left, next to the mayor."

"Thanks, Brad. I appreciate it. You guys really didn't need to do all this," Josh said, gesturing at the police escort.

"Since you guys donated the cruisers to the town, it was the least we could do," Brad said.

Josh looked at his watch: 0955. Right on time. His mom, Pops, and Jessica were walking up the stairs.

"Thanks again, Brad. I better catch up, or my mom will start without me."

Josh fell in behind his mom, and JJ brought up the rear of the procession. They climbed the steps, and Father Mattie was at the top of the stairs to greet them. He looked like George C. Scott with a full beard and glasses. Everyone in town thought he was his brother. Josh made a quick scan of the area to see if anything was out of place. There was a green State Police SUV parked across the street in front of the library, which was strange. The local trooper was Trooper Dale Murphy, who lived in Berlin. He already sent his regrets that he couldn't make it. Maybe this was his replacement. Josh reached the top step.

Father Mattie reached out his hand. "Josh, I'm so sorry for your loss."

Josh shook his hand. He had a firm Irish grip. "Thank you, Father," Josh said.

"And, this must be Syrin." He reached down and patted Syrin on the head, and Syrin licked his hand and wagged her tail.

"Thank you for letting Syrin be part of the ceremony. She's family," Josh said.

"All God's creatures are welcome into his house," Father Mattie said. "I think everything is ready to go, so if we can get inside, we can get started."

Josh followed his family inside, dipped his hand in the holy water, and made the sign of the cross. It had been awhile since he was last in this church. He had spent many a Sunday as a kid coming to Sunday Mass with his mom, dad, and sister, followed by Sunday brunch at the Lancaster diner. He was baptized here, made his first communion, first confession, confirmation, and on a warm sunny day on June 24, 2006, he married the love of his life. He remembered her walking down the aisle with her father, and now he was walking down the same aisle to say goodbye. Till death do us part. It came too early. He looked at the picture of Kat and Syrin on the easel, and the silver urn, which contained her ashes. A lifetime together, and it ends with a picture and a pile of ashes. He fought back the tears. Kat wouldn't want this to be a sad occasion, but a celebration of her life.

The place was packed. It was standing room only in the back, such was the respect for the family, which provided so much to the community going back generations. His mom, Pops, Jessica, and JJ moved into the first pew on the left. Father Mattie kneeled in front of the altar and the Thanksgiving display and took his seat in the back, behind the altar and to the right. Josh kneeled in front of the Thanksgiving display and the altar. He rose and went over to touch his wife's picture. He touched her on the forehead, feeling the canvas beneath his fingers and not her skin. He kissed her urn and tasted the metal beneath his lips and not the sweetness of her kiss. Syrin followed behind, not knowing what was going on. He could hear crying behind him. Hoping it wasn't his sister or mother, because he couldn't handle that. He walked behind the display to get to the marble lectern on the left of the church. Syrin sat down by a large pumpkin in the display and barked. Josh looked back to see Syrin seated by the pumpkin.

"Syrin, come," Josh said. She came over and sat by him. "Stay."

Josh looked at his watch: 1010. He had 10 minutes of prepared remarks, and then Father would start the ceremony. Hopefully, they would be out by 1100.

Josh looked at the crowd in front of him and paused. Connie, the mayor, in a black pants suit was seated behind his mom with the Chief of Police, Charley Parson, in his ceremonial uniform on her right. He spotted David and Audrey from the Littleton Dairy in the back. She was wearing a large black dress that was pulled tight over her growing stomach. It wouldn't be long now.

"Good morning, and thank you for coming," Josh said. "I wish it was under different circumstances. Before I begin, we have some ground rules. It's okay to laugh and smile. I know this is a solemn occasion, but Kat wouldn't want us to be sad. She would want us to remember her with joy in our heart and a smile on our face. Also, everyone is invited to the Maple Sugar House this evening for dinner, and a dance, in celebration of her life. All you need to bring is yourself and one canned good for the church pantry. We will have collection boxes in the Sugar House. Dress is casual."

Syrin padded back over to the large pumpkin in the display, sat down, and barked.

"Syrin, come," Josh said. She didn't move and barked again.

"Oh, shit," Josh said, under his breath. He walked over to Syrin and said, "Seek it." She turned around and nosed the box near the big pumpkin under a white cloth. Josh pulled back the cloth. There was a brown leather case next to the box.

"Good girl, Syrin." He patted her on the head.

He walked over to the front pew and leaned over to whisper in JJ's ear. "Syrin just indicated on the display. There's a large leather case next to the boxes. We need to get everyone out of here now."

JJ looked at Syrin seated next to the pumpkin. "Shit, okay. Let's move."

59

"Mom, something has come up. I need you and Jessica to leave now," Josh said.

"What is it, Josh?" his mom asked. "If it's Syrin, just let her sit over there. She'll be fine."

"No, Mom, it's not Syrin. I'll explain later. I need you to leave. Pops, can you please get her out of here? Head back to the house. Don't stay in front of the church."

"Let's go, Sarah," Pops said. He pushed her out of the pew.

Josh looked back at the Chief of Police. "Charley, can I see you for a minute up here?" He motioned with his hand for Charley to come up to the altar. There was murmuring in the crowd, as folks were trying to figure out what was going on, as they watched the Martin family leave the church.

JJ followed his mom out of the pew and stopped in the front of the church at the head of the aisle. "If I could please get everyone's attention," JJ said. "Something has come up. If we could please get everyone to leave the church, that would be great."

Everyone started looking around, some folks started leaving, and others stayed behind to see what was going on.

Charley Parson got around the mayor and walked up to Josh on the altar near the big pumpkin.

"What's going on?" Charley asked.

Josh lifted the white cloth to reveal the brown leather case. "Syrin indicated on the case," Josh said.

"For drugs or explosives?"

"Explosives. She lays down for drugs," Josh said.

"Holy Christ," Charley said. "The closest bomb unit is in Concord at the State Police Headquarters. They're about two hours away. What are we going to do?"

"You need to get everyone out of here quickly, and then clear everything, and everyone, away from the church for about a ½ mile," Josh said.

"What are you going to do?"

"I don't know, but I'll figure it out," Josh said. "Now get moving, we don't have much time."

"Right, fudge. Okay, people, we need to get everyone out of the church now. Brad, can you get these folks moving? We also need to clear all the vehicles from in front of the church," Charley said. "Let's go, folks…time to move."

The milling crowd now turned into a mass exodus, as they sensed something was wrong. JJ worked his way through the throng of people leaving and walked to Josh.

"What do we got?" JJ asked.

"Did you get everyone out of here?"

"Yeah. Everyone is in the limousine, and they're headed back to the house. Mom isn't very happy."

"I could have told you that."

Josh walked over to the big pumpkin and lifted it off the box and put it back on the altar away from the display. He pulled back the white cloth, which was an old bed sheet, to reveal the brown leather case. It was a large, brown, legal case with two brass twist latches holding the top flap in place. He made a quick scan of the case for any trip wires. It was clear.

He twisted both latches to align with the holes and slowly lifted the leather top to reveal a solid piece of clear ballistic gel-like plastic, which filled the entire case. Red lights blinked inside the plastic block, and hundreds of silver ball bearings were suspended throughout the block.

"Fuck me," Josh said.

"Not what I wanted to hear, brother. Do some of that SEAL shit and take care of this."

"Nothing I can do. I've never seen one of these. I've just read about them in some intel reports."

"What is it?" JJ asked.

"It's a gel bomb."

"A what?"

"A gel bomb. They make the bomb, and then encase it in this gel material, which hardens into a block." Josh rapped on the top of the plastic with his knuckle. "See? Solid. You also can add nails or any other shrapnel material into your mixture. In this case, they used ball bearings. Once it hardens, there is no way to diffuse the bomb, and it's also waterproof, so we can't dump it in a bathtub. It's usually on a timer for detonation, and they use a remote to start it. Once it starts, there are only two ways to turn it off. Use the remote, or it blows up. Do you have a remote?"

"No, I'm all the fuck out of remotes," JJ said.

"Well, we better figure something out quick, because I'm pretty sure this thing is going to go off soon."

"Sounds like it's time to go, bro. We can rebuild the church."

"Yeah, you're right. Let's go," Josh said. "Syrin, come." They both sprinted for the exit, pushed through the double glass doors, out into the street, and into a mob of people milling about. The traffic was packed on Main Street, as the beleaguered Lancaster police force tried to reroute traffic and clear the street of parked cars.

"Wait!" Josh said. "When that bomb goes off, all these people are gone." Josh turned and ran back into the church with Syrin close on his heels.

"Fuck me," JJ said. He followed his brother back into the church.

60

Director Santiago and Paul Ferguson watched everyone stream out of the church. Director Santiago looked at his watch: 1015.

"Kinda early for the ceremony to be over," Director Santiago said.

The Lancaster police tried to clear traffic out of the street and move cars parked at the curb. An older cop in his dress uniform approached the State Police vehicle.

"That's Chief Parson," Paul said.

Director Santiago lowered his window. "Good morning, Chief. What's going on?"

Chief Parson stuck his head in the window. "We got a bomb. Can you get the bomb squad and a forensics team rolling our way?"

"Sure, Chief," Paul said. He pulled out his phone and started making calls.

"Who's in there now?" Director Santiago asked.

"Josh Martin and his brother JJ. Josh is in the FBI, and he's a former SEAL. JJ spent eight years in the Marines, so they're the closest thing we got to experts, until the state guys get here. Can I get you to back up about a half mile down the road and block traffic?"

"Sure, Chief," Paul said.

"Thanks, guys. I gotta get back and sort this shit out." Chief Parson turned back and headed into the crowd.

Director Santiago put the window up and turned back to look at Greg, who was handcuffed in the backseat.

"Anything you want to tell me?" Director Santiago asked.

"I swear to god, we didn't know about this. We crossed the border in Pittsburgh and went straight to Littleton. We didn't want to raise any small-town suspicions about 12 strangers walking around town. We didn't stop for food or gas. I can tell you one thing."

"What's that?" Director Santiago asked.

"Somebody wants Josh Martin dead," Greg said.

Director Santiago turned back in his seat. *Ain't that the truth. This seems like more than a cartel issue. Blowing up two federal agents and two civilians is one thing. Blowing up a church full of God-fearing Americans attending a funeral service is a whole new level of stupid, unless you are a jihadist, and there is no indication of any terrorist involvement. Cartels may be evil, but at the basic level, they're businessmen trying to earn money. Blowing up a church is bad for business. That gets you a visit from the Marines, just ask the Mujahedeen. Something else is at play.*

Josh ran up to the case in the church and picked it up. "Fuck, it's heavy. How's your farmer's fitness?" Josh asked.

"What?"

"This bitch is heavy, so it's going to take both of us to tag team to get it out of here."

"Where are we going?"

"Away from here," Josh said. He picked up the case and headed for the rear door. JJ trailed after him and opened the door to the rear exit. They both fled out the door.

Josh ran about 50 yards across the back-church parking lot and stopped to put down the case. The case was dead weight, so it was difficult to run with. His arms, back, and shoulders screamed. Josh looked around for some place to leave the case to do the least amount of damage.

"JJ, take off. No sense both of us getting blown up! We don't have much time left, and no way we outrun this bitch. It must have at least 20 pounds of C4. Take Syrin with you."

"No way, Josh. We do this together."

"We need to find some place for this thing to go off to do the least amount of damage," Josh said.

They both scanned the area. A farm was on the right, which did mostly tractor repair. Some retail outlets were on the left, and the Colonel Town Recreation center with two ball fields, tennis courts, and a pool was straight ahead. They both looked at each other.

"The pool."

JJ picked up the bag and started running to the pool. He crossed a small field, and the pool parking lot, before coming to a 6-ft-high chain-link fence. The gate was locked, since the pool was closed after Labor Day weekend. Josh vaulted over the fence, followed by Syrin. JJ handed the case over the fence to Josh and started to climb over. Josh hit him square in the side of the head with a strong right punch, which knocked him back over the fence. JJ sprawled unconscious on the grass.

"Sorry, Bro. No sense Mom losing both boys."

Josh picked up the case and headed to the pool. He ran around the changing room, the office, and headed to the deep end with two diving boards sticking out over the pool. The pool was covered with a rubber tarp to keep leaves and debris out of the water, while it was closed for the winter. It was 16 feet deep at the diving end. Josh heaved the case just in front of the diving boards, but it didn't break through the tarp. It just bowed the tarp and sat there like a brick straining at the fabric. *Fuck, now what? Can't be much time left.* He looked around to see if there was something, he could use to pierce the tarp. Nothing. Everything was picked up and put away.

Slow down, six, slow breaths. Think. Gun. He drew his Glock and ripped off 15 shots as fast as he could pull the trigger at the tarp around the bag. The shots ripped holes in the tarp in a half moon. The sounds of the gunfire echoed around the concrete floor and the buildings of the pool. A flock of chickadees flew out of a nearby tree, swarming and flowing across the baseball field to get away from the perceived danger, and Syrin barked at the retreating birds. The shots shredded the tarp around the bag, and it slipped into the water. It bobbed momentarily and then sank.

Josh put his gun back into his holster and ran. He tore around the office building fully expecting to get hit in the back by flying debris. He ran to the fence and jumped over, followed by Syrin. JJ was just getting back to his feet. Josh pushed him away from the pool. They got another 20 yards and a large explosion shook the ground under their feet like an earthquake, and they both dove to the ground and covered their heads. Syrin kept running. The pool erupted in a giant fountain of water and debris shooting 50 ft into the air like a WWII depth charge movie and a loud thunderclap of the explosion echoed throughout the town, rattling windows. The water fell back into what was left of the pool like a wave crashing on rocks, and ball bearings started bouncing on the concrete pool deck like marbles dropping from the sky.

Josh shook his head to clear it from the concussion and sound of the blast. His ears were ringing. He looked at JJ, who was doing the same thing, plus recovering from getting knocked out.

"I owe you one for the sucker punch," JJ said.

"Bring your lunch."

Josh rolled over onto his back. Syrin ran up and licked his face. They both staggered to their feet. They could hear sirens in the distance getting closer. A crowd of people moved from Main Street to the recreation area to see what was going on. They walked over to the fence to look at the pool, or what was left of the pool. The deep end was gone. It was a dirt crater filled with water. The blast expanded the pool about 3 feet in every direction, cutting through the cement on all sides. The front half of the office building was gone, with wires and rebar hanging from the roof, and ball bearings covered what was left of the concrete floor.

"I guess we're buying the town a new pool," Josh said.

"I think you're right, brother." They turned and walked back to the church, weaving through the throng of people headed to the pool.

They entered the church through the back door. Syrin ran in and went straight to the urn and wagged her tail. Josh went to the front of the altar and picked up Kat's urn.

"She always knew how to go out with a bang," Josh said. The brothers laughed.

"Do you think anyone is waiting for us at the pond?" JJ asked.

"No, I think this was their shot, but I definitely need to find out who is not fond of Josh Martin."

They walked down the aisle and out of the church with Syrin in heel position. The Flex and the POS Chevy were still parked out front.

"I guess no one bothered to move the beauty and the beast," Josh said. "Probably thought they were doing you a favor in case that bomb took out the church and the rolling poster for a new truck."

"Not for long," JJ said. "Since my brother is going to buy me a new truck."

"Sorry, I think I just spent all my money on a new pool."

61

Robert Adams sat back in his recliner at the Ritz-Carlton Towers and took a sip of his third cup of coffee. He thumbed through some office expense sheets for the fourth quarter for the Boston office of Sea Island Security. *Damn, it's expensive to operate in Boston. Good thing, I'm not paying the bill.* He looked at his watch: 1045. Probably should be on the news now, although it may take a while for a news affiliate to get a reporter up there. Lancaster is about two hours from anywhere.

He picked up the remote and turned on CNN. A red breaking news banner flashed on the screen. Bomb blast in Lancaster, New Hampshire. He turned up the volume.

At around 1030 this morning, a device exploded at the Colonel Town Recreation Center, destroying the pool and the adjoining office and changing facility. There are no reports of fatalities. According to Police Chief Charley Parson, the device was planted at the All Saints Catholic Church during a memorial service for Katherine Martin, who was killed in a car bomb earlier in the week. Police do not know if there is a connection, and no one has claimed responsibility.

Robert turned off the TV. "Son of a bitch. That fucker has more lives than a cat."

He pulled out his cryptcell, punched in the number, and hit the green send button.

The caller picked up on the first ring. "Yes," came the reply.

"No joy on option one," Robert said.

"That is unfortunate," said the caller. "We paid you a great deal of money to solve this problem for us. Perhaps we need to find another problem solver."

"That won't be necessary. Option 2 is still in play," Robert said.

"For your sake, I hope it succeeds," said the caller, and he hung up.

"Fuck me. Maybe time to find a new line of work."

JJ climbed into his truck. Josh walked over to the back of the Flex, opened the rear hatch, and put the urn in the back. He walked back to the front and opened the driver side door. Syrin hopped in and assumed the shotgun position. Josh was just about to climb in, when a NH State Police trooper in full uniform waved to him and crossed the street.

"Agent Martin," the trooper said. "My name is Paul Ferguson." He extended his right hand.

Josh shook his hand. "What can I do for you, Paul?"

"Someone from Washington would like a few minutes of your time. He's sitting in the back of my SUV," Paul said. He pointed at the State Police SUV parked across the street with a dark blue Chevy Tahoe and a tan Suburban lined up behind it.

"Does this someone from Washington have a name?" Josh asked.

"He said to tell you White 55," Paul said.

Josh was speechless with a blank look on his face.

JJ stuck his head out of the truck window. "Everything okay?"

"Yeah, yeah, everything's fine. I need to go talk to the State Police for a minute. I'll be right back."

Josh checked traffic and followed Paul across the street. Paul opened the rear door of the SUV and gestured for Josh to get in. Josh climbed in and made a quick assessment of his companion; Hispanic male, 40ish, black hair, scar over right eye, dressed in woodland camo uniform, piercing brown eyes, command presence, not a paper pusher. A tier one operator. He had the look.

Paul shut the door and went back to the Tahoe parked behind the State Police vehicle.

"Good morning, Agent Martin," Director Santiago said. "You've had a busy morning. Nice job on using the pool." They shook hands.

"Thank you, and your name?"

"You can call me Vince. Vince Santiago." He handed Josh his White House credentials.

Josh looked at the credentials. They showed his photo, height, weight, hair color, name, and signature on one side, and his title, Deputy Director, Special Projects, White House Military Office superimposed over a print of the White House on the other side, with some verbiage about extending courtesies and assistance to the holder of this credential.

Josh handed back the credentials. "I'm guessing Delta."

Vince laughed. "A long time ago. What kind of device was it?"

"A gel bomb. And a big one, packed with ball bearings."

"So not a cartel special?"

"Not even close. So, what's White 55?"

"White 55 is your code name. We send you intelligence information every Saturday at 1900, and periodically throughout the week, if something comes up," Vince said.

"I never thought I'd meet you guys."

"Normally, you wouldn't, but every once in a while, we extend an invitation for certain individuals with certain skill sets and motivation to join our organization."

"The death of my wife."

"Unfortunately, yes," Vince said.

"So, what happens now?"

"We'd like you to come to DC to meet some folks, and we can brief you on our operation. Then, you can make the decision on whether to join us or not."

"What happens if I say no?"

"You won't hear from us again, and you can pursue whatever future you want. Twenty million, plus your inheritance, buys a lot of options."

"You've done your homework. Well, I can't see any harm in having a conversation. When do you want to do it?"

"Before we get into that, you have a little problem we need to solve," Vince said.

He reached for the tablet in the door pocket and touched the screen. The drone feed of Josh's Martin Meadow Pond estate appeared on the screen.

"Son of a bitch," Josh said.

62

"Charlie Oscar, this is Romeo One, Target is on the move. Headed in your direction, over," Greg said.

"Roger, Romeo One. Is he still driving the white Ford Flex?" Jim asked.

"That's affirmative. No Pax."

"Roger."

"All units, stand by. Target is on the move," Jim said. Both Zerbino and Villa keyed their mikes twice.

Josh headed out of Lancaster, driving the Ford Flex. Syrin was in the passenger seat. Dave Tuley and JJ were in the backseat. Both JJ and Josh changed into tactical uniforms. They were armed with M4 carbines with four extra 30-round mags in a tactical vest. They both wore Type IV conditioned body armor, which would protect against all pistol rounds and armor-piercing rifle rounds, including an AK47. Syrin, the war dog, also wore her ballistic vest. Trooper Paul and Director Santiago, along with a handcuffed Greg Bennett, followed in Greg's Chevy Tahoe. Director Santiago was in the backseat keeping Greg company.

It's five miles from the Israel River in downtown Lancaster to Martin Meadow Pond Road straight up Corrigan Hill. The two-vehicle caravan made it in about 10 minutes. Trooper Paul stopped the Chevy just short of the turnoff to give Josh time to make the turn down Martin Road, before following him.

Director Santiago held up the mike for Greg, who said, "Target just made the turn on Martin Meadow Pond Road."

Josh made the turn to Martin Meadow Pond Road, and both Dave Tuley and JJ ducked down in the backseat. The Flex windows were tinted, so it would be almost impossible to see anyone in the backseat, but they weren't taking any chances. Josh drove the two miles to Martin Road and made the right turn.

Aaron keyed his mike. "Target just turned on Martin Road. Confirm no passengers, his dog is in the front seat."

"Roger," Jim said. "Thousand bucks to anyone who pops the dog. Okay, everyone ready."

Trooper Paul made the turn on Martin Meadow Pond Road. As he approached the turn to Martin Road, a figure in a woodland camouflage uniform emerged from the woods to the edge of the road. He held an M4 carbine in a cross-chest carry. Director Santiago lowered the rear passenger window, before they came abreast of the target. He readied his Beretta 92F, just below the window edge. The target could still hose the SUV with the M4, if he thought something wasn't right. The vehicle stopped abreast of the target at about 7 feet. He brought the 92F up into a two-hand firing position, got sight alignment, and squeezed the trigger as the face of the target showed surprise and recognition that something was wrong and tried to bring the M4 around to fire. Too late. The Beretta fired, sending the 135 gr Hydra-Shok jacketed hollow point round spinning to its target at 1,145 feet per second. The round impacted in the center of the target's forehead, traveled through the brain, and exited out the back of the skull, spraying brain, blood, and bone on the dirt in the ditch like a summer shower. Aaron was dead before he hit the ground. His body fell back into the side ditch with the surprised expression still on his face, and the rifle fell by the side of the road. Director Santiago pushed the up button on his window, which closed.

"Jesus Christ," Greg said. "You didn't even give him a chance to give up."

"Like I told you before…scumbag elimination," Director Santiago said. "Today, we are not the cops."

Director Santiago keyed his mike. "Alpha Sierra, you are a go."

"Roger. Alpha Sierra is a go."

Lt Col. Dan Elmore kept the HH-60H Pave Hawk in a holding pattern at 2,000 feet elevation and about two miles from the eastern end of Martin Meadow Pond.

"Dave, are you set?" Lt. Col. Elmore asked.

"Yes, Sir, locked and loaded," Master Sergeant Dave Dixon said. MSGT Dixon moved the selectable fire rate from 4,000 rounds per minute to 2,000 rounds per minute on the door-mounted A/A49E-13 minigun. No sense running out of ammo. The six-barreled, air-cooled, electrically driven, rotary machine gun could run through its 3,000-round magazine in just over a minute of continuous fire. Dave brightened the LED reticle on the ring site system, until it glowed red. X marks the spot for a 7.62 MM wakeup call with a whole lotta friends along for the ride.

Lt. Col. Elmore pushed the stick forward into a dive and increased air speed to 150 kts. The helicopter dove and gained speed. The treetops flew by beneath the helicopter body.

"Over water," Maj. Paul Jackson said, as the Pave Hawk crossed the eastern end of Martin Meadow Pond. "1,000 meters to target. Weapons free. Fire at will."

"Roger, Sir," MSGT Dixon said.

Josh heard the roar of the helicopter as the engine echoed throughout the hills surrounding the pond. "Here we go, boys." He stomped on the accelerator, and the Flex gained speed. The trees flashed by in a blur, and the car rocked back and forth on the rough gravel road. The front tire hit a pothole, which rocked the car, and Josh corrected for a slight skid. JJ and Dave Tuley hung on in the backseat. Syrin swayed in the front. Keyed for action.

63

Jim Palmer kept his binoculars on the opening where Martin Road entered the estate. He heard a helicopter closing on them from the left. "What the fuck is that?"

"Sounds like a Black Hawk and close," Cam said, looking up from his shooting mat.

"What is a Black Hawk doing around here?" Jim asked. He looked through the binoculars to find the helo. He caught sight of the white Flex blowing into the estate clearing and sliding to a stop at a 45-degree angle in front of the main estate building.

"What the fuck?" He put the binoculars on the white Flex in time to see the driver side and rear door fly open and armed men and a dog spill out and sprint for the homes on the western side of the compound. The air was filled with the loud crack of machine gun fire in short bursts. The reports echoed in the surrounding hills

"We're taking fire, we're taking fire. Holy shit—" Zerbino said, on the radio.

"What?" Jim screamed.

Lt. Col. Elmore brought the helo into a low hover just over the water, with the gunner side to the edge of the clearing. MSGT Dixon put the red sight crosshairs on every pile of leaves on the edge of the stone wall. He fired in one-second bursts sending 50 to 100 rounds of 7.62 mm rounds at 3,200 feet per second into each pile at every squeeze of the trigger. The Legionnaires didn't stand a chance.

Zerbino had enough time to look left, see the helo slide into view, and watch the flash of the minigun. The first burst hit a pile of leaves to his left, kicking up dirt and wood. He had enough time to key his mike and give a warning. The second burst cut him in half with a string of 20 rounds tearing through his torso.

Turner Carriere watched Zerbino get cut in half, before he took nine rounds in his prone body. Bertrand Picard got to his feet, but he couldn't move very fast in the Ghillie suit, so all he did was give MSGT Dixon an upright and stationary target. He cut him down in a burst of fire. Turner did a little dance like a puppet on a string, as a fusillade of slugs tore into his body and decorated the ground with blood and bone. Arno Raymond had enough time to roll over and get off one wild shot, before he took a burst of slugs driving his body into the ground. The entire run took about 20 seconds.

Jim Palmer watched the Legionnaires get chewed up in his binoculars. "Son of a bitch. Time to go." He smacked Cam on the shoulder. "Let's go, let's go, let's go." He saw an object, which looked like a rock, drop to his left, roll into the leaves, and three rifle shots in quick succession cracked behind him. The rock exploded in a blinding flash of light and the boom of sonic sound. He grabbed his ears, closed his eyes, and fell to the ground. The world spun out of control, and he couldn't get it to stop. Strong hands grabbed his wrists and wrenched his arms behind his back, and handcuffs were snapped over his wrists. He could taste the dirt, as his face was pushed into the ground, before he was hauled to his feet. He still couldn't see or hear anything. *What the fuck is going on?*

Josh stood on the brakes, and the Flex slid to a stop. He jammed the selector into park and bolted out the door, dragging the M4 carbine with him. Syrin jumped past him and rocketed to the front of the first house. Dave Tuley and JJ bailed out of the back and sprinted to the side of the house to come in from the rear.

Syrin ran around the front of the house and let out a growl, as she tore into a target. Josh followed her around the corner and saw her latch onto the right arm of a figure dressed in a camouflaged uniform. A C8 carbine was at his feet, and he was trying to get his sidearm out of his front holster with his left hand, as Syrin chomped on his right arm with 195 pounds of bite force. The bones in the guy's arm snapped with the sound of breaking branches, and he howled in pain.

"Get the fuck off me, you fucking mutt," Juri Reimink screamed.

Josh raised his M4 and fired off two quick shots, which sent two 5.56 mm rounds into Juri's chest, just over his flak jacket. He pitched back into the dirt like he got struck in the head by a hammer. Syrin let go of his arm. Another figure in camo, behind Juri, raised his weapon to fire, when Juri hit the dirt. Josh tracked his sights right to the center of the target, when the target pitched forward in the dirt after jerking three times by bullet strikes in the back. Bojan Jovic fell face-first into the grass. Dave Tuley was behind Bojan with smoke wafting off his barrel. Josh gave him a thumbs-up. They headed to the last house to the west. They jogged past the north end of the tennis court and took cover behind the house. The last two targets were in the tree line. They would wait on the helo.

Villa watched everything play out in front of his eyes. The helo destroyed the Legionnaires on the stone wall. Some assault team got Palmer and Cam in the orchard with a flash bang and rifle fire. Juri and Bojan got smoked by three guys and a dog, and they were now on the other side of the house. He contemplated his options. The guys behind the house couldn't move on them, because there was nothing but open ground between the house and the tree line. Both Torai and he could smoke check them before they got 20 feet. Too bad he wouldn't get the extra grand for the mutt. The tact team was probably moving west through the trees to get north of them and pin them to the pond. *Fuck, not too many good options.* He looked across the field to the helo. The helo was now sliding west in his direction. The minigun would make quick work of them.

"Torai, fire at the helo," Villa yelled.

Both Torai and Villa started shooting at the helo, but it was too far, and too high to be effective. The minute they started firing, the team on the other side of the house returned fire from prone positions on either side of the house. A bullet grazed Villa's arm.

"Fuck," Villa said. He clutched his arm and ducked behind a tree. Bullets continued to strike all around their position. Villa looked up to see the door gunner outlined in the silhouette of the open helo door. There was a flash from the minigun, and a torrent of bullets annihilated Villa and Torai in a mist of blood and debris as the bullets tore through their bodies and splintered trees, sending dirt flying as some bullets struck ground. The helo stopped firing after 10 seconds, and Syrin ran for the tree line, followed by Josh, JJ, and Dave Tuley. They reached the tree line at a dead sprint, with JJ bringing up the rear. The bodies of two Tangos were laid out in the leaves riddled with bullets. Josh turned and gave a wave up to the helo. The helo banked left and gained altitude, disappearing to the east. The sound of the engines faded in the distance. An eerie silence filled the void. A squirrel chattered in the distance, and some leaves rustled through the trees pushed by a light wind.

"Nice place," Dave Tuley said.

"Thanks", Josh said. "My grandfather built it."

All three turned and started walking back to the Flex. Syrin ran out front.

"Pretty dog," Dave said. "Did you train her?"

"Yeah, I did," Josh said. "She's quite the dog, just don't let her hear you say it."

They walked up to the Flex and dumped their rifles in the back. Director Santiago was standing next to the dark Chevy Tahoe with some guy in handcuffs face-down on the hood. Five members of the tactical team milled around in a small circle to the left. Josh walked up.

"All down?" Director Santiago asked.

"Yes, Sir. We got two, and the helo smoked two in the tree line. Glad they're on our side," Josh said.

"Amen to that," Director Santiago said. "We dropped the guy at the entrance to Martin Road, the helo chewed the four on the stone wall, and our tact guys popped one in the orchard and rounded up this scumbag." He pulled Jim off the hood.

"You son of a bitch," Josh said. He stepped up and decked Jim with a strong right cross. Jim dropped to the driveway. Josh moved in to kill him. JJ and Dave Tuley held him back by each arm.

"Whoa, there, brother," JJ said. "Dial it back."

"That piece of shit is Nick Lacava," Josh said. "He was part of some CIA front company called Sea Island Security. He was with my SEAL team, when we were ambushed in the Caribbean. He was reported as dead. Motherfucker, I'm going to kick your ass. I bet that fat fuck Rob McDonald is also alive. At least, until I find that waste of space."

Director Santiago motioned to the tactical team. "Why don't you gentlemen take Jim Palmer, or Nick La whatever-the-fuck, and put him in the back of a vehicle, before Josh makes good on his threat. Don't worry, Josh. We have a special place for him at Camp X-ray in Cuba."

Two of the tact guys came over, pulled Jim to his feet, and half dragged and pushed him over to one of the tan Suburbans and stuffed him in the backseat. JJ and Dave let go of Josh.

"Sorry, guys. Brought back a lot of bad memories," Josh said.

Director Santiago pulled a phone out of his pocket and pressed a number in his contact list.

LCDR Kendall picked up on the first ring. "Good afternoon, Director, how can I help you?"

"Hi, Becka. How far out is the cleanup crew and forensic team?"

"They pre-staged in Whitefield, New Hampshire, at the airport. They're en route to your location. ETA is about 20 to 30 minutes. Also, the Pave Hawk recovered at the airport. They are in the process of refueling. They will be ready to depart, when you are ready to leave."

"Okay, great. Thanks, Becka. One other thing. Get anything you can find on Sea Island Security and any possible connection to the CIA and the La Libertad Cartel. This is a priority request."

"Roger, Sir. I'll get it started."

"Thanks, Becka. I'll let you know, when we are wheels up." He punched off the call. "Okay, folks, we need to clear out before the other crews get here. Let's roll." He walked over to Josh.

"We'll get this cleaned up today. You won't know anything happened by tomorrow. Can I expect to see you in DC?"

"Yes, Sir. I need to finish a couple of things, and then I'll be down. What contact number should I use?" Josh asked.

"I'll text it to you." He shook hands with both Josh and JJ. "Thanks for your help, boys." He walked over to the Chevy Tahoe and hopped in, and the vehicle drove out of the parking area.

Dave Tuley walked over and shook both Josh's and JJ's hand. "Enjoyed running with you guys. Maybe we will see you some time."

"Thanks, Dave," Josh said. "I hate to think what would have happened, if you guys didn't show up."

"No problem." Dave walked over to a tan Suburban and slid into the passenger seat, and the two Suburbans took off.

"Well, I guess that just leaves us, little brother," JJ said. "Do you think we get to keep the Tahoe on the other side of Jessica's house?"

"No, I think that will disappear soon, along with a lot of other stuff. What do you think we should tell Mom?"

"As little as possible. What do you say you buy me a beer, and we get our stories straight?"

"Sounds like a plan," Josh said. "Come on, Syrin. I think someone earned an ice cream cone." She ran over to the Flex at the mention of ice cream.

"She's riding in the back," JJ said.

"You tell her."

64

Robert Adams looked at his watch: 1600. "God damn. Where is that fuckin' Palmer? They gotta be across the border by now." Adams paced in his condo. His cell phone rang. He looked at the number. "Fuck." He pressed the green accept button. "Yeah?"

"Anything?" the caller asked.

"No, Sir. Nothing yet."

"Twelve shooters. How is that possible?"

"No idea, Sir. We checked with our law enforcement contacts. No reports of shootouts. No arrests. No accident reports, and no sign of our vehicles crossing back across the border. They checked out of their hotel this morning and just disappeared."

"I'll see what I can find out on my end. Call our South American friend. We may need some outside help on this."

"Yes, Sir." He pushed the red cancel button and did a mental calculation to figure out how much money he had stashed in his overseas accounts. It may be time to retire.

Josh and JJ headed down the driveway towards the house. The sun was starting to set, and the trees were throwing shadows across the road. They had stopped at Grandma's, a mom-and-pop restaurant on the way to Whitefield from the pond, for a beer, and the Martin Dairy in Lancaster for ice cream. Syrin got an extra, extra-large vanilla cone. She bounced around in the backseat as they approached the house. Bob and Brady ran off the porch, when they parked in front of the house.

"Those dogs are going to miss Syrin when you head back," JJ said.

"Which brings me to a favor. Do you think you could watch Syrin for a couple of days, while I head to DC?"

"Of course, whatever you need. You know Mom is going to spoil her."

"Yeah, I know. I'll have to break some bad habits when I get her back." Josh climbed out of the Flex. Bob and Brady danced around the rear door barking. "Easy, boys," Josh said. He opened the back door, and Syrin was off like a shot with Brady and Bob in close pursuit.

JJ rolled out of the front seat and walked around the back to get his stuff out of the rear of the Flex. "I'm gonna take my stuff up to my place. Do you want me to clean your gun?"

"Thanks, JJ, that would be great. I'll break the news to Mom."

Josh walked up the back-porch steps and into the house. The smell of fresh baked bread filled the room, and his mom was bent over the oven pulling out some fresh loaves. Four other loaves were on the counter under some dish towels cooling. She was dressed in jeans, sneakers, and a gray Navy sweatshirt. There was a white spot of flour over her left eye. Josh walked over and gave her a big hug. Nothing beats the embrace of your mom. He stepped back and wiped the flour from over her eye.

"I would weigh 300 pounds, if I lived here," Josh said.

"Well, why don't you get started in that direction and help yourself to some fresh bread. The two loaves on the right are honey wheat."

Josh walked over to the counter and cut three slices off. He got a plate out of the cupboard and a butter knife out of the drawer.

"Butter is on the island," his mom said.

He brought his bread to the island, slathered it in butter, and took a bite. "Mom, this is fantastic."

"Glad you like it. Where's your brother?"

"He's putting some stuff away at his place. He'll be down in a couple of minutes." Josh took another bite of fresh, hot bread and licked the melted butter off his lips.

"Charley Parson stopped by looking for you."

"What did Charley want?" Josh asked.

"He wanted to thank you and your brother for what you did at the church. He said, you saved a lot of lives."

"I also think we bought a pool."

"That's what I told Charley. I said we would pay whatever the insurance wouldn't cover. He wouldn't hear of it. He said the town would cover it. It was the least they could do. So, where were you and your brother all day?" his mom asked.

"We had to solve some problems." His mom gave him the look, which was not good.

"Related to what happened at the church this morning?"

"Yes. We took care of it, and it shouldn't be a problem in the future."

"When do you leave?"

"Tomorrow. I have to go to DC. JJ is going to watch Syrin while I'm gone."

"Well, take some bread for your trip, and we'll look after Syrin." She walked over and gave him another big hug. "Be careful."

"Always, Mom."

65

Director Santiago took the Pave Hawk from the Whitefield Airport to Coast Guard Air Station Cape Cod. An Air Force Gulf Stream G5 was waiting for him on the runway, when the helo landed. He was back at Andrews Air Force base in two hours. A White House car and driver were waiting for him at Andrews. Another hour, and he walked up the front steps of his town house in Crofton, Maryland. Given his work schedule, he should have a place in the city, but living in the suburbs gave him a chance to get away from work. Sometimes, he would take the Orange Line into the office, which gave him an uninterrupted hour to read the paper or a good book.

He walked in the front door and flicked on the hall light. He punched in the access code to his security system, which cleared the entry alert. He walked into the kitchen and put his overnight bags on the kitchen table. He got a glass out of the cupboard, some apple juice out of the fridge, and sat down at the kitchen table.

A Secure Terminal Equipment unit was on the table, plugged into the phone jack on the wall. The unit looks like an ordinary high-end office desk telephone. It can place unsecured calls to anywhere on the public switched telephone network, as well as secured calls, via the phone's backwards compatible STU-III mode. There is a PC card slot on the side of the unit. Director Santiago pulled his KSV-21 enhanced crypto card out of his jacket pocket and inserted it into the slot. When the NSA configured crypto card is present, secure calls can be placed to other STE phones. STE phones are "releasable" (unlike STU-III sets). All cryptographic algorithms are in the crypto card.

Director Santiago picked up the phone and pressed line one. There was a series of clicks, and the phone started ringing. It was picked up on the third ring.

"Yes," said the voice on the end of the line.

"Good evening, Mr. President. This is Vince Santiago."

"Good evening, Vince. How was New Hampshire? I saw some interesting stuff on the news and in the intel briefs. That was some quick thinking on the part of the unknown individuals in the church. Was that our boy?"

"Yes, Mr. President. It was. We also had an incident at his family estate on a pond just outside Lancaster."

"Did it involve the cartel?"

"Unknown at this time. Also, something came up that may involve our friends at Langley."

"Your old stomping grounds?"

"Yes, Mr. President."

"Is it bad?"

"Yes, Mr. President. I think it is."

"So, you need a meeting?"

"Yes, Mr. President. I do."

"Let me check my schedule. Okay, Tuesday, at 1400. I will put in a request for the others. Is our candidate going to be in town?"

"Yes, Mr. President. You can meet him after the meeting."

"Excellent. So, he passed your initiation?"

"Yes, Mr. President. Flying colors."

"All right, then. Tuesday, 1400. See you then, Vince."

"Yes, Mr. President. Have a good evening."

He hung up the phone and got his secure cell phone out of the side pocket of his overnight bag. He typed a phone number into the message center and hit send. So, the dance begins.

66

Josh got up at 0430, took a shower, and dressed in jeans, boots, and a red canvas shirt. He put on his brown leather bomber jacket and walked down the steps behind the garage from the guest suite carrying his overnight duffel and his garment bag. He tossed both into the back of the Flex. He had said his goodbyes last night, after a family dinner. Syrin had a sleepover in his mom's room last night with Bob and Brady, so she was happy. He hopped in the front seat and started down the road. Kat was still in the back. Tough to let go.

It was early, so there was virtually no traffic. He cruised through Lancaster, Whitefield, and Littleton, and picked up I93 south. He listened to some Phil Collins, Eagles, and Billy Joel, and switched to Golic and Wingo on ESPN at 0600. It was 175 miles from Lancaster to the Cape Sands Resort and Casino. He made the trip in about four hours. He stopped for breakfast at a Cracker Barrel in Londonderry, New Hampshire, off I93. He checked his messages during breakfast and found the text from Vince Santiago with a contact phone number. He called him and told him he would be in DC on Monday morning at 1000. Vince told him to come to his office at 1400 and gave him his address. Josh pulled into the second-floor VIP high rollers valet area just before 0930.

Josh pulled the Flex into one of the valet slots and got out. Nick pushed a luggage cart in his direction.

"Hey, Nick," Josh said, and he waved him over.

"Good morning, Mr. Martin. Welcome back. We're all really sorry to hear about Kat. Everyone really thought the world of her. It won't be the same around here without her. If there is anything you need, please let me know," Nick said.

Josh could see the tears starting to well in his eyes, and Nick rubbed his eyes with the back of his uniform sleeve.

"Thanks, Nick. It's been a tough couple of days." Josh gestured at the Flex. "This beauty is from the rental fleet. Could you please call over to guest services and have someone return it for me? Also, please have someone take the stuff out of the back and bring it to my office."

"Sure thing, Mr. Martin."

Josh handed him a hundred and the key fob for the Flex.

"You always over-tip, Mr. Martin."

"I know, Nick, but you're my favorite." He patted him on the back, and reached into the Flex, and took out the silver urn.

Josh headed up to his office carrying the urn under his right arm, hoping he didn't run into anyone he knew, which was unlikely this early on a Sunday. He made it safely to his fifth-floor suite, walked through the reception area, and into his office. He went to the back bar and put the silver urn on the display shelf, which was supposed to hold his future championship ring collection. He moved the card for the 2004 Red Sox World Series Championship ring and put the urn in its place. "Sorry, babe. I will get you home, soon enough."

He went over and sat in one of the recliners, flipped on the TV, and started watching the NFL pre-game shows, switching between channels during commercials. The Pats didn't play until 1630, so he had time to kill. First time, in a long time, that he had nothing to do. *Man, this sucks.*

He spent the rest of the day in his office and apartment watching football and avoiding people. He watched the NFL Red Zone at 1300, until the Pats game started at 1630. The Pats played in Denver, so it was a close game. The Pats finally pulled it out at the end on a last-minute drive by Tom Brady, the GOAT. That's one guy who has it all—beautiful wife, beautiful family, and a great career. Josh clicked off the game. He had had everything at one time, and someone took it away. *Time to start playing some offense. Defense sucks. Sitting in this chair, feeling sorry for myself, sucks. Time for some payback. To find that piece a shit Rob McDonald, or whoever the fuck he is, and put a bullet in his bald head. To find that waste of breath Juan Pablo Rodriguez and put a bullet in his head, and any other motherfucking member of the La Libertad Cartel. Fuck them. Fuck them all. Hell hath no fury like a motivated*

SEAL with nothing to lose. Time to fight like the third monkey on the ramp to Noah's Ark, and brother, it's starting to motherfuckin' rain.

Josh got out of his recliner and went into his apartment, put on his workout clothes, and headed to the gym. *Time for the Joshua Chamberlain Martin revenge tour to start. Shit, I used my middle name.*

Josh was up early at 0500. He had already packed the night before. He showered and put on tan khakis with a light blue shirt and the leather bomber jacket. He would change into his DC go-to meeting clothes at the hotel. The casino valet picked up his stuff at 0530, and he followed him down to the lobby. A hotel executive car was waiting to take him to the airport. He caught a 0900 flight out of Boston's Logan airport, landed at Reagan National around 1100, and caught a taxi to the St. Regis Hotel in DC, on 16th Street, a few blocks from the White House. He waved his room key at his door key pad, just about noon. Good timing. He had about 90 minutes to get ready, which would give him about 30 minutes to make the walk to the New Executive Office Building.

He opened the door to the Caroline Astor suite and walked in. The suite was named in honor of "Mrs. Astor," the celebrated mother of St. Regis founder John Jacob Astor IV. The suite was large by DC standards with a separate bedroom and living room area. It also came with a butler, which is why Josh chose the room. He might need some help with stuff over the next couple of days. Kat would have flipped out, if she saw the room rate: $700 a night. Josh laughed at the thought. He could just hear her now, "You could stay at the Embassy Suites near the convention center for $150 a night." *Yes, but I wouldn't have butler service.*

The room was done with a royal blue print carpet, light blue wallpaper, and white drapes with a light blue floral print. There was a circular wooden table with two Queen Anne chairs set against a window that looked out on the Astor terrace, directly in front, when you walked in. A light blue fabric couch was on the left, complete with end tables and lamps, and a padded armchair set to the right of the couch. They both faced a large wooden entertainment center, which encased a 42" flat-screen TV on top, and the suite's fully stocked minibar on the bottom with two wooden double doors for access. A large writing desk with chair, Wi-Fi, and multiple outlets were on the right upon walking into the room.

The entrance to the bedroom was to the right of the entertainment center. It had a king-size bed with a sitting bench at the foot with a white cushion on top, two nightstands with lamps, and a walk-in closet. The marble bathroom had two sinks, a large soaking tub, and a separate walk-in shower to go along with the toilet. Not a bad setup. He had the bellman put his luggage on the bed and hang his two garment bags in the closet. He tipped him a twenty, thanked him, and the bellman left. Time to take a quick shower and suit up.

67

Robert Adams leaned back in his chair and swiveled to look out the window behind his desk, which gave him a view of the Boston waterfront. Sea Island Security occupied the entire 22nd floor of the Benjamin Franklin Building, next to the Intercontinental Hotel, on Atlantic Avenue. A couple of tugboats pushed barges in the harbor, and some recreational sailboats crisscrossed the channel with their white sails catching the wind. He turned back to his desk and opened his right-hand desk drawer. He pulled out the cryptcell phone and pressed the green send button.

The call was answered on the second ring.

"Mr. Smith, so good to hear your voice," Juan Pablo Rodriguez said.

Mr. Smith hesitated. "Eh, yes…yes, Sir. I wasn't expecting you to pick up the phone."

"Our well-connected friend said you may be calling. Apparently, you have misplaced some of your employees."

"Yes, Sir. We were hoping you may be able to check around to see if your folks can find out what happened to them."

"I'll see what I can do. I also hear our Navy friend is still walking around. Is that true?"

"Yes, Sir. That is true. That motherfucker has more lives than a cat."

"That is unfortunate. He poses a great risk to us and our other friend who asked me to personally insure our Navy friend does not see the sun come up tomorrow. Any idea where he may be? I have some friends watching his house at the Old Naval Air Station. He has not been back."

"No idea. We tracked him to his childhood home in Lancaster, New Hampshire, two days ago, and our welcome committee went missing."

"If you hear anything, please let me know, and I will try to find out what happened to your friends."

"Thank you, Sir."

"Oh, and Mr. Smith? Remember, there is only one way out of our business. Retirement is not an option." The phone went dead.

"Shit." Mr. Adams put the phone back in the drawer.

Director Santiago walked into his office, took off his gray wool overcoat, and hung it on the coat rack to the left of his office door. His office was small for someone who had 24/7 personal access to the president of the United States. There was a sitting area to the left with a leather couch on the wall and two leather chairs facing the couch with a glass coffee table between them. A 55" flat-screen TV hung on the wall over the couch. It was tuned to CNN. Every intelligence office in the DC, Virginia, and Maryland area had a TV tuned to CNN. The goal was to always get information to the boss, before he saw it on CNN. A cherry conference table with eight chairs was next, followed by two leather executive chairs that faced his desk. There were no windows in his office, because it was a Sensitive Compartmented Information Facility (SCIF). In fact, the entire third floor of the New Executive Office Building was a SCIF.

He looked at his watch: 1230. He had about 90 minutes to prepare for the Josh Martin meeting. He punched up his computer to check on the status of the Sea Island Security analysis. He scrolled to his inbox and saw the email from LCDR Kendall marked Top Secret NOFORN. He opened the email, clicked on the attachment, and the document opened. He started reading the two-page executive summary.

"Son of a bitch." *That explains the gel bomb and the overkill to take out Josh. This should get interesting.*

Josh walked over to the TSA-approved aluminum, weapons, transportation case. As a credentialed FBI agent, he could carry a firearm on a plane, but he needed to have a reason to carry it, such as for dignitary protection or prisoner escort. Otherwise, he must check it through. He dialed the combination on the approved lock and jerked it open. He opened the case and found a red TSA inspection tag for inspector 67. The case contained his Glock 22 and his Sig P938, plus three, 15-round, loaded magazines for the Glock. He pulled out the Glock, inserted a clip, and jacked a round into the chamber. He slipped it into his shoulder holster and snapped the keeper tab shut. The P938 went into the belt holster in the small of his back, and the two extra clips went in the pouches under his right arm. He picked up the dark blue suit coat off the bed and slipped it on. He gave himself one more check in the mirror. The dark blue, sable wool suit from Zegna was a perfect fit, which contrasted perfectly with a French cuff, 100 Figo white shirt, and matching red tie. The cuff links were 18 kt gold squares with a monogrammed M. They were a gift from his mom when he graduated from the Coast Guard Academy. Not bad for a hick from New Hampshire. He slipped on his long, black, wool overcoat and headed for the door. He was the picture of a DC professional and not a highly skilled Navy SEAL on a revenge tour.

Josh exited the Saint Regis, turned left on 16th Street, and headed to the White House. He crossed over I and H streets and entered Lafayette Park on the north side. He walked across the park, past the statue of Andrew Jackson on horseback, honoring the Battle of New Orleans, and walked to Pennsylvania Avenue in front of the White House. Tourists posed along the edge of the black iron fence in front of the north lawn fountain to get a picture with the White House in the background. Pennsylvania Avenue was now a large, open-air, concrete, walking mall with a cross-section of the world trying to get a picture of the White House.

Josh turned right on Pennsylvania Avenue and walked past the Blair House, which is the president's guest house. It's also the world's most exclusive hotel, because it is primarily used to host visiting dignitaries and other guests of the president. It is larger than the White House and, unlike that building, closed to the public. He paused at the bronze plaque on the front steps, which commemorated the memory of Leslie Coffelt, who was killed on this spot defending President Harry Truman from an assassination attempt by two Puerto Rican Nationalists in 1950. He walked around the corner to the red brick New Executive Office Building, 725 17th Street NW, the address given to him by Vince Santiago.

He stood in front of the revolving doors and looked up at the large 725 in black letters on the front of the building. He had an uneasy feeling in the pit of his stomach, like walking through that door would change his life forever. He remembered the feeling twice before: walking into Chase Hall at the U.S. Coast Guard Academy, and driving on Naval Amphibious Base, Coronado, to begin SEAL training. Both were life-changing events for him. He mulled the decision. Walk in, or go check out the Smithsonian Museum of American History.

68

Matt Richards badged through the security turnstile at the Langley Campus and hustled down the gleaming corridor to his office. The meeting at the State Department took forever, and he needed to check his computer. He turned right and entered his suite. "Director Transnational Desk" was stenciled on a placard to the left of the door.

"Good afternoon, Director," Barbara said. She had been his secretary for the last three years. She was a heavyset woman with dyed brown hair and wire-framed glasses. She was in a gray pantsuit with a white shirt.

Anyone call?" Matt asked.

"No, Sir."

Matt pushed through his office door and put his brown tweed sport coat on a hanger on the back. He wore matching brown dress pants, a light-yellow shirt, and a tan tie with yellow stripes. He was 45 with curly red hair, a slight paunch that draped over his belt, and the look of a college professor tired of his life.

The alert on his Cayman account pinged his phone while he was at the State meeting. Someone had accessed the account. He half expected security to be waiting in his office when he got back.

He punched up the Bank of Cayman on his computer and entered his account name, password, pin, and answered a security question about his first pet. His balance flashed on the screen: $1,850,000.65. He sat back with relief. *They hadn't touched it. But who was they?*

He clicked the transfer tab and highlighted his account at the Bank of Ireland. He entered the entire amount and hit send. The balance on the account registered 0.00. He pulled up the next tab for account services and selected cancel account. He hit cancel account, and the prompt said his account would be closed in seven days.

That fucking Adams, thought Matt. *Can't get rid of one frickin squid with 12 shooters and a gel bomb.* The gel bomb was probably a mistake. He should have used a conventional backpack or IED. They'll eventually trace the bomb back to him. In three days, it won't matter. *In three days, I'll make my quarterly visit to the Station Chief in Colombia, and I won't come back. They can take the Deputy Director of Operations job and shove it up their ass. Fuck me, none of this would have happened if I didn't apply for that job.*

Josh stepped into the revolving door and entered the lobby of the New Executive Office Building. A uniformed Secret Service officer stood at the entrance of a security line that snaked right to go through a security check and a metal detector. Josh handed the officer his FBI credential. He flipped open the case, checked the photo against his face, and then compared the name to a list on a clipboard. He waved his hand, and a gentleman in a gray, pinstriped suit walked up. The haircut and bearing screamed military.

"Special Agent Martin, my name is Pete Sessions. Director Santiago sent me down to get you," Pete said, extending his hand.

Josh shook his hand. "Pete Sessions. Did you go to the Academy? Your name sounds familiar."

"Class of 99."

"Well, thanks for coming down to get me. I thought the Coast Guard only had Mil Aides at the White House."

"We've got both the President and Vice President Mil Aides, and we have one commander billet assigned to the White House Military Office, and a lieutenant assigned to the White House Communications Agency," Pete said. He handed Josh a badge with a big red V on the front.

Josh took the visitor badge and put the lanyard over his head. They started walking over to a bank of elevators at the back of the lobby.

"So, what do you do?" Josh asked.

"I work at Presidential Contingency Programs. We ensure the President can be Commander in Chief, Head of State, and Chief Executive no matter where he is in the world, and all that it entails," Pete said.

The elevator door opened, and they got in. Pete hit the button for the third deck.

"Sounds like an interesting job," Josh said.

"It definitely has its moments, but it's a lot of travel. I have more fre-quent flyer miles than I know what to do with."

The elevator dinged and opened on the third deck. They both stepped off the elevator into a tile foyer. There were two doors on the right as you stepped off the elevator, on either wall, and a single door on the left, at the end of the foyer.

"Our offices are over there," Pete said, pointing to the doors on the right. "The one on the left goes to our director's office, and the one on the right is for the staff. You're going over here to the left." He nodded his head to the door on the left at the end of the foyer.

They walked to the end of the foyer and opened the door into an outer office. A secretary's desk was on the right. Four office waiting chairs were on the left, and there was a single set of elevator doors straight ahead with a mural on the doors. Gates of Hell was written in bold red letters over a scene of hell complete with the devil, fires, and lost souls. There was also a door on the right, just past the secretary's desk.

"What's up with the elevator doors?" Josh asked.

"Military guys, idle hands, and one of them is a pretty good artist," Pete said. He pointed to the secretary's desk. "Lisa's at lunch. Vince said to bring you right in." He walked over, knocked twice on the door, and opened it. "Director Santiago, I have Josh Martin with me."

"Great, send him in," came a voice from inside.

Pete stood back and let Josh walk by. "Maybe we can catch a beer or dinner, if you have some time after your meeting."

"That would be great. I'm staying at the Saint Regis." Josh shook hands with Pete and walked into the office. Pete shut the door behind him.

69

Director Santiago walked around his desk to greet Josh. "Hey, sailor, welcome to DC. I take it you've been here before?" Vince asked. He walked up and shook Josh's hand.

"Yes, Sir. A few times, but never to the White House complex."

"The 18 acres. That's what we call the White House, the Eisenhower Building, and the New Executive Office Building. Come in, please have a seat." Vince gestured to the conference table.

Josh took a seat at the conference table, and Vince sat across from him. On the table in front of Vince was a folder marked Top Secret NOFORN, a small dish with a blue and white pill capsule in it, a silver watch with a black face that looked like a Rolex, and an antique object that looked like a small type of urn or oil lamp. It was brown with green patina from age, and it really looked like a small ugly Stanley Cup.

"So, before we begin, let me tell you a story," Vince said. "Do you know William J. Donovan?"

"Yes, Sir. He was the Director of the OSS during World War II."

"Correct. How about Colonel Ned Buxton, Jr?"

"I think he was Donovan's Deputy."

"Correct again," Vince said. "Well, at the end of World War II, Director Donovan and Col. Buxton proposed the creation of an organization that would take certain actions to preserve our democracy and way of life, which may be outside our normal standard of laws, ethics, and regulations. Have you heard of the 38-cent solution?"

"Yes, Sir. The idea of what the world would look like if someone put a bullet in Hitler's or Stalin's brain, when they were first coming to power."

"The idea that a single bullet, which costs 38 cents, could potentially save millions of lives and billions of dollars. But, the question always remains the same. Without the benefit of hindsight, who decides? Do we shoot Martin Luther King Jr. in the head, because he is changing our society? Do we take out Putin, or Kim Jong-un, because we differ with their policies and politics?"

"So, who does decide?" Josh asked.

"We'll get to that in a minute. Also, at the end of the war, we created a professional intelligence apparatus that provided significant information on many things, not just military related. Financial, law enforcement, agricultural, manufacturing, international relations, and politics, and not only in the foreign arena, but also at home. So, what do we do with that? How do you provide information to help convict a bank robber, but protect the sources and methods of how that information was obtained?"

"White 55 and the weekly intel dumps," Josh said.

"Exactly. Our White Program provides information to select individuals across a broad spectrum of America, who can use that information to improve our society. But like you, and Agent Randolph, you can't use that information in a court of law or tell anyone how you got it."

Vince reached out and put his hand on the Top-Secret folder. "Now, Josh, you need to make a decision. Our Executive Committee voted to invite you to join our Black Program. Our Black Program provides support to highly trained, and select, individuals with a wide range of backgrounds to perform certain operations to 'Preserve the democratic institution which is the United States of America and the defense of our Constitution against all enemies foreign and domestic' to quote our founding document. In fact, you met one of our black operatives."

"Dave Tuley," Josh said.

"Yes. That operation was your initiation into our program."

"What's in the folder?" Josh asked.

"This folder contains everything you want to know about what happened to your SEAL team on Mangle Island, who planted the bomb in the church, and who killed your wife. Join us, and it's yours, and eliminating those people responsible will be your first assignment."

"What do I need to do to join?"

Vince reached out and slid the dish with the pill across the table to Josh. "Take this pill."

"What's it for?"

"It insures loyalty. In the infancy of our program, we had some issues with members not following the rules or having doubts about performing some of the operations we asked of them. That is how the theories about the military industrial complex and the shadow government got started. So, our technical branch created this." Vince tapped the pill dish. "The pill is encased in a plastic Nano polymer that is mixed with your DNA, so your body will not reject it, or attack it. When you swallow it, it will attach to your stomach wall. The polymer casing will protect it from your stomach acid, and it will absorb any imaging scans from X-rays, an MRI, or CT scans."

"What does the invisible pill do?"

"Its purpose is threefold. First, it contains a universal GPS transmitter. We can track your location, via satellite, anywhere on the planet. Second, the pill acts as an identifier." Vince pushed the watch over to Josh. "This is yours."

Josh picked up the watch. It was a Rolex Oyster Deep Sea ultra-resistant divers' model, waterproof down to a depth of 4,000 ft. Silver with a black face. "What…you couldn't afford the Sea-Dweller?"

Vince smiled. "If you need to go down to 12,800 ft, I'll get you the other watch."

"How does it work?"

"The pill marries to the watch. If you come within 100 ft of one of our members, you'll get a tiny shock on your wrist. One shock, if it's a White member, and two, if it's a Black member. You will find this is a great asset when you are working across the country with many of our members, who are unknown to you. You will always know if the person you are meeting is one of us," Vince said.

"No imposters, or moles."

"Exactly."

"What is the third feature?" Josh asked.

"Opposite the GPS transmitter is an electronic pulse generator," Vince said. "It ties into the GPS unit. I can send it a command from anywhere in the world via the GPS link, and stop your heart in a second."

"Holy shit," Josh said. "Who decides that?"

"It must be a unanimous vote of the Executive Committee and myself. Usually, I don't get a vote on operations, but in this case, I do."

"Who's on the committee?"

"That, I can't tell you, unless you are one of us. I can, however, assure you, that getting a unanimous vote out of them is extremely difficult," Vince said.

"How many times have you used it?"

"I have never used it during my tenure. It has been used fourteen times in the past, and they were before 1970."

"I'm sure the Civil Rights Movement and the Vietnam War was a difficult time."

"So, sailor, you have a decision to make. You can walk out of here, and remain White 55 for as long as you are an FBI agent, or you can take the pill, join us, and make a real difference for our country. What's it going to be?" Vince asked.

70

Robert Adams reviewed some operation requests from customers. The CEO of Energy Quest was making a trip to the Middle East and wanted a security detail, and another, Transport International, was looking for some help with demonstrators who were blocking construction of an oil pipeline. He approved both requests and put them in his out box.

Robert drummed his fingers on the desk. He still couldn't shake the last conversation with El Jefe. *El Jefe, fuck him, Colombian piece of shit. Retirement is not an option. What the fuck is that? Ah man, I never should have listened to the fucktard Richards. I was making good money running legit operations in the Caribbean. But no, I had to go for the brass ring. It was more like a gold ring at a little over 10 million dollars, but money is no good unless you can spend it, and where is that fuckin' Lacava? The little bitch is probably on some South Sea Island sipping little umbrella drinks and enjoying his retirement.*

The phone in his right drawer started to ring and vibrate. "Shit, now what?"

He pulled open the drawer, retrieved the phone, and hit the green accept button.

"Yes," Robert said.

"Good afternoon, Mr. Smith," Juan Pablo said. "Your target spent last night at the Casino Sands Resort. He flew to Washington, DC, this morning. He's staying at the Saint Regis Hotel. We are sending a couple folks to say hello."

"That is good news."

"No word on your missing employees. We had some people check out the estate on Martin Meadow Pond. There was no sign of any disturbance. The place was closed up tight. Employees at the Littleton Motor Inn confirmed the presence of your people, but they checked out. Again, nothing to indicate any type of law enforcement action. We also checked all the credit cards and familia of everyone involved. There were no transactions on anyone's credit card, and significant others have not been contacted," Juan Pablo said.

"Okay, thanks."

"We'll eliminate Agent Martin, and then we can go back to making money. I'm sure your friends will turn up somewhere, and then we can handle them."

"Yes, Sir. That sounds great," Mr. Smith said. The line went dead. He put the phone back in the drawer.

Well, that is good fucking news. Agent Martin will meet an unfortunate end in the crime-ridden city of DC, far from me and Sea Island Security, and any chance of exposure of our little arrangement with Matt Richards is gone. It may be time for a vacation to recharge. Maybe I can find Lacava on a beach and kick his ass.

Barbara stuck her head in the door, and Matt looked up from his desk.

"Mr. Richards, you have a Mr. Aten to see you."

"Great, send him in," Matt said.

"He will see you now," Barbara said to a man behind her.

Mark Aten walked into the office and shut the door behind him. Mark worked on the Latin American desk. He was about 35 with very short black hair, dark large-frame glasses, a brown Hispanic complexion, and he spoke with a South American accent. He walked over and took a seat in one of the two leather chairs in front of Matt's desk.

"What are you doing here?" Matt asked. "Now is not the best time to be seen together. Someone accessed one of my accounts this morning."

"Any idea who?" Mark asked.

"No, but at least they didn't touch anything. So, what is so important that you had to see me in person?"

"Our Colombian friend wanted me to pass a message. He didn't want to use a phone or computer," Mark said.

"And?"

"Your FBI friend is now in DC. He's staying at the Saint Regis. We're going to send him on a vacation, so you need to be around people who can verify your presence, when the issue is done."

"Oh, that is good news," Matt said.

71

Josh picked up the blue-and-white pill and held it in his right hand between his thumb and forefinger. "Do you have anything to take this with, or is choking it down part of the initiation phase?"

"Oh, yeah, that would help," Vince said. He got up and walked over to a mini-fridge behind his desk on the wall. He came back with a Diet Coke. He popped the top and handed the can to Josh.

Josh took the can in his left hand. Put the pill in his mouth, took a big swig of Diet Coke, jerked his head back to get the pill in the back of his mouth, and swallowed. He set the can down on the desk. "Well, I don't feel any different," Josh said.

"Believe me, you are." Vince extended his hand. "Welcome to the Black and White Club."

Josh shook his hand. "Now what?"

"Now, I finish my story, and then you can look at this folder," Vince said, tapping the folder with his hand. "First, put on the watch."

Josh took off his Fitbit silver Blaze watch and set it on the table. He picked up the Rolex, opened the clasp, slipped on the watch, closed the latch, and immediately felt three zaps on his wrist.

"What does three zaps mean?" Josh asked.

"Three zaps are me," Vince said. "The Director of the Black and White Club. When, or if, I'm replaced, you'll always know the identity of the director by three zaps."

"That is a neat security feature," Josh said.

"So, back to the story."

"Wait, before you begin, what is the purpose of the ugly Stanley Cup replica?"

Vince laughed. "I guess it does look a little like the Stanley Cup." He picked it up.

"On January 17th, 1945, President Roosevelt signed our founding document, which was contained in Addendum A to Executive Order 9513."

"What was Executive Order 9513?" Josh asked.

"It Extended the Periods of Service or Training and Service of Persons Inducted Into or Assigned to the Navy, Marine Corps, or Coast Guard. It was not important. It was just a cover for Addendum A, which created, funded, and staffed our organization." Vince turned the oil lamp in his hand. "So, when Roosevelt signed our founding document, Stanley here was on his desk. Col. Ned Buxton was the only person present, other than Roosevelt, when the document was signed. He became our first director. Roosevelt gave him this beauty to remind him of the light of freedom. 'May it always shine on all our decisions.'"

"How many directors have held the lamp?"

"Six counting me."

"So, who makes up the Black and White Club Executive Committee?" Josh asked.

"There are six members: The President, Vice President, Speaker of the House, President Pro tempore of the Senate, and the Chief Justice of the Supreme Court."

"Wow, they are all part of this?"

"Yes. Since FDR, everyone who has held these positions, regardless of party affiliation, has been a member of the Black and White Club."

"What happens if they say no?"

"There has only been one."

Josh thought for a moment. "President Kennedy," he said.

"Unfortunately, yes," Vince said. "This program is more important than one man's life, regardless of his position. The vote was unanimous."

"Even Lyndon Johnson?"

"Yes," Vince said.

"Oswald was a Black and White member?"

"No, he was a shooter of convenience. The second gunman was one of ours," Vince said.

"And Jack Ruby?"

"His mother was very sick. We paid him. To get serious for a moment, the question you must ask yourself is, could you kill the President of the United States, if you were directed?"

Josh paused. "I don't know."

"I bring this up to illustrate a point," Vince said. "If you refuse an assignment, you'll be terminated, and I don't mean fired. Do you understand?"

"Yes, Sir. I do."

"Any other questions?"

"A couple. How do you get access to such great intelligence?"

"During the Eisenhower Administration, they prepared to fight a nuclear war with the Soviet Union. So, they built a Continuity of Government Program to keep the government operating in case of a nuclear exchange. All the information nodes of the U.S. Government: intelligence, politics, financial, social security, military, international relations etc. funneled into a single secure facility, which would house a shadow government to keep the business of government functioning after a nuclear war. The Legislative Branch used the Green Brier Resort in West Virginia as their facility, until the *Washington Post* exposed its existence in a 1992 story. We had an office in that facility with access to all the information nodes of the government."

"What did you do, after 1992?" Josh asked.

We kept all the intelligence and information links and remotely sent them to our two intelligence facilities: Naval Air Station Jacksonville, FL, and the other at Naval Base San Diego. We have secure underground bunkers, and we run a 24/7 intelligence support watch at each location. The Jacksonville Center generated your information," Vince said.

"What about funding?" Josh asked. "This has to take some serious cash to keep all this running."

"Our primary funding comes from a line item for Presidential Support in the General Defense Intelligence Program's classified budget for Intelligence activities. We also have our own asset forfeiture program, just like the Treasury Department. Any money we uncover, earned from illegal activities, is deposited into our general operating fund, which we run through several shell companies. For example, Nick Lacava had a little over 8 million dollars stashed in a couple of offshore accounts. That money is now ours," Vince said.

"How is that douche bag doing?"

"He is enjoying his accommodations at our wing at Camp X-Ray in Cuba. This folder contains his debrief." Vince slid the folder over to Josh. "Why don't you start reading this."

Josh opened the folder and started reading. Finally, some answers.

72

Anthony Jaimes and Nathan Velasquez were attaches assigned to the Venezuelan Embassy. They were both members of the Venezuelan Intelligence and Preventive Services Directorate (DISIP), and they were problem solvers for the La Libertad Cartel. They stood across the street from the New Executive Office Building away from the sidewalk to get out of the flow of pedestrian traffic, but still keep an eye on the front of the building. They followed Josh here from the Saint Regis.

Anthony wore a long, black, leather overcoat with a white scarf, over a navy-blue Brooks Brothers suit with a silenced Browning High Power 9 mm in a shoulder rig under his left arm. He had dark black hair, full black mustache, and a prominent mole on his right cheek. Nathan was wearing a long, black, wool overcoat with a gray scarf, over a navy-blue sports coat with gray pants. He carried an identical Browning, standard weapon for the DISIP. He was bald, with a red rosacea patch on his right cheek, and a black mustache with a touch of gray.

"We can't hang out here forever," Anthony said. "Too many cameras. And dark-skinned males loitering in front of a White House facility draws police interest."

"Think he's going back to the hotel?" Nathan asked.

"No idea. He's dressed to go anywhere," Anthony said. "We can't stay here. Our best bet is to go back to the hotel. He has to return sometime."

"Okay, let's go," Nathan said.

They joined the crowd heading south on 17th Street, crossed the road, and walked down Pennsylvania Avenue to Lafayette Park.

Matt Richards walked out of his office, carrying his coat.

"I'm going to take off, Barbara. You can also go home," Matt said.

He walked out of the office suite and into the hallway with a smile on his face, imagining Barbara being interrogated by CIA Security, about how could she possibly not know her boss was a traitor. He headed to the south parking lot to get his car. He needed to find a place to be conspicuous. Couldn't go home, since there was no one home, after the divorce. Probably best to find a bar, have a couple of drinks, order dinner, and tip well, so he was remembered. He would also use his credit card for the receipt.

Barbara picked up the phone after Matt departed, and dialed the CIA Inspector General's Office, Internal Affairs Division.

"He just left," Barbara said.

"Any idea where he's going?"

"No. He did have a visit from a Mark Aten. He works on the Latin American Desk. I looked him up. He was not on today's visitor list."

"Okay, thanks, we'll get someone on him."

Barbara hung up the phone. *I can't wait to the see the expression on Mr. Dumbass's face when he goes down. Time to do something a little more exciting than babysitting the absent-minded professor. Can't believe he hasn't gotten caught before this. Must be good at avoiding the polygraph.* She gathered her things, and her coat, and walked out the door.

Josh put the folder down. "Son of a bitch, all this over a fucking job, and Rob McDonald, or Robert Adams, or Mr. Smith has an office in downtown Boston. Unbelievable," Josh said. "Also unbelievable is the level and specific detail in this report. I've never seen anything like it; phone calls, locations, transcripts, specific dates, and times, across the globe. How is that possible?"

"As you know, we're excellent at collecting vast amounts of intelligence from communication intercepts, emails, intelligence reports, etc. The problem has always been sorting through all the information to find the one piece needed. We're tied into the new, reprogrammable, quantum computer at the University of Maryland, and we have reconfigured their computer to our system. We call the new configuration the Buxton D-Wave Quantum Computer in honor of our first director. We have links at both of our intelligence sites. The Buxton D-Wave runs our new GNOSIS system.

Think of it as Google on a global scale for intelligence, which provides keyword searches on anything," Vince said.

"So, let me see if I get this straight," Josh said. "A few years ago, when Matt Richards worked on the Colombian desk at the CIA, he made a deal with Juan Pablo to provide information on the Venezuelan government, the FARC, and Colombia, in exchange for Richards providing information on U.S. patrol tactics, patrols areas, and schedules for drug interdiction operations."

"Yes," Vince said.

"And, as things progressed, the cartel paid Richards for names of agents, raid times, and strike locations. He then used the CIA to hire Sea Island Security, so he had someone who could deal directly with the cartel to keep him clean."

"Yes," Vince said, "and he specifically hired Robert McDonald and Nick Lacava to be his representatives. So, it was Robert and Nick who tipped off the cartel on your SEAL raid on Mangle Island."

"They knew we were coming," Josh said.

"Yes. If you weren't taking a leak, you wouldn't be here now."

"And, Matt Richards is a candidate for Deputy Director of Operations for the CIA. So, when he finds out I'm an undercover FBI agent investigating the La Libertad Cartel in Boston, where it just so happens Rob McDonald is the Boston Director of Sea Island Security, he moves to eliminate anything that could tie him to Sea Island Security and his ties to the cartel," Josh said.

"Yes."

"Well, what happens now?" Josh asked.

"There's a meeting of the Executive Committee tomorrow at 1400. I'm going to brief them on what happened in New Hampshire and present the case on Matt Richards. They'll determine whether we just arrest him, take him to Cuba, or put him in the ground. They already approved a sanction on Juan Pablo and anyone connected to the La Libertad Cartel, including your Rob McDonald."

"I volunteer for that job," Josh said.

"That's what I thought. We also want you to remove Juan Pablo."

"In Colombia?"

"In a matter of speaking. I'll brief you on the op when we know what we're going to do about Mr. Richards. Also, we noticed you made a good show of flying into DC and staying at the Saint Regis. Fairly easy to find you."

"I was tired of playing defense and wanted to start playing some offense."

"Get any bites?" Vince asked.

"Two South American types followed me from the Saint Regis over here. They were waiting across the street. One was wearing a black leather overcoat with a white scarf, and the other had a black wool jacket with a gray scarf. Looked Venezuelan or Colombian to me."

"They were leaning on the building across the street. We picked them up on the surveillance cameras. They left via Lafayette Park," Vince said. "Probably heading back to the hotel to wait on you."

"Do you want me to leave them alone?"

"I don't think we want them to disappear. That might raise some more suspicions because we have disappeared the 12 shooters in NH. We don't want Juan Pablo going underground. Why don't you put your FBI hat on and arrest them for espionage?"

"Will do," Josh said. He stood to leave.

"Come by tomorrow about 1530. There's someone I want you to meet," Vince said.

"Yes, Sir. See you tomorrow." They shook hands, and Josh left.

73

Matt Richards exited the CIA campus and eased into traffic on the George Washington Memorial Highway in his silver Ford Escape. Traffic was heavy with all the commuters starting the evening slog to get home. Washington traffic sucked. He turned right on Dolley Madison Blvd, and then right on Tysons Blvd, crawling along with the flow of traffic. He pulled into the parking lots for the Tysons Galleria Mall. He parked near Neiman Marcus and walked into the store. He avoided the lady at the perfume counter trying to spray him with the latest concoction and exited into the mall. He threaded his way through the mall to Legal Seafood and walked over to the bar. The usual business and political crowd were standing at the bar waiting to get a table. He got a seat at the bar and struck up a conversation with Larry, the bartender. A 40% tip would get him remembered. He checked his phone. No texts yet. *I wonder if they have malls in Bora, Bora.*

Josh pushed through the revolving door and exited on 17th Street. He did a quick scan to see if his company had returned. No one in sight, and no one interested in him. He turned left and retraced his steps, walking back through Lafayette Park. The sun was starting to go down, and the crowd around the White House began to turn from tourists to a more unsavory lot. The weight of the Glock was always a welcome feeling when walking in unknown territory. Although he could kick the ass of anyone on the street, he couldn't kick the ass of street kid with a gun. The park was not well lit, but he made it across without any problems. Crossed I and H streets, and headed back up 16th. He could see the overhang of the Saint Regis Hotel up on the right, and a dark blue Suburban parked just inside the drop-off loop. Josh walked up to the Suburban, and the driver lowered the window.

"Agent Martin?" the driver asked.

"Yes, Sir, thanks for coming out," Josh said.

"No problem, this is Jerry Sloane," he pointed at his passenger, "and I'm Patrick Sullivan. We're working counterintelligence. What do you have?"

"I'm down here from Boston, on an assignment for the White House, and I picked up a tail on my walk over to the White House. I'm not sure why, but I was hoping you guys could take them off my hands."

"Sure thing. What do they look like?" Patrick asked.

"One's wearing a black leather overcoat, black hair, black mustache. The other guy is in a black wool jacket, bald, and both look like they're straight from central casting for a South American drug dealer."

"How do you want to play it?" Patrick asked.

"How about I go in and ID them, and you guys follow for cleanup and transportation."

"Sounds good to us," Patrick said. Jerry nodded in agreement.

Josh walked through the entrance doors of the Saint Regis and into the lobby. It was like walking into a palace in Paris. The lobby was decorated in French provincial with large hanging red drapes on the windows, crystal chandeliers, and ornate gold ceilings. Josh stopped in the center of the lobby and scanned the area. He quickly spotted the two targets. They lounged in red upholstered chairs to the right of the entrance, near one of the large windows with the red drapes. They both pretended to read a paper. Josh went over and sat on a matching red couch to the left of the chairs and looked at their shoes. You could always tell a lot about people by their shoes. This place screamed money. So, if you were staying here, your shoes would look brand-new with a fresh coat of polish. Since rich folks don't walk much, they would also be free of creases. The shoes on these guys were rode hard and put up wet with heavy creases and a faded shine with scuff marks.

"Your shoes are a dead giveaway," Josh said.

"Excuse me, no English," said the bald guy on the right looking over his paper. The man with hair lowered his newspaper and looked at Josh. He looked like he wanted to draw a weapon.

"Okay, no English. Maybe you can understand this. If either of you moves a muscle, I'm going to start beating on you, until you learn perfect

English," Josh said. The recognition in their eyes was there in an instant, and they began to move their hands inside their jackets.

"Easy, boys," Patrick said. Both Patrick and Jerry were standing on either side of the non-English-speaking gentlemen with their guns drawn. "How about you put your hands back on the armrests and don't move."

They both complied.

"I guess your English is pretty good with a gun pointed at you," Josh said. He got out of the chair, walked over to the bald guy, and patted his left jacket pocket. Felt a hard object like a gun, reached his hand in, and retrieved an automatic, a Browning High Power. He pressed the mag release button and slid out the magazine. Then he jacked the slide open, caught the 9 mm bullet, and locked the slide open. He put the round in his pocket and set the gun on the couch. He did the same thing with the guy with hair.

Patrick holstered his gun. "Okay, bald guy, get up, and put your hands behind your back." The bald guy stood, and Patrick handcuffed him. Jerry did the same thing with the guy with hair. Patrick reached into each guy's pocket and pulled out his ID.

"Anthony Jaimes and Nathan Velasquez attaches assigned to the Venezuelan Embassy," Patrick said.

"So, now you know we have diplomatic immunity," Anthony said.

"Wow, you can speak English! It's a miracle," Josh said.

"What I know," Patrick said, "is that I have two guys with a one-way ticket out of our country with illegal firearms."

Jerry and Patrick started to perp walk the two out of the lobby. Josh collected the Brownings off the couch and followed them out. They packed the two would-be assassins into the back of the Suburban and shut the door.

"Thanks for the help, guys," Josh said.

"Sure thing, Josh," Patrick said. "If you need us to pick up anyone else, just give us a call. Easiest arrest I've ever made." Patrick climbed into the Suburban along with Jerry, and they pulled through the Saint Regis drop-off lane and headed down 16th Street.

Josh called Vince. "My two shadows are gone. They were attaches from the Venezuelan Embassy."

"By gone, you mean arrested?" Vince asked.

"Yes, Sir. Arrested. I got a couple of agents from counterintelligence to pick them up. They were happy with the arrest."

"Excellent," Vince said. "You'll find that helping others look good goes a long way in our line of business."

"Roger that. I'm going to catch some dinner and turn in. I'll see you tomorrow at 1530."

Matt Richards put the finishing touches on the seafood platter. The shrimp, scallops, calamari, and clams were good, but even a deep frying couldn't make the whitefish edible. *What the hell was a whitefish, anyway? Probably whatever flopped out of the net that wasn't cod.* He took a final sip of his third glass of Riesling and felt his phone vibrate in his pocket. He fished it out and saw the symbol for a text message. He pressed the message button, and the text popped up.

No Change. Go Home.

"Fuck me." Trying to kill this guy is like winning the war on drugs. A lot of people are putting in a lot of effort, and no one is getting the job done. Well, there goes Larry's big tip. No need to be remembered for this. He counted out $78 and left the cash on the bill tray. He twisted out of the bar stool and swayed out of the restaurant. *In two days, this will all be a bad memory. It will be warm sunshine, an ocean breeze, and a different hooker every night.*

Robert Adams was just sitting down to a Hungry Man, turkey frozen dinner when a similar text came in on his phone. He looked at it and put the phone back in his pocket. *Fuck El Jefe. I'd rather take my chances with the cartel than a motivated SEAL. Time to put the exfil plan into action.*

74

Josh got up early at 0500 and ran five miles through the quiet streets of DC with a lap around the Mall, before coming back to the hotel. He showered and got dressed in jeans, a blue Henley shirt, and his brown leather jacket. He had tenderloin, two eggs, and an English muffin for breakfast in the Decanter restaurant in the hotel.

After the meal, he walked over to the American History Museum to see the original Star-Spangled Banner that flew over Fort McHenry the morning after the Battle of Baltimore during the War of 1812 and inspired Francis Scott Key to write the words that would one day become our national anthem. He went up to the Civil War exhibit and found the white towel that Lee used at the surrender at Appomattox Court House along with the letter Grant wrote for the terms of surrender for Lee's army. The chairs and table Lee and Grant used to sign the terms of surrender were also on display. After the American History Museum, he headed over to the National Portrait Gallery to see the official portrait of General Joshua Chamberlain. An identical portrait hangs over the family fireplace at the house in Lancaster. When he was done playing tourist, he headed back to the hotel. Time to catch some lunch, change clothes, and head back to the New Executive Office Building for his meeting with Director Santiago at 1530.

At exactly 1405, the elevator doors of the Black and White Club's secure conference room opened, and President Brian C. Byrne walked in carrying the football. He wore a dark blue suit, red tie, white shirt, and looked every bit presidential. He set the football down by the door.

"Sorry I'm late, and I apologize in advance to you Donna, but Senator Lopez, from your good State of Florida, does not know how to shut up. My God that woman can talk. Cruise ships calling in Cuba are not going to be the end of the world as we know it. Please, everyone, be seated," President Byrne said.

"I usually have to put a timer on her for meetings," Donna Alonzo, President Pro Tem of the Senate said. She was dressed in a dark blue pant-suit with a white shirt and a string of pearls.

President Byrne laughed. "I must try that in the future. How is every-one doing today? Mr. Chief Justice, how is the Supreme Court?"

Chief Justice Carlo Virgilio rubbed the top of his bald head. He was dressed in a white shirt with a solid magenta tie and black pants. He did not have a suit coat with him, since he came straight to the meeting after a court session, and he was going straight back after this meeting.

"Pretty busy, Mr. President, since the fall term started. We hear about 24 cases in a sitting."

"Well, then, let's get started," President Byrne said. "Vince, are you ready?"

"Yes, Mr. President."

President Byrne opened the black binder and started to read:

Under the purview of Executive Order 9513, Addendum A, this meeting of the Black and White Club is called to order. All actions taken by this committee must be by unanimous decision and based on the best judgment of each member without consideration to position, political affiliation, or current United States law. The only guiding principle is the preservation of the democratic institution which is the United States of America and the defense of our Constitution against all enemies foreign and domestic. All the proceedings, and decisions, made during this meeting shall never be divulged beyond these founding members. Does everyone agree?

There were nods around the table.

"Okay, Vince, all yours," Brian said.

"Thank you, Brian," Vince said.

Vince pressed his remote, and a frame grab from the drone video over Josh's estate on Martin Meadow Pond appeared on the screen with the infrared overlay showing the position of 12 shooters arrayed around the estate.

"As you recall during our last meeting, this committee authorized the use of force against the La Libertad Cartel and all agents working on their behalf. The gentlemen you see here are contractors for a company called Sea Island Security. They were working for the La Libertad Cartel to eliminate Special Agent Josh Martin, after the ceremony for his wife. With a Tactical Team out of Boston, a Pave Hawk out of Andrews, and the help of Agent Martin, and his brother JJ, we neutralized the threat. We took down 10 and seized two. The two captured personnel are currently our guests in Guantanamo," Vince said.

"What were the contractor nationalities?" Amelia asked. Vice President Amelia C. Evelina was wearing a green skirt with a white top and a green jacket.

"Four Canadians, four French, and four Americans," Vince said. "The two we have under detention are Americans; a Mr. George Schneider, aka Greg Bennett, and a Mr. Nick Lacava, aka Jim Palmer."

"What about the attempted church bombing?" Katherine asked. Katherine Rich, the Speaker of the House, wore a red, green, and blue plaid wool skirt with a light blue shirt.

"Thanks for the lead-in, Katherine," Vince said. He pushed the remote, and a picture of the bombed-out Lancaster pool came on the screen.

"Wow," Brian said.

"This bomb was intended for this church," Vince said. He clicked the remote and a picture of the All Saints Church in Lancaster, New Hampshire, came on the screen. "At the anticipated detonation time, the church would have been filled with about 300 mourners, including Agent Josh Martin and his family."

"Who's the son of a bitch responsible for that?" Carlo asked.

"This son of a bitch," Vince said. He hit the clicker, and Robert Adams' official picture for Sea Island Security appeared on the screen. "This is Robert Adams, aka Rob McDonald, the Boston director for Sea Island Security. The parish priest identified Mr. Adams as being in the church the night before the bombing. Also, a waitress recognized Mr. Adams meeting with DEA Agent Quinn Christy on several occasions."

"Did Agent Martin actually run from the church carrying a bomb?" Amelia asked.

"Yes," Vince said. "Josh and his brother JJ carried the bomb out of the church and dumped it in the deep end of the pool."

"Somebody raised those boys right," Katherine said. "Did he join us?"

"Yes, he did," Vince said.

"Probably should extend an invitation to his brother," Donna said.

"Crossed my mind," Vince said. "He's a former sniper with the US Marines."

"So why are we here, Vince?" Brian asked. "From what I have seen, you already have the authorization to eliminate these scumbags. What's new?"

"This," Vince said, and he flashed a picture of Matt Richards on the screen in his official CIA portrait with the American flag over his right shoulder.

"Shit," Carlo said.

"This is Matt Richards. He's currently the Director of Transnational Issues at the CIA. A few years ago, Mr. Richards was an operations officer on the Colombian desk. He set up a deal with Juan Pablo Rodriguez to exchange information on anti-narcotic operations, plans, patrols, etc., in exchange for information on the FARC, Venezuela, and Colombia. He also was on the payroll with about $10.2 million in offshore accounts. We pinged his Cayman account to see where he would move the money. We have another account in Ireland," Vince said.

"How bad?" Brian said.

"This bad," Vince said. He flashed a composite shot of the car bombs that killed Katherine, Agent Li, and Agent Britt. He clicked on a shot of a CIA gel bomb and the aftermath of the pool bombing. "Mr. Richards provided the bomb to Mr. Adams to blow up the church in New Hampshire."

"The CIA provided domestic terrorists with a bomb to blow up a church full of people in New Hampshire, at a funeral service for the wife of an FBI agent, who they also blew up?" Katherine asked.

"Yes," Vince said. There was audible exhale around the table.

Carlo broke the silence. "So, what do you propose, Vince?"

"I don't know. That's why I called the meeting. We have a plan in place to remove Juan Pablo and Mr. Adams. The issue is Mr. Richards. We alerted the CIA's Inspector General's office on our suspicions, in case Mr. Richards tries to take an early retirement. We also froze his passport, so he can't leave the country," Vince said.

The committee discussed the issue for a while and finally reached a unanimous conclusion.

"Are you clear on our instructions, Vince?" Brian asked.

"Yes, crystal," Vince said.

"Is there anything else, Vince?" Brian asked.

"You meet with Agent Martin at 1530, right after this meeting."

Brian looked at his watch. "Okay, I guess we're done. Meeting adjourned."

75

Josh read the proposal on the Phillips Brook project from JJ, while he waited in Vince's office for the 1530 meeting. His walk over from the Saint Regis was uneventful. No more South American escorts. JJ's proposal looked good, plus his mom wanted to do it. However, 7 million was a lot of money, but at the worst, they would just sell the land.

Lisa, Vince's secretary, stuck her head in the door. "They're ready for you now." Lisa was pretty with long brown hair, a beautiful smile, and she filled out a blouse.

Josh walked out of Vince's office. "Thanks, Lisa, what do I do now?"

"Walk over to the elevator and put your hand on the scanner. Then just step in, when the door opens."

Josh walked over to the elevator doors with the gates of hell mural. He put his hand on a blue pad to the right of the doors with the outline of a hand. A blue light scanned his hand like the view of a copier scanning a document. The elevator doors opened, and he stepped in. Then the doors closed.

A computer voice from a speaker in the ceiling said, "Please state your name."

"Joshua Chamberlain Martin," Josh said.

"Identity confirmed," said the computer voice, and the elevator started to descend. It was a little disconcerting, since you couldn't watch the floors tick off. You just got the sense of falling. The elevator stopped, the doors opened, and Josh walked into a room with the President of the United States and Vince Santiago. Josh felt three zaps on his wrist from his watch, with a pause, followed by two more. *Holy shit, the president was tagged*, thought Josh.

"Hey, Josh, come on in," Vince said. "Let me present the President of the United States."

"Mr. President, it's a distinct honor to meet you."

The president walked up and extended his hand. "Welcome to the club, Josh." Josh shook his hand. "I wish it was under better circumstances. My condolences on the loss of your wife."

"Thank you, Mr. President."

"Please come in and sit down," Vince said.

Josh walked in and sat at the round conference table to the left of the president. Vince sat on his right.

"I always like to meet our new Black Club Members," President Byrne said. He rubbed his hand across the table. "I want you to know two things: that Director Santiago speaks for the committee, and that I'm in this with you. I saw the expression on your face when you walked in. You realized I'm tagged, just like you."

"Yes, Mr. President. It did come as a surprise." He still couldn't believe he was sitting next to the President of the United States having a normal conversation.

"We created the pill technology, after the issue with President Kennedy," Vince said.

"We didn't want another member to face the ethical dilemma of pulling the trigger on the President of the United States."

"And after reviewing your record, and the report from Director Santiago, I don't want you on the other side of a firearm pointed at me," President Byrne said.

Josh shifted in his seat at the president's statement. "No, Mr. President. I'm here to serve my country."

"Of that, I have no doubt," President Byrne said. "Also, just like in the military, I got your six. I'll do whatever it takes to support you on your assignments, and if something fucks up, I'll get you back. On that, you have my solemn vow."

"Thank you, Mr. President," Josh said.

"Well, gentlemen, I won't take up any more of your time." President Byrne got to his feet, followed by Vince and Josh. "I'd better get back topside. My detail isn't too happy with these meetings." President Byrne shook hands with Vince and Josh, stepped over to the elevator, and picked up the football. He walked into the elevator when the doors opened. He gave a thumbs-up as the doors closed.

Vince and Josh sat back down.

"Ever meet the president before?" Vince asked.

"Not like that. I shook hands with President Bush at my graduation from the Coast Guard Academy, but that's it. Nothing like this."

"Well, get used to it. He likes you, and more importantly, you impressed him."

"So, what now?" Josh asked.

"We move forward on Adams and Juan Pablo. I also just got our marching orders on Richards. Let's head back to my office, and I'll give you the details." They both stood and walked over to the elevator.

I hope those orders include me putting a bullet in his brain, thought Josh.

76

Matt Richards took a sip of coffee and looked around his kitchen for the final time. The exposed logs of his home gleamed with a fresh coat of preservative. *Who even lives in a log home in a suburb of DC?* he thought. It was his wife's idea to build a log home, and then she decided to run off with the car executive across the street and move to Detroit. He put his mug down and shook his head. "Stupid bitch." *I'll have to send her a postcard from the South Pacific with a naked babe lying on a pile of Benjamins.*

He took yesterday off, so he could pack and prepare for his trip to Colombia. He was scheduled to leave on American Airlines flight 1038 at 0600 to Miami, where he would hop on flight 913 for the journey to Bogota. It was a round-trip ticket, but he wouldn't be using the return leg. He would catch a flight from Bogota to the United Arab Emirates, who didn't have an extradition treaty with the U.S. Get a new identity and documents, and then off to French Polynesia; the land of sun, fun, and no cartel, Sea Island Security, or Josh "fucking" Martin.

He dragged two duffel bags full of clothes and some personal items and tossed them into the back of his Escape. He was dressed in jeans, sneakers, and a blue polo shirt, with a light gray jacket. He called it his don't-get-mugged-in-Colombia outfit. He could care less about the clothes and the personal items, but he divided up $9,000 in U.S. currency in hiding spots throughout both bags, and he had $995 in his wallet. Even if Customs and Border Protection found all the money, which was very unlikely, he would still be below the $10,000 threshold to file a declaration. He walked to the front of the car and got in, started the engine, and turned on the headlights. He pushed the opener on the visor to open the gate at the top of the driveway, shifted into drive, and headed out. "Goodbye, motherfuckers," he screamed, and he hit his steering wheel three times. "I made it. I'm out of here. Thank you, Jesus."

Josh walked out of the Saint Regis a little after 0100. He had a beverage tray with four large coffees with some cream containers, sugar, and stirrers in a separate bag. Room service delivered it to his room. The dark blue Suburban was waiting just under the check-in canopy. Josh opened the passenger side rear door and climbed in. He handed the coffee tray to a female Asian agent sitting behind Jerry Sloane, who was driving. Patrick Sullivan was in the front passenger seat.

"Now this is what I call a partner," the Asian agent said, taking a coffee and handing the tray back to Josh. Josh took a coffee and gave the tray to Patrick in the front seat.

Josh extended his hand across the seat. "Josh Martin."

"Amy Chow. Pleased to meet you." She shook hands with Josh. Everyone was wearing dark blue FBI raid jackets with large FBI in yellow letters on the back.

"Thanks for coming out," Josh said.

"No problem," Amy said. "The boys in front told me you deliver felony busts without wanting any credit. My kinda partner."

"I do what I can," Josh said.

"Where to?" Jerry asked.

"16017 Garriland Drive, Leesburg, Virginia," Josh said.

Jerry plugged the address into the GPS and pulled the Suburban into traffic, turning right on 16th Street. The streets were empty, so they made good time. They took the Dulles Greenway from the city out to Leesburg, took Exit 1, to Route 15 north, and turned left on Montressor Drive, about 7 miles north of Leesburg, into a residential development called Selma Estates. Two miles down Montressor, they turned left on Garriland Drive. Garriland was open fields on either side of the road for about a half-mile, until they started seeing executive homes on both sides of the road. They found the mailbox for 16017 and turned down the driveway and parked. A gate was closed, which shut off the driveway from the house.

"Now what?" Jerry said.

"We wait," Josh said.

"Who is this mutt?" Patrick asked.

"Matt Richards," Josh said. "He's with the CIA. They want him for espionage."

"No shit," Patrick said. "We're going to be on their Christmas card list this year. They were looking for some bargaining chips to negotiate an exchange of agents with Venezuela, and we showed up with old Anthony and Nathan. They were ecstatic. Now, we pick up someone on their watch list. Doesn't get any better than this."

"When the gate opens, drive up and block the exit. We hop out and take him down. He's got nowhere to go. We have him boxed into the vehicle, so he's got no choice," Josh said.

"Any weapons?" Amy asked.

"Not that I know of," Josh said. "He's an analyst and not an operator, so I don't think he will be a problem. Plus, he looks like your fat Uncle Fred."

"How did you know I had an Uncle Fred?" Amy asked.

"Lucky guess," Josh said.

"Showtime," Jerry said. The lights in the house came on. "He's up early."

"He's supposed to catch a 0600 flight out of Dulles," Josh said. "I don't think he's going to make it."

They waited another 20 minutes and saw Matt drag a couple of duffels out to the car, which looked like a silver Escape. Then he climbed in, started the vehicle, and the driveway gate began to open.

Matt started to approach the gate when a car's high beams came on directly in front of him blocking the road. He raised his arm to shield his eyes. "Son of a bitch, what the fuck is this?" The realization started to dawn on him. "No! Fuck no! How did they find out?"

There was movement on either side of the car with figures approaching from the shadows.

"FBI. Show me your hands," said a voice out of the dark. Matt raised his hands up to the ceiling of the car, feeling the interior material on his hands. His driver side door opened.

"Don't move," a voice said. He still couldn't see anything in the blinding light.

"With your left hand, slowly unlatch your seat belt and exit the vehicle."

He reached down with his left hand, pressed the seat belt latch, and let the seat belt retract to the side of the car. He swung his legs left out of the car and lifted himself out.

"Now, get down on the ground, cross your legs, and interlock your fingers behind your head."

Sounds like a female voice, he thought. He got down on his hands and knees, and then flattened to the ground on his stomach. He put his hands behind his head and crossed his legs. A firm grip grabbed his left wrist and twisted his arm behind his back. He felt the cold metal of handcuffs snap on his wrist. He felt a tap on his back.

"Other hand," came the voice. He put his right arm behind his back, and his right wrist was handcuffed. Strong hands grabbed him on either elbow and dragged him to his feet.

"You're making a terrible mistake. My name is Matt Richards, and I work for the U.S. government."

Josh stepped up closer and whispered in his ear. "No, scumbag. You used to work for the CIA. Now, you're going to be a pin cushion for some Cuban terrorists looking for love in all the wrong places."

"Who the fuck are you?" Matt asked.

"I'm the guy who lost his wife because you wanted a new job."

Matt felt the blood drain from his head and his balls shrink up to his ass.

"Oh, shit. It wasn't my idea."

"I'll make sure you get a chance to explain it to a few friends of mine. All you boys and girls, enjoy." Josh turned and started walking up the driveway. "Call the CIA Inspector General's office, when you get to holding."

"Aren't you coming back with us?" Patrick asked.

"No, I got my own ride," Josh said, with a wave of his hand. He walked up to the end of the driveway, and Pete Sessions from Presidential Contingency Programs pulled up in a green Dodge pickup truck.

Josh climbed in. "If I knew you were going to pick me up in a Dodge piece of shit, I would've walked," Josh said.

"I can stop if you want," Pete said, hitting the brakes.

"No. Keep driving. It's dark. No one will see me." He pulled out his phone and dialed the number for Vince, who answered on the second ring.

"How did it go?" Vince asked.

"He's on his way to holding. No issues," Josh said.

"Great. Sorry we couldn't go with the 38-cent solution. They want to find out how much he knows, and how much information he passed."

"Yes, Sir. I understand. I'm heading back to Boston to close the loop on Mr. Adams. I'll call you when mission complete." He clicked off the call.

"Where to?" Pete asked.

"Andrews Air Force Base, and I'll pay for any speeding tickets. I want to get there before it gets light, so no one sees me in this Dodge."

Pete shook his head, chuckling, and stepped on the gas.

77

Rob Adams walked into his office with his briefcase and a mug of coffee. He set the briefcase on the floor next to his desk, took a sip of coffee, and set the cup down on his desk. He sat in his chair and looked out at the harbor. Traffic was going up and down the Boston Ship Channel in its own little world. Delivering cargo and people to all points in the Boston waterfront, and sending and receiving cargo and people from all over the world. *Maybe time to be one of those people heading out of Boston. Passage on a freighter may be a good way to go,* he thought. Not much scrutiny on commercial vessels leaving Boston. A few greased palms, and he would be invisible. Something to think about. Probably sooner, rather than later.

He attended a couple of meetings on new hires, reviewed the quarterly reports, and answered his overnight email. He looked at his watch. It was just about noon. Time for lunch. The phone in his right, top desk drawer rang. "Shit." Never good news, when it was unexpected.

He pulled the phone out of the drawer and pressed the green to accept button. "Yes, Sir."

"Richards did not make the flight to Miami, and he's not on the flight to Bogota," Juan Pablo said.

"That's not good," Rob said. "They must have picked him up."

"My thoughts exactly. Time to go."

"Okay, I'm going to get out of the country. I'll get in touch when I have a new location."

"Good luck."

The phone went dead. Rob put the phone in his coat pocket and got up to leave. He put on his jacket and walked out of his office. "I'm going to lunch, Kerri."

"Yes, Mr. Adams," his secretary said.

Pete Sessions took Josh to Andrews Air Force Base. A Gulfstream 5 was waiting on the tarmac for his arrival. Once he was aboard, it was a straight shot to Hanscom Airfield, about 18 miles northwest of Boston. The flight took about an hour and a half to cover the 440-mile trip.

An executive town car was waiting for him at Hanscom Airfield. It took him into the city and deposited him at the Ritz-Carlton Towers. The bellman opened the door, and Josh stepped out.

"Welcome back, Mr. Drake. I hope you had a successful trip."

"I did Wayne, thank you."

Josh walked into the lobby. The front desk clerk looked up as he walked in. "Welcome back, Mr. Drake. How do you like the new condo?"

"It's great Francis, thank you." Josh walked over to the bank of elevators and pressed the up button. The doors opened. He stepped in and pushed the button for the seventh floor.

Capt. Dana Gordon, USAF put the Reaper MQ-9 drone into a reconnaissance holding pattern over Bogota, Colombia, a few minutes after 1200. The drone was armed with two MMW radar Longbow Hellfire (AGM-114M) air-to-ground missiles. It also had two external fuel tank pods, which gave it about 24 hours of on-station time. *More than enough to accomplish this strike mission,* she thought. *Nothing to do now but wait.*

Adams grabbed a taxi back from the Sea Island Security office to the Ritz-Carlton Towers. He stepped out of the taxi and walked through the lobby to the front desk clerk. "Could you have them bring my car around to the front?" Robert asked.

"Yes, Mr. Adams, right away." The clerk picked up the phone. "Could you please bring Mr. Adams' car around front? Unit 702. All set, Mr. Adams."

Adams walked over to the bank of elevators. The doors opened. He stepped in and hit the button for the seventh floor. *Okay, grab the go bag. Get the car and drive west. Hang out off the grid for a couple of days. Pick up a new ID in Kansas City, and then head north to Michigan to cross the border. A few days and all this shit will be behind me. 10 million bucks, a new ID, and a new life. I think a few days in Aruba are looking good.*

The elevator stopped on the seventh floor, and the door opened. He turned left and stopped at his door. He fished the key out of his pocket and stuck it in the lock. He glanced at the door to unit 703. He was hoping the new tenant was a smoking hot blonde. Oh, well, not going to find out.

He pushed the door open and walked in. Then he turned, closed the door, and caught a shadow and movement out of the corner of his eye, and then he felt a searing pain in the center of his chest from two punches, like getting kicked by a mule. The donkey kicks threw him against the wall, and he fell on the floor. The room was spinning, and he fell on his back, gasping for breath that wouldn't come. *What the hell?* He tried to focus on the looming shadow. *I recognize that face.* "Oh, fuck." The shadow flashed a stab of flame, and the world went blank.

"So long, asshole," Josh said. He slipped the silenced Glock back into his holster. He stepped to the door and opened it to check the hallway. Nothing. He closed the door, checked Rob's pockets, and found the crypt-cell phone. "Bingo." He walked into the kitchen, which was to the left of the front door, and set the phone on the counter. He reached into his pocket and pulled out a black plastic cube about 2 inches square. He flicked a switch on the left side of the cube to on and set it next to the phone.

He pulled out his own phone and dialed the number Vince gave him.

The caller answered on the second ring. "Agent Martin, this is Becka Kendall, do you have the phone?"

"Yes."

"Okay, turn it on." Josh pushed the power button, and the cryptcell turned on. "I need a password, pin, and finger swipe key," Josh said.

"Is the phone next to the cube unit?"

"Yes."

"Stand by. I'm sending the signal now." The cube next to the phone made a series of beeps, and the cryptcell flashed twice and went to the call screen.

"I'm in," Josh said.

"Okay, initiate the call."

Josh scrolled to the contact list. There was only one number. He high-lighted the number and pressed send. The cell started to ring. "Come on, come on, you scumbag…answer the phone and win the prize." On the fifth ring, the phone answered.

"What is it? I didn't think you were going to call until you were out of the country."

"Juan Pablo?" Josh asked.

"Who is this?"

"Is this the head of the pussy brigade, otherwise known as the La Libertad Cartel?"

"We got it," Becka said.

The GPS coordinates flashed on Captain Gordon's screen. She punched them into the drone fire control system and pressed the red fire button. Two MMW radar Longbow Hellfire (AGM-114M) air-to-ground missiles dropped off the missile pods, and the solid fuel rocket engines ignited. The semi-active laser targeting system locked onto the programmed target coordinates and the weapons started their glide path to the target. The missiles quickly reached their terminal velocity of about 995 mph.

"Whoever I am speaking to is a dead man," the caller said.

"No, I'm looking at the dead man. He has two in the chest and one in the head. It improves his appearance if you ask me."

"Agent Martin, I presume," Juan Pablo said.

"You get a gold star, dickhead. I'm just happy that my voice is the last voice you will ever hear."

"What the fuck are you talking about? I'm going to—"

The missiles punched through the roof of Juan Pablo's villa and the two metal-augmented, 18-pound, shaped charge warheads exploded, vaporiz-ing Juan Pablo, the villa, plus another 10 members of the cartel.

"Drone pilot confirms destruction of the target," Becka said.

"Outstanding," Josh said. "Is the cleanup crew en route?"

"Yes, Sir. They're walking into the building now."

"Okay, thanks." Josh hung up the phone and looked at the body of Rob Adams.

"That, my friend, is for SEAL Team 4, Agent Li, Agent Britt, Ellen Page, my wife, and my unborn child. May you rot in hell with Juan Pablo." Josh opened the condo door and walked out into the hallway, just as the cleanup crew stepped off the elevator.

"Thanks for your help, guys," Josh said, as he passed the crew in the hallway. He stepped into the elevator and hit down.

78

Josh clicked send and transferred $7,000,000 into the Martin Company account from his personal account for the down payment on the Phillips Brook purchase. *I guess Mom is now a land baroness.* He closed the laptop, slipped it into his backpack, and put it behind the front passenger seat. Josh turned out of his driveway in Lancaster and stepped on the gas. The Maserati, ruby red, Gran Turismo convertible launched forward from 0 to 60 in 4.5 seconds. Josh had just taken delivery of two blue, fully loaded, Ford F150 Platinum Crew cabs. He parked them in front of the house with big red bows and lottery winner sized cards, marked for Pops and JJ. Syrin was doing her happy dance in the front seat. Glad to be riding shotgun with Josh.

Josh eased off the gas and turned right to head back to town. Once he cleared town, he stepped on the gas and rocketed over Corrigan Hill, slowed at the crest of the hill, and turned right on Martin Meadow Pond Road, and then right on Martin Road. He pulled into the lot in front of the main house and got out of the car. Syrin jumped out and ran over to water some grass on the side of the house. Josh reached in behind the driver seat and pulled out the silver urn. He started down the path, worn smooth by countless trips to the water, through the field in front of the house to the water's edge. A steady 20-knot wind blew across the water, and the white caps were running from the west across the pond. He reached the water's edge and walked out on the dock which stuck about 30' into the water. The sound of waves lapping on the dock, and the wind blowing through the trees, filled the air. Syrin paced back and forth on the dock, looking into the water, her nails scuffed on the wood. Josh stood on the edge and looked across the water.

What a peaceful place. So many good memories. You couldn't tell that a few days ago, evil visited God's country. Josh took the lid off the urn and opened the plastic bag that contained Kat's ashes.

"Sorry, babe. I guess we didn't stick to the plan to die in each other's arms when we both turn 100. I always wanted to go first, or die exactly one minute after you, when we were old and gray. I've got to be honest with you. This is tough. I miss you so much. So does Syrin." Syrin came over and sat down next to him at the mention of her name, and he stroked the top of her head. Josh opened the bag and dumped the ashes into the pond. They mixed with the water, and the dust was carried away by the wind. "Till we meet again, sweetie. You will always be in my heart. May God keep you safe until we're together again." Josh heaved the urn into the pond. It landed about 15' out from the end of the dock with a splash. Syrin barked at the sound.

Josh and Syrin walked back to the Maserati, climbed in, and headed down the road. He had to be in DC in a week and needed to finalize things with his household goods and the club before he got back to work at the new job. They stopped in Littleton, bought Syrin an ice cream cone, and left a little something in the tip jar. He cruised through Littleton, picked up I93, and put the hammer down. Why own a sports car, if you don't drive fast?

Audrey's shift was just about over. She waddled over to the tip jar to get her tips for the day. It looked like someone left a note. She opened the note. It was a bank check. Pay to the order of Audrey and David Watkins, the sum of Twenty-Five Thousand Dollars and no cents. Signed, Joshua C. Martin. Tears filled Audrey's eyes. "Dave! Dave, you're not going to believe this."